Bridging the Border

WITHDRAWN

FORSYTH LIBRARY
FORT HAYS STATE UNIVERSITY

WITHDRAWN

Bridging the Border

Transforming Mexico–U.S. Relations

Edited by
Rodolfo O. de la Garza
and
Jesús Velasco

ROWMAN & LITTLEFIELD PUBLISHERS, INC.
Lanham • Boulder • New York • Oxford

ROWMAN & LITTLEFIELD PUBLISHERS, INC.

Published in the United States of America
by Rowman & Littlefield Publishers, Inc.
4720 Boston Way, Lanham, Maryland 20706

12 Hid's Copse Road
Cummor Hill, Oxford OX2 9JJ, England

Copyright © 1997 by Rowman & Littlefield Publishers, Inc.

All rights reserved. No part of this publication may be reproduced,
stored in a retrieval system, or transmitted in any form or by any
means, electronic, mechanical, photocopying, recording, or otherwise,
without the prior permission of the publisher.

British Library Cataloguing in Publication Information Available

Library of Congress Cataloging-in-Publication Data

Bridging the border : transforming Mexico–U.S. relations / edited by Rodolfo O. de la
 Garza and Jesús Velasco.
  p.   cm.
 Includes bibliographical references and index.
 ISBN 0-8476-8438-5 (cloth : alk. paper). — ISBN 0-8476-8439-3 (pbk. : alk.
paper)
  1. United States—Foreign relations—Mexico. 2. Mexico—Foreign relations—
United States. 3. United States—Foreign relations—1993– . I. De la Garza, Rodolfo
O. II. Velasco, Jesús.
 E183.8.M6B75   1997
 327.72073—dc21   97–19263

ISBN 0-8476-8438-5 (cloth : alk. paper)
ISBN 0-8476-8439-3 (pbk. : alk. paper)

Printed in the United States of America

⊗™ The paper used in this publication meets the minimum requirements of American
National Standard for Information Sciences—Permanence of Paper for Printed Library
Materials, ANSI Z39.48–1984.

For Sofia Elena and Rodrigo

Contents

Figures and Tables

Acknowledgments

This volume was made possible through the support of Dr. Carlos Elizondo, director general of the Center for Economics Research and Training (CIDE) of Mexico City, and Dr. Sheldon Ekland-Olson, dean of the College of Liberal Arts, the University of Texas at Austin.

Introduction

Rodolfo O. de la Garza and Jesús Velasco

Since the 1980s, Mexico's foreign policy and especially its bilateral relations with the United States have changed substantially. From the postwar years to the 1970s, Mexico maintained a foreign policy based on four basic principles: nonintervention in the internal affairs of other states; the right to national self-determination; the peaceful solution of controversies; and the judicial equality of nations. These principles were very useful for a country relatively isolated from the outside world. In the domestic arena, Mexico has been governed since 1929 by a pseudo-democratic authoritarian regime that provided political and institutional stability. In the economic sphere, the system was closed and ruled by the strategy of import substitution. In foreign affairs, the international environment was essentially indifferent to Mexico's domestic and foreign policies. This is a major reason why the Mexican government was free to maintain a decidedly nationalistic and independent foreign policy posture.

However, beginning in the 1970s economic difficulties and significant changes in the international arena propelled the government to modify these traditional policies. The "economic miracle" of the 1960s showed clear signs of deterioration by the 1970s when the economy slowed and began experiencing unusually high inflation rates. Mexico's international debt increased considerably, and the peso was devalued in 1976 and 1982. The collapse of the Bretton Woods system and the protectionist tendencies adopted by the United States during those years also contributed to Mexico's economic decline.

This was the context within which President Luis Echeverría (1970–1976) decided to search for a new approach to the international arena. He energetically participated in multilateral organizations such as the United Nations and some

Latin American forums, and he formulated an active policy defending the interests of the so-called Third World countries. The economic breakdown of 1982, which, among other things, revealed that Mexico was more vulnerable to the outside world than most officials wanted to admit, forced the government to initiate even more radical transformations. Deregulation, privatization of important governmental enterprises, and the liberalization of the Mexican economy were the main measures the government adopted to deal with its economic crisis. These economic initiatives solidified Mexico's connection with the outside world and ushered in a new foreign policy era.

Historically, Mexico conducted its foreign policy via the official activities of its embassies and consulates in their respective posts, and through its participation in international forums. In other words, Mexico's involvement in international affairs was basically confined to formal diplomatic relations with governmental and international agencies. This was in keeping with the principle of nonintervention. Beginning in the 1980s, Mexican officials moved beyond these formal activities to also develop linkages with various types of political actors abroad.

This book is about how this new Mexican foreign policy has been implemented vis-à-vis the United States. It is an examination of the interactions between the Mexican government and American governmental and civilian institutions. This analysis is both pertinent and necessary. It is pertinent because it gives an account of the new manner in which the Mexican government is developing its most important bilateral relation, its relation with the United States. It is necessary because it focuses on the contemporary nature of Mexico's activities abroad, a topic poorly explored by the academic community.

Alan Knight opens this volume by offering a historical account of U.S.–Mexican relations from 1910 to 1995. Knight examines the bilateral relation in terms of four categories: salience, congruence, attitudes, and actors. He uses the first two to examine the moments in which Mexico has played an important role in U.S. politics (salience) and the degree to which Mexico has constituted part of "U.S. hopes, prejudice, and expectations (congruence)." For him, "salience and congruence have usually been the product of given circumstances largely beyond Mexican control, whereas attitudes and actors have been susceptible to a degree of Mexican massaging."

According to Knight, there are three main periods in the history of U.S.–Mexican relations. The first, from 1910 to 1940, was permeated by the Mexican revolution, its consequences, and the ambitions of the United States to constrain and control the revolution. During this period the factors shaping the relationship—such as the 1938 oil expropriation—were more conjunctural than structural. The emergence of World War II shifted the focus of U.S. concerns to Europe with a consequent deterioration of the presence of Mexico in American politics. Finally, the third period, which started in the 1980s, has been characterized by an increasing interdependence in which bilateral relations have become closer but more hostile.

After his journey through the history of the bilateral relationship, Knight concludes that although Mexico and the United States have had several conflicts, they have been "limited in scope and impact." This is because both countries "share certain political ideas and experiences" and because the Mexican revolution was a "'bourgeois' revolution that the Americans could understand, endorse, and even massage." He concludes that for most of this century the bilateral relation has been structured by opposite positions, that of U.S. pressure and Mexican resistance. Historically this has left both sides with limited autonomy. In the post–cold-war era, however, Mexico's increased salience may lead to greater tensions in the relationship, or it may reproduce the Newtonian dynamics of the 1920s. The latter would be conducive to Mexico's new foreign policy approach.

Contrary to Knight, who analyzed the bilateral relation over a long period of time, Jorge Chabat concentrates his analysis on Mexico's foreign policy within the context of the North American Free Trade Agreement (NAFTA). Chabat argues that strong countries use foreign policy instruments such as war to promote their interests, while weak states tend to use negotiations and diplomacy. Chabat also shares the view of those scholars who argue that the interdependence of two states contributes to negotiations rather than to the use of military instruments. In other words, the "mutual vulnerabilities" between two countries in a relationship of interdependence facilitate negotiation rather than military conflict.

For Chabat, the main reason for Mexico's historical ability to resist the United States is not that Mexican foreign policy is based on respect for international law, but that the Mexican border established the primary nexus of interdependence of the two countries. Chabat considers that Mexico's negotiating capacity was evident in the oil expropriation of 1938. In his opinion, however, Mexico has gone from passive interdependence (1930s–1980s) to active interdependence in its relations with the United States.

Chabat argues that the administration of Carlos Salinas de Gortari marked a considerable transformation in the foreign policy of the country. During the Salinas presidency and in the NAFTA debates in particular, Mexico initiated an active foreign policy dependent on new foreign policy instruments to accomplish its goals. As evidenced during the NAFTA negotiations, this new policy included efforts by the Mexican government to promote its own interests within American society. To that end, Chabat argues that Mexico targeted four basic groups in the United States: a) the general public, and Hispanics in particular; b) American investors; c) President Clinton and his cabinet; and d) Congress and congressional staffers. To get its message across, Mexico used the mass media, especially television, and invested in the most expensive foreign lobbying effort in the history of the United States.

Chabat notes an inconsistency between Mexico's new foreign policy instruments and its domestic practices. The new international endeavors represent a significant change from the traditional position of nonintervention that had been used to defend the nation's sovereignty. To attenuate the impact of this change, the government has promoted a political discourse that equates actively promoting Mexico's interests abroad with defending the nation's sovereignty. At the same time, President Salinas initially rejected the participation of international observers in Mexico's 1994 elections. To defend his position, Salinas, the architect of the new foreign policy instruments, resorted to the traditional discourse that equates national sovereignty with noninvolvement in the domestic affairs of other nations. According to Chabat, that international visitors ultimately were present during the 1994 Mexican elections demonstrates the decline of the legitimacy of the traditional discourse. Furthermore, public pressure in favor of democratization is also compatible with the rules of interdependence that govern Mexico's new economic program. In the not too distant future, therefore, the "logic of interdependence will end up modifying what remains of Mexico's second post-war foreign policy."

Carlos González Gutiérrez's chapter examines one of the modern instruments of the new Mexican foreign policy—the consulates. The role of consulates in Mexico's foreign policy has changed substantially as a result of both a closer relation with the United States and the government's decision to use these offices to promote its newly defined interests, including its new economic relationship with the United States. González Gutiérrez argues that the Salinas administration adopted four measures to invigorate the consulates: 1) designating distinguished politicians to direct these offices; 2) appointing specialized personnel to staff them; 3) allocating additional resources for the protection of Mexicans in the United States; and 4) establishing the Program for Mexican Communities Living in Foreign Countries (PMCLFC).

Mexico's new economic program has accelerated the integration of the U.S. and Mexican economies, and this has stimulated the proliferation of channels of communications between both countries as well as an increase in potential conflicts. Mexican officials, therefore, have begun to deal with a variety of nongovernmental organizations, interest groups, and distinct agencies of local governments on a daily basis. Under these conditions, traditional diplomatic relations, asserts González Gutiérrez, were not enough to maintain a harmonious bilateral relation. As a result, the consulates became very useful instruments for dealing with the numerous political actors that now participate in the bilateral relation.

González Gutiérrez concludes by arguing that consuls in the United States are, in the final analysis, the implementors of the strategy focusing on the Mexican diaspora. Indeed, he sees the diaspora as "the primary clientele" of the consulates. This has forced consuls to redefine the traditional concept of nonintervention in U.S. domestic affairs. Today, therefore, Mexico must find a way to expand its relations with this group without becoming overly involved in domestic American affairs.

Rodolfo de la Garza studies one of the themes commented on by González Gutiérrez, the Program for Mexican Communities Living in Foreign Countries (PMCLFC). His study examines three related themes: the origins of the program, its possible consequences for Mexican domestic politics, and its effect on U.S.–Mexican relations. The birth and growth of PMCLFC, de la Garza argues, can be explained by the domestic political transformations experienced by Mexico and the modification in U.S. foreign policy-making processes. For him, the opening of the economy, the Chiapas revolt, and the political struggles within the Partido Revolucionario Institucional (PRI) have paved the way for the participation of new important political actors in Mexico. Likewise, de la Garza argues that Mexico's foreign policy toward the United States has changed so considerably that "by the early 1990s, nationalism and sovereignty were redefined so that the United States became an ally rather than the enemy."

The United States has also experienced important changes. Starting with the Vietnam War and culminating with the end of the cold war, the American foreign policy agenda changed from its traditional anticommunist focus to include issues such as drugs and immigration. Domestic issues, de la Garza argues, currently dominate the U.S. foreign policy agenda. Thus, changes in the American foreign policy process and the objectives of Mexican foreign affairs have transformed the bilateral relation. Today, Mexico's relations with the United States are closer than perhaps they have ever been, and Mexico is undoubtedly a first priority issue for American decision makers. PMCLFC must be understood within this context.

According to de la Garza, the establishment of PMCLFC may be more relevant for Mexican domestic politics than for U.S.–Mexican relations. He argues that PMCLFC has three main goals: to reinforce relations with Mexican emigrants, which in the final analysis will strengthen the "economic links between émigrés and home-country counterparts;" to show Mexico's concern for its diaspora; and to encourage naturalization and therefore "stimulate the development of an ethnic lobby." However, de la Garza notes that PMCLFC is having only a marginal impact on U.S.–Mexican relations. He notes, for example, that Mexican emigrants are the principal target of the cultural and educational projects. Thus, de la Garza's view differs only somewhat from González Gutiérrez, who maintains that the main goal of the Mexican government "is not to use its diaspora as a device for pressuring the United States."

De la Garza argues that NAFTA has not realized the ambitions of the Mexican government to strengthen economic ties with the Mexican American community. Instead, NAFTA connected both economies and facilitated the access of Mexican entrepreneurs to the American market without the need for

Mexican Americans. Moreover, for a variety of reasons Mexican entrepreneurs may prefer to do business with Anglos rather than with Mexican Americans.

Finally, de la Garza argues that the interests of the Mexican American community often differ from the those of the Mexican government. Of four immigration issues, for example, Mexican Americans and the Mexican government agree on only one. Moreover, when both parties agree, as in the case of Proposition 187, it is coincidental rather than the result of Mexican mobilization of the Hispanic community. Furthermore, although Mexican American political influence in the United States is growing, Mexican American officials and legislators are responsive to their domestic constituencies rather than to Mexico. Also, Mexican Americans are not especially interested in Mexican politics, and, given the support Mexico receives from the Clinton administration and other major U.S. political actors, it is not clear how much Mexico needs an ethnic lobby. Overall, de la Garza concludes that "while PMCLFC is a key example of Mexico's new foreign policy, it may be an even better indicator of how Mexican domestic politics are changing."

Todd Eisenstadt also examines one of the clearest examples of the new Mexican foreign policy toward the United States: the Mexican lobby. In his view the main accomplishment of the Mexican lobby was to establish an alliance with American big business and, to a lesser extent, with the Latino community. He also argues that only powerful countries like Japan are capable of developing a strong negotiating position. Thus, Mexico's position of "asymmetrical interdependence" reduces its margin of influence in the United States.

As Alan Knight notes, Mexican officials have tried to influence the American government since the time of the Mexican Revolution. However, Eisenstadt reminds us that since the mid-1980s Mexico has been more systematic and tenacious in such efforts, especially with regard to the U.S. Congress. To that end, and especially during the NAFTA negotiations, Mexico has recruited high-priced lobbyists. However, he concludes that such efforts have been of limited impact.

Eisenstadt explores the origins, evolution, and strategy of the contemporary Mexican lobby. In 1986, for example, the Mexican government paid over $400,000 to promote President De la Madrid's visit to the United States and to publicize Mexico's war on drugs. The NAFTA negotiations provided a major boost to the expansion of the Mexican lobby in Washington, and by 1991 Mexico had the second biggest foreign lobby (in terms of expenditures declared) in the United States. In the same year, President Salinas designated the Secretariat of Commerce and Industrial Development (SECOFI) as the main agency responsible for the bilateral relation, and hired several lobbying agencies such as Burson-Marsteller to conduct Mexico's public campaign in the United States.

The Mexican government also employed other lobbying firms to influence specific sectors of the American population and to promote Mexican interests across the country. For example, Mexico recruited Latino lobbyists such as Toney Anaya, Jerry Apodaca, and Eduardo Hidalgo, and designed a general campaign to mobilize Latinos, border region communities, and the American private sector, especially through the pro-NAFTA U.S. business coalition. Nonetheless, Eisenstadt argues that despite the $37 million spent by Mexico in its lobby over a three-year period, NAFTA's approval was the result of President Clinton's congressional-vote-buying campaign.

Eisenstadt concludes that lobbying in Washington no longer guarantees a favorable outcome. A better way to influence the legislators, he argues, is through direct contact with their constituencies, especially given today's communications technology. Nevertheless, because of the complexity of the bilateral relation, he concludes that Mexico's lobby has become a key instrument in defending Mexican interests in Washington.

Jesús Velasco further analyzes Mexico's lobbying effort by exploring the alliance between the Mexican government and American think tanks. Velasco shows that a central component of the Mexican strategy to promote NAFTA in the United States was to have Mexican perspectives penetrate American think tanks. He concentrates his analysis on five institutions—the Center for Strategic and International Studies, the Heritage Foundation, the Hudson Institute, the Institute for International Economics, and the Brookings Institution—while also considering the activities of individual researchers and other academic institutions.

To place his analysis within the proper historical context, Velasco analyzes the contemporary American political environment to demonstrate that during the current political era ideas have become an important variable in the American decision-making process. He notes, for example, that in the 1970s think tanks emerged as powerful institutions. Velasco also shows the role played by corporations and foundations in the birth and development of think tanks, and he points out that some of the corporations that financed these institutes also supported NAFTA. Thus, he makes clear that ideas—in this case pro-NAFTA ideas—have material interests. However, he argues that while the corporations did not impose their views on the think tanks, the ideology of the latter quite often coincide with their benefactors' views.

In the second half of his chapter, Velasco examines the Mexican strategy to promote NAFTA in the United States. Mexico believed that think tanks would be very helpful as promoters of Mexican interests in the United States because of their close contact with U.S. members of Congress and their staffs, and because they can organize study groups involving legislators and business organizations. In a similar vein, Mexican officials believed that think tanks and their researchers were both creators of public opinion and able to influence public opinion leaders. Therefore, American think tanks were included in two key areas of the Mexican strategy: congressional relations and the communications campaign.

Velasco reveals the way that Mexico established its first contact with think tanks, how the Mexican government courted key members of these organizations and other academics, and the kind of advice these scholars provided to Mexico. He also presents evidence of the kind of events sponsored by these organizations and the type of arguments presented by them to promote pro-NAFTA viewpoints in the United States. Likewise, Velasco describes the rewards offered by Mexican officials to think tanks and academics.

Velasco also evaluates the impact of think tanks on the enactment of NAFTA using two empirical tests. First, he discusses the outcome of an electronic search of approximately 580 American newspapers from 1990 to 1994. In this, he examines the number of citations in which the five think tanks he studied and two anti-NAFTA think tanks were quoted in relation to NAFTA. He also analyzes the use of "think tankers" as congressional witnesses. His findings reveal that think tanks were not central actors in the NAFTA decision. Nonetheless, Velasco argues that the think tanks helped build the intellectual arguments that shaped pro-NAFTA public opinion. He concludes that the "level of attention Mexico conferred on U.S. scholars was a unique episode in recent Mexican history."

In the next chapter, Victor Godínez examines recent negotiations between the Mexican government and the American financial community. Godínez focuses on the Mexican financial crises of 1982, 1986, and 1995. He argues that beginning in 1982, Mexico established a "recurrent pattern of financial negotiations" with the American government and U.S. banking and financial institutions. The main purpose of this chapter is to demonstrate that these negotiations have not only shaped the changes experienced by Mexico's economy since the 1980s, but also the rise to power of the technocrats.

According to Godínez, Mexico's periodic economic breakdowns have produced a stable relationship between Mexican officials and the American financial community. A central feature of this relationship is the absence of disagreements between the two sides. Thus, Mexico and the American financial community have established a regime of "cooperation and understanding." Godínez also explores one of the structural causes of this cooperative regime— Mexico's negotiating position.

After the crisis of economic import substitutions, Godínez argues, a new political group seized power in Mexico. This group unanimously supported a market-oriented economic position and implemented the so-called Mexican "modernization project." One of the main features of this group is that its members share the viewpoints of the American financial community, thus reinforcing the interests of both parties.

Subsequently, Godínez explores the pattern of the Mexican negotiations. He asserts that Mexico entered into them in 1982, 1986, and 1995 from a weak economic position and urgently in need of help. Moreover, he argues Mexico has lacked a rigorous international economic policy design in these negotiations, and that the negotiating power of the Mexican officials diminished with each consecutive crisis. In 1995, he adds, the terms of U.S. aid were determined by the Clinton administration and the U.S. Congress in the face of passivity among the Mexican negotiators.

Edward Williams' chapter examines one of the most fragile and obscure issues of the bilateral relation—labor cooperation. Williams asserts that recent times have witnessed the intensification of U.S.–Mexican relations and the creation of a new nexus of cooperation between the two countries. The exception in this new political climate is organized labor. The Confederation of Mexican Workers (CTM) and the AFL-CIO have refused to work together. Williams examines the North American Agreement on Labor Cooperation (NAALC) with the aim of showing that this agreement has not improved that relationship. Furthermore he argues that the agreement has accentuated the differences and complicated the relationship.

For Williams the debility of the labor movements in Mexico and the United States explains the lack of cooperation between the CTM and the AFL-CIO. The causes of this weakness are varied, but at least three features are shared by the two countries: the emergence of "neoliberalism, the changing characteristics of the two nations' economies, and the disreputable image of labor leaders."

Williams also notes that NAFTA accentuated the issue of jobs. The major labor unions, however, have different perspectives on the issue. While American labor organizations opposed the agreement because of the threat of job losses, the CTM went along with the Mexican government on the assumption that NAFTA would create jobs in Mexico. The job issue, together with the nationalism of both labor movements, the protectionist impulse of American labor organizations, and the authoritarian nature of the Mexican political system mix in a fertile ground to explain the absence of agreements between the AFL-CIO and the CTM.

In other words, NAFTA and the NAALC have further polarized the fragile relationship between the labor organizations. Williams concludes that three factors may alter the relation between the two movements: "the increasing influence of binational social action groups in the relationship; an evolving sense of community encompassing U.S. and Mexican workers; and a change of leadership and policies emanating from the top of the two union movements."

Jorge I. Domínguez's concluding chapter analyzes this volume's contributions from the perspective of state-based explanations, society-based explanations, and institution-based explanations. According to Domínguez, state-based schemes explain presidentialism and the principal decisions taken by both governments concerning NAFTA. Society-based frameworks complement state-based arguments, illuminating topics such as immigration and the "capacity of Mexican Americans to influence their communities of origin in Mexico." Institution-based approaches help us understand the increasing presence of the Mexican agenda in the United States, the changes in Mexico's political

institutions that have facilitated the participation of nongovernmental organizations in the decision-making process, and the creation of new international
institutions to mitigate the new American influence in Mexico.

Domínguez conducts a journey through the different essays included in this
book, noting how they can be studied using the lenses of these three approaches.
He reads the chapters of Knight, Chabat, Eisenstadt, Velasco, and Williams
through the eyes of the state-based approach. He understands the work of de la
Garza and Godínez using the society-based explanation, and reviews the work of
González Gutiérrez employing the institution-based framework. He concludes
that, despite the significant convergence of the elites of both countries, we can
expect considerable conflicts at the nonelite level, which will provide "the
political foundations for intergovernmental conflict."

Together, these chapters plainly indicate how substantially Mexican foreign
policy has changed since the mid-1980s. Clearly, Mexico will no longer be able
to withdraw behind the rhetoric of sovereignty and nonintervention. How
effective will its new policy be? We leave that question for future studies, but
we hope that the issues raised in this volume will lay a foundation that will
benefit those who try to answer it.

Chapter 1

Dealing with the American Political System: An Historical Overview 1910–1995

Alan Knight

By way of contributing to the theme of this important volume—the Mexican factor in U.S. politics—I shall attempt a brief résumé (analytical rather than narrative) of U.S.–Mexican relations through the "short" twentieth century, roughly 1910–1995. The scope is, of course, excessive, hence the coverage will be superficial. I also admit to two failings (there are others about which I will keep quiet): first, a relative lack of expertise concerning the latter half of the period; second, a patchy knowledge of the inner workings of U.S. politics. This is not exactly a surprising confession for a historian of revolutionary Mexico, but it means that I am frequently trespassing on unfamiliar ground. If there is a compensating advantage in having the perspective of a historian of Mexico, it might be to provide a longer-term perspective of the problem, and thus to avoid "immediatist" ahistorical distortions. There may also be some point in a European participating in a volume dominated by gringos and Mexicans (Middlebrook and Rico 1986: 4).

I shall organize the discussion under four headings: salience, congruence, attitudes, and actors. The first two headings relate to the general pattern of U.S.–Mexican relations in the period and address major—perhaps "structural"—questions: how big a part has Mexico played in U.S. politics (that is, its salience) and to what extent has Mexico conformed to U.S. hopes, prejudices, and expectations (its congruence)? The third and fourth headings involve a closer look at U.S. politics, and the part played by the Mexican factor in U.S. politics; the attitudes and actors are largely American and the analysis tends to be less structural, more conjunctural. It may seem that the first two themes (salience and congruence) are less relevant to the specific topic of this book. However, I would justify their inclusion in terms of their structural importance. Salience and congruence have usually been the product of given circumstances largely beyond Mexican control, whereas attitudes and actors have been susceptible to a degree of Mexican massaging. An analysis that placed great emphasis on agency—on the Mexican capacity to mold opinions, processes, and events—would focus squarely on attitudes and agencies. However, I tend to take a more structural view of the U.S.–Mexican relationship, hence I think that the capacity of purposive agents to achieve their goals is often quite limited. (This applies particularly to Mexican agents, but also, to a lesser extent, to U.S. agents). Roughly, structures impose definite preconditions, within which agents have to work. Or, we might say, "men make history, but not in circumstances of their own choosing." It is therefore logical to start with the structures, then proceed to the agents.

One additional clarification is required. Historians are very keen on periodization. They do not like "timeless" analysis; they insist on locating arguments within historical narratives. Historiography advances to the beat of an insistent chronological drum. (Incidentally, on reading or re-reading a number of studies of U.S.–Mexican relations—not written by historians—I am struck by the extent to which the authors are also shackled to a narrative approach). Narrative is certainly a safe and sound approach. However, it often overlooks—or diffidently leaves to the reader—the crucial problems of evaluation and causality. We learn that a crisis or a détente occurs, but we are not told explicitly what was at stake, who was responsible, how significant the process was, and whether alternative outcomes were possible. While I do not claim to answer these questions here, I think they can best be raised—and history can best serve contemporary concerns—by preferring analysis to narrative. However, especially in view of the scope and complexity of the topic, analysis may require some preliminary narrative, or periodization. I shall therefore begin with a rapid synopsis that stresses the pivotal importance of the decade of the 1940s.

Prior to the 1940s, Mexico experienced first armed then institutional revolution; a major civil war was fought; an effective revolutionary state was gradually and painfully established. The revolution affected most areas of Mexico's national life, including its foreign relations: it was, as Robert Freeman Smith argues, the "first important challenge to the world order of the industrial/creditor powers and capitalistic nations made by an underdeveloped nation trying to assert control over its economy and reform its internal system" (Smith 1972: x). Mexico thus anticipated a challenge that the United States would repeatedly face in the decades to come (Blasier 1976; Kolko 1988). For about a generation, U.S.–Mexican relations were chiefly determined by the revolution, its aftermath, and American efforts to control, co-opt, or come to terms with this pioneer Third World challenge. The petroleum dispute was the extreme example (Meyer 1972). However, the United States which confronted the Mexican Revolution was, as yet, an incipient rather than an established great power. "Imperialist" in its relations with the nations of the Caribbean area, it was not yet an "imperial" power in the Western Hemisphere, still less the world as a whole (Aron 1974: 252–260; Poitras 1990: 11–19).

The decade of the 1940s marked a decisive transformation in two respects. Mexico's phase of revolutionary reform came to an end, and a new political generation—civilian, technocratic, industrializing, anticommunist—took power. Belatedly recovering from the depression, the United States emerged as the arsenal of democracy, the chief belligerent and beneficiary of World War II. In 1895 Secretary of State Richard Olney had hollowly proclaimed U.S. hegemony in the Western Hemisphere ("today the United States is practically sovereign on this Continent and its fiat is law"); fifty years later his boast rang more true (Smith 1979: 30). U.S. economic power dwarfed its rivals (the British had beaten a final retreat from the southern cone) and U.S. military power, latent for most of the century, was now supreme. The United States controlled a third of world trade, a third of world production, and a third of world arms expenditures (Lowenthal 1992: 69). What is more, the sequence of World War and cold war helped to generalize U.S. cultural and economic norms throughout the continent. U.S. aid to Latin America was paltry—until the late 1950s Latin America received less than the Benelux countries—but U.S. corporations now accelerated their penetration of the continent; the U.S. government, having successfully deployed "cultural" weapons, such as film, in the service of the war effort, maintained its cultural offensive during the ensuing years of fragile peace (Lundestad 1990: 48; Fein 1995; Rabe 1988: 18, 33). U.S. hegemony was, of course, contested—the Cuban Revolution being the most recalcitrant case—but it proved durable, especially compared to U.S. hegemonic pretensions elsewhere, for example in Southeast Asia. Despite recurrent nationalist challenges, sporadic Soviet probes, and its own supposed economic decline during the 1970s, the United States reserved and, in the 1980s, arguably reasserted its hegemony in Latin America. Debt negotiations and direct interventions in the circum-Caribbean displayed that, if U.S. hegemony had declined, it nevertheless remained formidable.

This was particularly true in the case of Mexico. U.S.–Mexican détente, incipient in the 1920s, tested in the 1930s, forged ahead during the decade of the war, producing what Howard Cline called "a ripe mature social entente that does not require public lovemaking to assure the participants and the world that all is well" (Cline 1965: 388). The heated controversies of the revolutionary era—oil, land reform, anticlericalism—gave way to more mundane and manageable issues: trade, migration, the Chamizal, foot-and-mouth disease, shrimp, tuna, dolphins, and drugs (Schmitt 1974: 193–256). The threat of intervention, which last reared its head in 1927, disappeared; U.S. pressure now took more discreet, though not necessarily less effective, forms, in which economic leverage combined with what Centeno calls "intellectual isomorphism" (Centeno 1994: 23, 119). NAFTA and the Washington consensus were the logical conclusions. Confrontation thus gave way to détente and integration, and with recent integration came a subregionalization of Latin America whereby, even if Brazil or Argentina diversified their external links, Mexico opted for closer economic, financial, political, and even cultural ties with the United States (Whitehead 1986: 89).

We can therefore note some initial paradoxes. The early period (c. 1910–1945), punctuated by conflicts, gave Mexico a higher profile in U.S. politics, even though the U.S. economic presence in Mexico was threatened and declining. (Rippy [1958: 36–43] gives figures of U.S. investment in Mexico, at current prices, as: 1914: $853 million; 1930: $710 million; and 1943: $422 million). After the war, conflict receded and détente flourished. The United States, "imperial" and interventionist elsewhere in Latin America, especially the circum-Caribbean, coexisted amicably with Mexico and U.S. economic penetration forged ahead. Yet, as economic hegemony deepened, Mexico became a nonissue in American geopolitical thinking, which for some twenty years after 1945, displayed a remarkable cold war consensus (Middlebrook and Rico 1986: 32; Schoultz 1987: 13–14). Compared to Europe and Asia, Latin America was a lesser battleground of the cold war and, within Latin America, Guatemala, Cuba, and the Dominican Republic attracted more U.S. fear and loathing. Mexico— "something of a sideshow for the cold war"—enjoyed the benefits of anonymity (Niblo 1995: 211). Even when the U.S. foreign policy consensus began to fracture, as a result of Vietnam, Cuba, and Nixon's détente with both China and the USSR, U.S.–Mexican relations underwent no significant change, and—relatively speaking—Mexico still failed to capture headlines or provoke debates. It was not, in fact, until the (renewed) cold war petered out in the 1980s and Mexico itself weighed its traditional anchors and began to chart a new neoliberal course across a choppy sea, that U.S.–Mexican relations, typified by NAFTA, began to achieve a renewed salience in U.S. politics. The shift from salience (1910s–1940s) to low profile (1960s–1970s) and back to salience (1980s– present) thus depended principally on Mexican trends, but the changing capacities and perspectives of the United States, as well as the global geopolitical context, clearly affected the reactions of the *coloso del norte* to trends taking place south of the border.

Salience

With this rough periodization established, I will now enter somewhat more deeply into the whole 1910–1995 period, starting with the question of salience.

Sometimes Mexico was headline news in the United States, sometimes it scarcely figured. News coverage, of course, is far from being a balanced reflection of current issues; it is shot through with assumptions and prejudices. U.S. reporting on Mexico was often lurid and sensationalist (Mexican reporting on the United States was far from balanced and objective itself). Cornelius Vanderbilt described an antigovernment demonstration taking place on the Paseo de la Reforma on election day in July 1940, when, he claimed, "shots went wild" and "scores bit the dust;" one victim, conforming to the western style, toppled into the street from a two-story building. However, it was all "pure fiction;" Vanderbilt had left Mexico City four days before the election (Niblo 1995: 81). If this was freelance sensationalism, there were also concerted campaigns. Powerful U.S. interests, like the Hearst press, the oil companies, or the Catholic hierarchy, could determine what Americans read, though what Americans made of what they read is another matter (Britton 1988). Mexicans, applying their own experience abroad, sometimes assumed that the U.S. press obeyed government directives. Although this was usually mistaken, the U.S. government did impose tighter controls—both positive and negative—in wartime. Avila Camacho's lackluster image was therefore deliberately polished up by the spin doctors of the day.

Throughout the period down to the present, press coverage of Mexico tended to reflect major conjunctural events (rather than deep structural processes); it naturally focused heavily on American angles and it was also strongly affected by rival claims to Americans' attention (e.g., perceived threats to U.S. lives, property, and interests). During the armed revolution, the *New York Times* coverage of Mexico soared, especially with the 1914 Veracruz landing and the 1916 Punitive Expedition. Thereafter, it declined, as the European War absorbed attention and—overt, military—American involvement in Mexico receded (Knight 1987: 16).[1] There were later, lesser blips on the screen: the 1919 crisis, the 1927 war scare, and the 1938 oil expropriation. During the 1940s, as the United States and Mexico forged unusually tight bonds of political and economic cooperation, Mexico dropped from sight: unspectacular processes, however profound, were not the stuff of headlines. After 1945, other Third World countries and issues predominated: China, Cuba, Vietnam. Political crises within Mexico (e.g., 1968) stirred only a smidgen of interest, and it was not until the late 1980s and 1990s—with renewed political and economic crisis—that Mexico again started to figure as a lead story.

This pattern of coverage is reflected in political memoirs and standard international relations analyses. Wilson, Bryan, Lansing, Coolidge, Kellogg, Hull, and Roosevelt all had to pay ample attention to Mexico, which was both proximate and problematic. From Truman on, however, Mexico could, to an extent, be taken for granted. "After the Allied victory," Niblo writes, "U.S. diplomats quickly shifted their priorities, much to Mexico's consternation. A highly valued ally became a neighbor of minor importance" (Niblo 1995: 284).

Eisenhower, campaigning for office in 1952, admitted as much: having "frantically wooed Latin America" during the war, the United States "proceeded to forget these countries just as fast" (Rabe 1988: 6). As president, however, Eisenhower only partially remedied the situation: his first administration "neglected and took for granted U.S. neighbors in the western hemisphere;" his memoirs "gave only a cursory and defensive review of inter-American relations" (Rabe 1988: 3). Latin America as a whole was less vexatious than Europe and Asia (hence the lack of a Marshall Plan for the Americas), and statesmen nurtured in a northeastern Europhile environment had difficulty focusing on their own hemisphere. George Kennan, the intellectual begetter of "containment," made his first trip to Latin America in 1950 ("I had never been there. I wanted to see something of it before I left government.") and he did not like what he saw. Mexico City was "disturbed, sultry, and menacing;" Caracas, "jammed in among its bilious-yellow mountains, appalled me with its screaming, honking traffic jams, its incredibly high prices, its feverish economy debauched by oil money." Rio was "repulsive," Lima prompted the "reflection that it had not rained in the place for twenty-nine years and . . . that some of the dirt had presumably been there, untouched, for all that time" (Kennan 1967: 476–479). Twenty years later another cerebral statesman, Henry Kissinger, was no less forthright when he slapped down the Chilean foreign minister at a White House lunch: "Mr. Minister, . . . you come here speaking of Latin America, but this is not important. Nothing important can come from the South. History has never been produced in the South. The axis of history starts in Moscow, goes to Bonn, crosses over to Washington, and then goes to Tokyo. What happens in the South is of no importance. You're wasting your time" (Francis 1988: 30).

Kissinger's recent magnum opus, *Diplomacy*, confirms these assumptions (Kissinger 1994). Mexico gets five references in 912 pages, compared to 26 for Bulgaria. Argentina and Brazil get two each, Peru and Paraguay none. The one partial exception, as might be expected, is Cuba (19 references). Latin America achieved salience in U.S. politics to the extent that it entered cold war politics: Guatemala, Cuba, the Dominican Republic, Chile, and Nicaragua were therefore exceptions to this tale of neglect, although, save for the Cuban case, U.S. attention was short-lived and crisis-driven.

Mexico's relative obscurity, or low salience, depended partly on its own good behavior (in 1951 the Alemán government assured the State Department that "the United States could count on its support in the event of a showdown with the Soviet Union") (Niblo 1995: 249), partly on the bad behavior that distracted U.S. attention elsewhere and made Mexico seem safe in comparison. These two factors—Mexico's reputation and the global context—therefore need to be analyzed in conjunction. Since the enunciation of the Monroe Doctrine, the United States had sought to ward off European incursions in the Americas, while claiming a supposedly "special relationship" with its hemispheric neighbors. A series of perceived external threats jarred American sensibilities: in the 1820s it was the Holy Alliance; in the 1860s, the French Second Empire; in the 1890s, British imperialism; in the 1910s and again in the 1930s, German and Japanese ambitions; after 1945, Soviet expansionism. Throughout, O'Donnell observes, the United States displayed a "paternalistic desire to monopolize or jealously control any relationship between its wards and third countries—which, given the terms of the relationship, are necessarily viewed as hostile intruders" (O'Donnell 1986: 355). Such external threats, often grossly exaggerated, sometimes for electoral reasons, could provoke American retaliation against supposed Latin American clients/victims of foreign imperialism: hence McKinley's, Roosevelt's, and Wilson's interventions in the Caribbean and Central America; the ousters of Arbenz and Bosch; Reagan's war against the Sandinistas.

In the case of Mexico, however, the outcome was different. First, Mexico was much less easily "intervened" than Cuba, Haiti, or Nicaragua (and they were no pushovers). Even gung-ho gringo imperialists thought twice about invading Mexico; they remembered Pershing's fruitless pursuit through the sierras of Chihuahua in 1916–1917. The Nicaraguan intervention of 1927–1928 had required six thousand military personnel; an invasion of Mexico, it was reckoned, would need half a million (Knight 1987: 123). Second, though Mexican leaders were skillful at playing off U.S. and Old World powers against one another, they did not carry their Old World flirtations too far. Carranza had no truck with the Zimmermann telegram (Gilderhus 1986: 89); Cárdenas was prepared to sell boycotted oil to the Axis powers, but he left the United States in no doubt that he was a staunch antifascist (Knight 1987: 17) and post–1940 administrations readily distanced themselves from Moscow—though not from Havana (Blasier 1987: 22–27). Mexico therefore avoided touching that most sensitive of U.S. nerves: fear of foreign subversion close to home, of "trouble in our backyard" (Diskin 1983: xv). Mexico was sometimes troublesome, but this was homegrown trouble, as Mexican as cactus and tequila. Hostile U.S. interests—the businessmen and Catholic spokesmen of the 1920s and 1930s— tried to incite fear of a Red Mexico taking its orders from Moscow, but in the face of massive evidence to the contrary, they could never convince a skeptical or indifferent public (Knight 1987: 128–129, 134–136). This was a lesson Arbenz or Castro would have done well to learn: domestic reformism was much more likely to elicit American hostility and aggression if a presumption of Soviet interference was permitted. After 1945, U.S. fears of Mexican radicalism were few; they were stirred, only briefly and fitfully, by Echeverría's Third World posturing. By now, in fact, Mexico was seen as a bastion of capitalist—and maybe democratic—stability. Even the CIA gave Mexico a clean bill of health: "only in Mexico," the agency reported in 1951, "is the existing political machine . . . proof against overthrow by demagogic opposition" (Niblo 1995: 200). If, in the 1920s, a radical Mexico seemed to be subverting a conservative Nicaragua, sixty years later the pattern was neatly reversed. Even when Mexico displayed its independence in foreign policy—toward Cuba or Central

America—shrewd Americans realized that this was, for the Mexicans, good domestic politics, and something the United States could manage to live with (Meyer and Vásquez 1982: 206).

Size, coupled with prickly nationalism, made Mexico a tough proposition to coerce; Mexico's stance on major geopolitical issues (the two world wars, the Cold War) also deterred aggressive U.S. action. During World War I, Ambassador Henry P. Fletcher commented, his task was "to keep Mexico quiet, and it was done" (Smith 1972: 93). During World War II, which followed a period of deepening détente between the United States and Mexico, Ambassador Messersmith and his rapidly expanding embassy staff went much further, enveloping Mexico in the U.S. war effort, promoting political, economic, and cultural relations, thus ensuring a safe southern flank for the duration—and beyond (Niblo 1995). Domestic political trends in Mexico, combined with intelligent U.S. diplomacy, thus ensured that Mexico would not only evade outright U.S. intervention but also turn global conflicts to its own advantage.[2] U.S. hemispheric paranoia—what we might call the Monroe syndrome—which doomed Arbenz and debilitated Castro, served to deter rather than provoke U.S. intervention in Mexico, even when Mexico was pursuing reformist and nationalist policies. It helped, of course, that Mexico pursued these policies prior to 1945, when the chief external threat came from Germany and Japan and that, after 1945, as the Soviet Union supplanted the Axis powers, Mexico obligingly shifted to the right. This leads me to my second consideration: congruence.

Congruence

Following Howard Cline, I have elsewhere argued that Mexico's capacity to co-exist relatively peacefully with the United States is in part a product of the congruence of the two political systems (Cline 1965: 214; Knight 1987: 4–14). Throughout the twentieth century Mexican and U.S. politics have tended to march roughly in step. Of course, neither country is a political monolith, hence I am not postulating neat sequences. Rather, I am pointing to comparable shifts in the political center of gravity on both sides of the border. This can be seen most easily by comparing administrations, although, of course, congruence goes deeper than that and relates to phases of global political economy. The *Porfiriato* roughly coincided with America's Gilded Age, the era of big business, of populist defeat, and of Republican hegemony (hence Presidents Hayes through Taft, 1877–1913). Madero came to power as Progressivism peaked in the United States; his program displayed a distinct Progressive tinge, being democratic, reformist, concerned for social evils, yet reluctant to challenge the logic of capitalism. Madero shared Woodrow Wilson's liberal idealism, as well as his disappointment as idealism ran aground on the rocks of war and power politics. The Sonorans, Obregón and Calles (though certainly more radical than their Republican contemporaries Harding and Coolidge), had a high regard for the organizing principles and entrepreneurial opportunities of the market; Sonoran politics also placed considerable emphasis on forms of "status" politics (anticlericalism, temperance, nationalism) which, *mutatis mutandis*, had their North American counterparts (e.g., nativism, Prohibition, anti-Catholicism).

On both sides of the border, however, the 1930s depression curtailed "status" politics and induced new economic measures: greater state intervention in the economy, collectivist experiments, a government alliance with organized labor, hence conflicts with capital, a shakeout of the Supreme Court, and a measure of party realignment (Hofstadter 1955: 302–304). Cárdenas was, as Jean Meyer put it, *el FDR mexicano* who, like other Latin American leaders, professed a profound regard for the president of the United States (Meyer 1979: 11; Rabe 1988: 12; Blasier 1976: 121). With World War II and the cold war, Mexico and the United States again experienced comparable transformations: a retreat from the pro-labor, collectivist measures of the 1930s; a switch to policies favoring business; a political repudiation of the "official left" (Cardenistas and New Dealers); the proscription of Communists in both politics and the unions. This shift, spanning the crucial decade of the 1940s, was—as I have already suggested—particularly profound; it helped ensure the "ripe mature social entente" of the 1950s and 1960s. But the long postwar period can be seen as well in terms of loosely congruent subperiods: stable, low-inflation growth during the 1950s (Ruiz Cortines, Eisenhower); a modest shift to the left with Kennedy and López Mateos, both of whom had to confront the challenge of the Cuban Revolution; radical challenges to the status quo in the later 1960s and 1970s, which in turn contributed to the conservative (neoliberal) agenda of the 1980s, characterized by stateshrinking, an abandonment of entitlement policies, and a new reverence for the market (hence PRIstroika, the "Reagan Revolution," NAFTA). Perhaps now, in the mid–1990s, as the Salinas miracle is debunked and President Clinton takes the fight to a faltering conservative Congress, we are witnessing the turning of the neoliberal tide and the beginning of a new chapter in this long story of qualified congruence.

I stress "qualified" because I am not, of course, arguing for carbon-copy congruence in societies as diverse and different as the United States and Mexico. The collective *ejido* was a very different proposition from the New-Deal–era Agricultural Adjustment Administration's farm support policy; U.S. students' protests directed against an overseas war were not the same as Mexican students' protests, which targeted domestic abuses. The killings at Kent State and Tlatelolco must be differentiated as well as compared. So, too, in today's era of neoliberal consensus: even if rhetoric and prescription are similar on both sides of the border, the United States has the luxury of diluting the strong medicine it prescribes for others. Hence the U.S. deficit drags on, while Mexico has twice in fifteen years slashed government spending with Draconian commitment. The United States' fiscal hypocrisy—"do as I say, not as I do"—bears comparison with its better known political hypocrisy.[3] Despite these caveats, the fact of political congruence is striking and, I think, it helps explain why U.S.–Mexican conflicts have been less fierce and less frequent than they might otherwise have been.

The potential for counterfactual apocalypses is considerable. It was, for example, providential that Cárdenas governed while FDR was in the White House—and Josephus Daniels in the U.S. embassy in Mexico City. One need only substitute the names of, say, Ronald Reagan and John Gavin, to see how things might have turned out differently. This may be a somewhat phony comparison, since each of these actors was a product of his time: FDR and Cárdenas could coexist because both lived through and were influenced by the Depression and the rise of fascism. To a large extent, congruence was generated by common experiences rather than direct mimicry. Mexico did not slavishly follow the United States (still less vice versa); rather, both groped toward roughly common solutions to shared problems. However, different—often worse—outcomes were feasible: the Argentine response to depression and fascism contrasted with that of Mexico; it was also much less congruent, or isomorphic, with the North American response. From the 1930s through the 1950s Argentina stuck in the American craw in a way Mexico rarely did (Rabe 1988: 13–14, 29, 36).

This comparison raises the interesting but difficult question of causality. If congruence smoothed the path of U.S.–Mexican relations, what caused congruence? The most obvious argument is that sheer proximity compelled Mexico, consciously or not, to toe the U.S. line, not just in foreign policy, but also in broader areas of domestic politics. Mexican policies roughly resembled American ones because Mexico had no choice. Either the United States forced Mexico to follow suit, or Mexican policy makers were ineluctably drawn to emulate U.S. norms and policies. Emulation was proof of U.S. hegemony: "elites in secondary states buy into and internalize norms that are articulated by the hegemon and therefore pursue policies consistent with the hegemon's notion of international order" (Ikenberry and Kupchan 1990: 283). This argument is only partially valid for the pre–1945 period, since, of all the Latin American countries, it was precisely Mexico, on America's doorstep, that pioneered radical policies of social reform and economic nationalism that the United States disliked. American pressure certainly inhibited those policies, but it could not abort them. The United States had to come to terms with the Mexican Revolution, and—although the revolution also had to come to terms with the United States—the final arrangement did not represent a craven sellout of revolutionary principles.

Furthermore, to the extent that the United States was capable of blunting the revolutionary thrust, it did so less by outright coercion than by "constructive engagement."[4] The period of violent revolution, which saw several U.S. armed interventions in Mexico (1914, 1916–1917, 1919), was not a success story for U.S. coercive policy. Neither the Veracruz landing nor the Punitive Expedition achieved their goals. On the other hand, as the revolutionary state began to consolidate itself—and governments sought to secure arms, recognition, loans, and investment—so U.S. approval counted for more. Obregón incurred fierce criticism for the Bucareli agreement with the United States; Calles was obliged to compromise with the oil companies; and Cárdenas, boldly expropriating those companies, had to pay a heavy financial and political price (Knight 1992). To the extent that the revolutionary state remained a committed actor in the capitalist world economy—and did not, like Cuba, retreat into the socialist bloc—so it was bound to experience similar economic cycles (recession, recovery, boom) and experiment with similar economic policies.

The United States was not afraid to use economic leverage against Mexico, and generally found it more effective than the threat of coercion: "the use of loans to mold Mexican policies was far more effective than force" (Niblo 1995: 202). U.S. banker Thomas W. Lamont summed this up in tones of plutocratic paternalism: "you could lead them [the Mexicans] around the world with a lump of sugar but you could not drive them an inch" (Smith 1972: 190). U.S. influence over Mexico therefore grew in periods of détente and economic collaboration: the 1920s, 1940s, 1980s, and 1990s. (We may note that, with the possible exception of the 1920s, these have also been periods of socioeconomic polarization in Mexico; when the rich got richer, the poor poorer). The height of Mexican "dependency" was probably achieved during World War II; however, the U.S. government exerted its economic power cautiously—first, because it feared offending an important wartime ally, and second because it was blessed with unusually shrewd representatives and policy makers: George Messersmith, Laurence Duggan, Merwin Bohan. After 1945, as Mexico receded from importance, the quality of representation slumped (Niblo 1995: 284). Today, U.S. economic leverage has obviously grown apace, dramatically accelerated by NAFTA and the 1994 bailout of the Mexican economy. Now, however, no wartime imperatives prevail; cold war considerations have faded; and, I would argue, Washington's contemporary "lumpen intellectuals and policymakers" are less shrewdly statesmanlike and probably more afraid of electoral retribution than were their counterparts of fifty years ago (Petras and Morley 1990: 44–45). Conceivably, U.S. hegemony today will be cruder, brasher, and more capricious in its impact than it was fifty years ago.

So long as the Mexican state—even during its most "revolutionary" days—was content to remain within the fold of capitalism, U.S. economic leverage was bound to count. What Nora Hamilton, analyzing Cardenismo, terms the "limits of state autonomy"—the limits beyond which the Cardenista state could not go without upsetting the capitalist applecart—were set in part by the United States, as well as by Mexican capitalist interests (Hamilton 1982). To put it differently, the "structural dependence of the state on capital" necessarily involved a degree of Mexico depending on the United States. During the 1930s and 1940s, this economic dependence was somewhat offset by U.S. geopolitical concerns (fear of the Axis powers), as well as Mexican "backwardness" (the large rural sector cushioned recession and Mexico was already debarred from international credit). On both counts, Mexico today appears to be more dependent, and more vulnerable.

While the United States was well aware of its economic leverage and exploited it repeatedly, this did not necessarily incur Mexican resentment and resistance. Or, at the very least, Mexican policy makers regarded this leverage as a fact of life against which it was pointless to rail. As a result, the congruence that has characterized U.S.–Mexican relations, especially in the economic field, has often been the result of Mexican initiatives, not simply U.S. impositions. Obregón and Calles genuinely admired American industry and favored American investment. Cárdenas equated his own project with that of the New Deal, stressed that the oil nationalization was exceptional, and "recognized that foreign technology was central to the industrial push" (Niblo 1995: 40–42, 48–50). The repudiation of "socialism" and "exotic doctrines" and the espousal of probusiness policies on the part of Avila Camacho and Miguel Alemán were autonomous decisions, the products of domestic class and sectoral alignments. Americans naturally applauded these outcomes (and waxed lyrical about Avila Camacho) (Niblo 1995: 152), but they did not single-handedly bring them about. The best example is also the most recent: the intellectual isomorphism generated by U.S. higher education and the (economic) *cursus honorum* that top Mexican decision makers—Salinas, Aspe, Serra Puche, and Zedillo—now characteristically pursue and which has made them, in neoliberal terms, more Catholic than the Pope (Centeno 1994: 23–24, 119–120). NAFTA was not forced on Mexico—certainly not by the United States; it was less an "imperialist imposition" than a "profoundly domestic" turnaround, the result of "a massive shift in the ideological orientation of key political and economic actors" in Mexico (Pastor and Wise 1994: 463, 469–471).

The U.S. role in these policy shifts was significant, though subtle and unspectacular. Ambassador Morrow allegedly "took the Secretary of Finance under his wing and taught him finance" (Smith 1972: 263). In the late 1940s, Robert Gardner, vice-president of the World Bank, similarly tutored PEMEX executives (Niblo 1995: 251–252). Nelson Rockefeller, as both statesman and entrepreneur, inculcated liberal capitalist values in Latin America in general and Mexico in particular. Today, such individual efforts have given way to the collective pedagogy of Ivy League universities. In all these cases, of course, tuition would have been futile had not the pupils shown willing. Why, though, did Montes de Oca or PEMEX executives bother to listen? Why did Calles and even Cárdenas accept a greater degree of American tutelage than, say, Peron or Castro? Why does the Mexican elite now choose to send its sons (less often its daughters) to Stanford, MIT, or Harvard? Why, to rephrase the question in more impersonal terms, did the Mexican political system, for all its revolutionary origins, permit this recurrent congruence between Mexican and U.S. policies/ projects?

Geographical proximity, cultural osmosis across the border, the gravitational pull of a powerful and rich society that appeared to offer both collective models and individual advantages—all these are valid reasons that could be explored. Niblo's comment on the 1940s rings even truer for the 1990s: "it was when dominant theories of development interacted with vested interests that a truly formidable combination emerged" (Niblo 1995: 224). There is, however, a danger of exaggerating direct Mexican dependence and mimicry. After all, Cuba was geographically close and culturally even more intimate with the United States, yet ended up repudiating the suffocating embrace of the United States. I would therefore suggest two additional factors.

First, the Mexican Revolution served over time to fortify a vigorous domestic capitalism; or, in grand, over-simple and distinctly unfashionable terms, it constituted a "bourgeois" revolution (Knight 1985). It helped integrate a national market, broke up particularist—even some "feudal"—obstacles to growth, and promoted free wage labor. Though there were moves toward a more collectivist, quasi-socialist economy in the 1930s, these were limited and reversible. Unlike the Cuban Revolution, but like the Bolivian, the Mexican Revolution bolstered capitalism, and made collaboration with the capitalist United States feasible and even mutually attractive. Thus, particularly in its pre–cold war, pre-"imperial" days, the United States found that this was a revolution with which one could do business, both literally and metaphorically. Indeed, some Americans (not necessarily rabid socialists) welcomed it: even President Wilson applauded the Mexicans' efforts to achieve their own emancipation through revolution; in the 1930s New Dealers like Josephus Daniels convinced themselves that Cárdenas was doing much the same as FDR. Needless to say, no one saw Peron as a southern cone liberal; and, though Castro was briefly seen in these terms by some U.S. analysts (not, of course, by the percipient Richard Nixon), the honeymoon did not last. The United States certainly sweetened the Mexican—and Bolivian—Revolutions, thus making them more palatable to American tastes. But sweetening was possible only because these were "bourgeois" revolutions, dedicated to goals that American statesmen understood: a Jeffersonian promotion of democracy and an independent farmer class; a Hamiltonian development of national industry; a Franklinesque emphasis on education and the separation of church and state. The American Revolution itself was a relevant precedent, which U.S. observers like Wilson had in mind. In short, the Mexican Revolution was, at least to a degree, a "Lockean" revolution, of the kind that the United States approved.[5] Hence the contrasting Wilsonian responses to Carranza and Mexico on the one hand, and Lenin and Russia on the other. Hence the Mexican Revolution escaped the fate of the Cuban.

Comprehension and congruence were all the more feasible since, prior to the 1940s, the cold war had not yet diluted and distorted America's revolutionary sympathies. The United States could still identify, to a degree, with democratic, popular, and nationalist struggles. After the 1940s watershed, however, such struggles tended to assume more Marxist forms and—more important, perhaps—they were seen in such terms by an increasingly paranoid United States. Bolivia, being distant, landlocked, and economically marginal, got away with it; Guatemala, in contrast, became an early victim of cold war conservatism, even though Arbenz's policies were not radically different from Cárdenas'. Cuba also escaped, but not for want of American trying, and at the cost of a debilitating boycott. Thus, both the character and the timing of the Mexican Revolution guaranteed it a more tolerant response from its northern neighbor.

But a second feature was also important. Compared to the states of Central America and the Caribbean, Mexico was not only larger (hence harder to "intervene"), it was also a more culturally autonomous nation-state, and the Mexican Revolution, like other "bourgeois" revolutions, served not only to transform the political economy, but also to reinforce the political culture of the nation-state. Building on older precedents—Creole patriotism, Guadalupismo, Juarista liberal nationalism—the revolution helped *forjar patria* (forge a nation), making mid-twentieth century Mexico a more integrated nation-state than many of its Latin American counterparts (Mallon 1995; Knight 1985). This process—helped along by recurrent conflicts with the United States—gave Mexico the discursive weapons with which to resist U.S. cultural hegemony, even as U.S. economic hegemony was consolidated. Both revolutionary and nonrevolutionary (e.g., Catholic) traditions played a part; there were, crudely put, both left- and right-wing, Jacobin and Catholic, versions of patriotic anti-imperialism. The revolutionary Left, pledged to the nationalist constitution of 1917, harked back to 1810 and 1857, to Hidalgo and Juárez. Though they sympathized with some progressive aspects of American society—Obregón and Calles admired the U.S. model—in the 1920s and 1930s returning migrants brought with them not only radios and sewing machines but also radical notions about citizenship, political participation, and union organization (Craig 1983: 91–94). They also resisted perceived U.S. interference and, quite logically, their attempts to implement U.S. democratic norms brought them into conflict with U.S. interests, such as oil companies and landowners. (We have here a specific example of a global phenomenon, whereby the export of American ideals—which has been a staple of U.S. foreign policy—paradoxically constitutes a threat to U.S. interests overseas.)

March 1938 was, of course, the apotheosis of this revolutionary nationalism. Although thereafter it went into decline and, by the 1990s, it appears as a quaint period piece,[6] it played an important historical role in buffering Mexican sovereignty at a time when smaller, neighboring countries were experiencing U.S. interventions. Where Central American and Caribbean

elites had been prepared to flirt with U.S. intervention—even conniving with
invasion—Mexican elites were restrained by a vigorous nationalist tradition. On
the contrary, Mexican elites were constantly afraid of appearing as *vendepatrias*
cats-paws of the gringos. The historical list is long (Knight 1987: 31–33);
Castañeda argues that, even today, "American support in Mexican politics . . .
continues to be more a liability than an advantage" (Pastor and Castañeda 1988:
37). Perceptive U.S. observers realized this and made allowances: hence
Morrow's preference for cajolery rather than coercion (Smith 1972: 244–265) or
George Messersmith's tactful approach to wartime collaboration (Niblo 1995:
89–91). Mexican sensitivities were the greater because of the existence of a
strong Catholic, "conservative" nationalism, which competed with its revolutionary, Jacobin counterpart. Mexican Catholics could invoke a set of counter-
symbols, drawn from colonial New Spain, such as the thought of Lucas Alamán
and the example of Agustín Iturbide, and from the twentieth-century phenomenon of Hispanism—including Franquismo. For some Catholics, the
revolution was traitorously gringophile and pro-Protestant. Vasconcelos therefore
blamed the revolution for polluting Mexico with a degenerate cultural *pochismo*,
and the Cristeros accused Calles of selling out to Mexico's hereditary Anglo-
Saxon enemy (Knight 1987: 39–46).

Two consequences followed. First, Right and Left, revolutionaries and
Catholics, vied with each other to prove their patriotic credentials. Odd
arguments ensued. During the 1920s, the Catholics accused Calles of colluding
with the oil companies, while Calles accused the oil companies—with some
justification—of favoring the Cristeros (Meyer 1973: 276; Bailey 1974: 120).
March 1938 was crucial not just as an example of spontaneous patriotism (which
it was, to a degree), but also as a convenient rendezvous for these rival
nationalisms. Right and Left, church and state, were able to come together on
common patriotic ground, each cautiously recognizing the legitimacy of the
other, thus paving the way to the more durable détente of the 1940s (Knight
1992). Meanwhile, the existence of these competing patriotisms—unusually
strong, it would seem, in Mexico—acted as an insurance policy against
entreguismo (neither side wanted to be seen as selling out to the United States).
Even as economic collaboration forged ahead in the 1940s, Mexico jealously
defended her territorial sovereignty, of which the presence of Cárdenas in the War
Ministry was a reassuring guarantee.

In later years, of course, church and state came together, and their shared
antipathy to Communism inclined them more favorably to the United States.
Catholic and PANista opinion shed its anti-American, Franquista trappings,
while the postwar PRI broadly opted for collaboration with the United States—
most enthusiastically and unreservedly in the 1990s. I do not share the view,
common among critics of NAFTA, that economic integration per se poses a
mortal threat to Mexican nationality. The latter, fertilized during decades of
historical struggle and cultural invention, is too strong a plant, too deeply

rooted, to wither in the heat of a free trade agreement. However, there can be no doubt that the neoliberal project, of which NAFTA is an integral part, involves some diminution of Mexican political autonomy, which in turn touches sensitive nationalist nerves. The Zapatista rebellion obeyed many causes, many of them specific to Chiapas, but the timing and rhetoric of the uprising clearly reflected concerns about NAFTA, which drew upon these old traditions of Mexican nationalism. Zapatismo, like neo-Cardenismo, could justifiably and effectively play the nationalist card. The problem that both faced—and face—is that contemporary nationalism in Mexico and elsewhere runs counter to the imperatives of a hegemonic economic liberalism. In contrast to the 1930s, there is no credible economic nationalist project that can rival neoliberalism, while providing an economic counterpart to political or cultural nationalism. Today's neoliberals may seem like traitors but unless today's would-be nationalists can come up with an economic alternative—thus disproving the familiar refrain, "There is no alternative"—their nationalist critiques will continue to lack credibility.[7]

Attitudes

Thus far, the analysis has focused a good deal—perhaps excessively—on the Mexican side. I now wish to turn to the United States. It is a commonplace that nations are complex entities, and that assertions of U.S. interests, goals, policies, or achievements involve a large dose of reification. "The United States is hardly monolithic," Pastor reminds us; "its objectives are diverse" (Pastor and Castañeda 1988: 85). Any analysis of the role of Mexico in U.S. domestic politics and decision making must recognize the multiplicity of factors, even if (a) their complexity is such that precise conclusions are impossible and (b) the causal chains that result in particular decisions are often shrouded in obscurity. (Obscurity may result from lack of documentation or more basic epistemological problems).

As I have argued elsewhere, U.S. policy toward revolutionary Mexico was subject to multiple pressures and lobbies (Knight 1987: 91–101). In trying to make sense of this multiplicity, we may usefully distinguish between U.S. attitudes toward Mexico and U.S. actors, i.e., institutions or lobbies. The first could be discussed at enormous length. The analysis of U.S. foreign policy is replete with big umbrella concepts: moralism, realism, exceptionalism, pragmatism, providentialism, paranoia (Hunt 1987; Kissinger 1994: 36, 44, 48; Lundestad 1990: 11–17, 117, 139). A conventional distinction contrasts "realist" (realpolitik) and "idealist" approaches to U.S. foreign policy (in this case, toward Mexico). Wilson, FDR, and Carter (all Democrats, of course) are seen as more idealistic, i.e., influenced by normative notions of democracy, self-determination, sovereignty, human rights, while Taft, Coolidge, Eisenhower,

Nixon, and Reagan (all Republicans) would be seen as exponents of a realist concern for American self-interest, viewed geopolitically and/or economically. While there is some mileage in this familiar approach, it is open to question. Idealistic presidents did not neglect American power and self-interest (Wiarda 1986: 326). Even Wilson, I would argue, blended idealistic and realistic motivations, which were not necessarily incompatible and may even have been mutually reinforcing. Wilson's espousal of the revolution and repudiation of Huerta responded not only to (inflated) fears of British imperialism but also, and more importantly, responded to his considered belief that a stable, representative Mexican government (i.e., a revolutionary rather than a Huertista regime) was a better prospect for the United States, both economically and geopolitically (Knight 1987: 107–114). In this, I think, he was right. The Mexican regime did not conform to Wilson's liberal democratic principles, but it was more stable and representative than the *Porfiriato* (not to mention most other Latin American regimes), and, given the bourgeois nature of the revolution that gave it birth, it could profitably coexist with its capitalist northern neighbor. FDR's "idealism" was even more pragmatic: respect for Mexican sovereignty was strongly reinforced by fear of Axis expansion. Today, we find advocates of an idealistic human rights policy invoking self-interest as well as morality: an active policy on human rights in Latin America "is likely to promote global stability and, hence, U.S. interests" (Crahan 1986: 412, 428, 432–433).

Conversely, the roster of Republican realpolitikers reveals some strikingly unrealistic assumptions as well as a tendency, typical of U.S. diplomacy, to cloak power politics in moralistic garb, and thus to incur the charge of humbug and hypocrisy (Lundestad 1990: 24, 118). During the 1910s, Republicans berated Wilson for his feeble stance on Mexico and urged either the recognition of Huerta (who, I think, was bound to fall whatever the United States did) or, more egregiously, a hard-line policy involving U.S. threats and intervention—a policy that was advocated with scant regard for the scale of the operation or the likely consequences (Knight 1987: 116–130). During the 1920s, Republican administrations again flirted irresponsibly and counterproductively with intervention, branding Mexico a Bolshevik fellow-traveler which, in Kellogg's words, was "on trial before the world" (Knight 1987: 83; Smith 1972: 234–241). This hard line responded to several motives: the supposed defense of U.S. economic interests in Mexico; the exploitation of party advantage; the thirst for votes or newspaper circulation. It did not necessarily respond to a calm, realistic analysis of U.S.–Mexican relations. The chief exponent of real realism was Dwight Morrow who, in his shrewd, pragmatic, banker's way, took Mexican grievances seriously, flattered rather than threatened, and worked—successfully—for détente and cooperation. More recently, it is a moot point whether Republican critiques of the PRI or endorsement of the PAN in the 1980s served the real interests of the United States—economic, geopolitical—or, rather, responded to domestic political concerns and arbitrary ethnocentric U.S.

assumptions, of the kind that Howard Wiarda has amply discussed (Wiarda 1986). Did Jesse Helms' diatribes against Mexican corruption (Pastor and Castañeda 1988: 34, 71), or the tendency to equate the PAN with "people power" in the Philippines, represent a rational appraisal of the United States' real interests in Mexico?

For, as these examples illustrate, U.S. perceptions of Mexico (and other countries) often depend on crude assumptions and simplistic categories. The phenomenon is not new, nor is it purely an American phenomenon. In part it reflects the inevitable tendency of people—policy makers in particular—to insert complicated and unfamiliar problems into convenient, stereotypical pigeonholes, thus rendering a messy and intractable universe neat and comprehensible (Schoultz 1987: 11–33). Analysts need filters; policy depends a good deal on the filters through which information is refracted. Between 1910 and 1940, American perceptions of Mexico varied to the extent that some observers saw the revolution as a justifiably progressive and popular movement, not lacking in American parallels and inspiration, and some, in contrast, chose to see aimless violence, mayhem, xenophobia, and imported "Bolshevism." Both sides took liberties with Mexican reality (as we all do), and the political impact of rival interpretations did not necessarily depend on their accuracy; often, it was their appeal within the United States that counted. Thus, Wiarda comments, policy often depended on U.S. factors and fashions (1986: 327–328).

Over time, the filters have varied. In the earlier period racist stereotypes were commonplace and unashamed; more recently they have, perhaps, been driven underground rather than thoroughly eliminated. In the 1940s a corporate executive of Anderson, Clayton & Co. complained that the Mexicans "do not want their country to be a White Man's country, which is what we would like to make of it" (Niblo 1995: 213). In the 1950s Dean Acheson blamed Latin America's problems on "Hispano-Indian culture—or lack of it" (Rabe 1988: 209). WASPish racism often conspired with an ancient anti-Catholicism—"the Roman Catholic religion is incompatible with free government," as John Adams had laid down in 1818 (Rippy 1958: 8)—thus generating the notion that a population of swarthy idolaters could hardly aspire to democracy or economic development. (Interestingly, some Mexicans agreed: only by assimilating Indians and combating Catholicism could the country hope to advance.)

If racist and religious stereotypes faded over time, new filters took their place. The most obvious was anticommunism—a theme that affected U.S.–Mexican relations from the outset of the revolution, but which became increasingly dominant as the USSR established itself as a major power. If, during the 1930s, fears of Communism were offset by more pressing fears of fascism, by the later 1940s things had changed; the crusade against the Axis had neatly metamorphosed into a crusade against the Soviet Union; Communist "totalitarianism" replaced fascist "totalitarianism" as the official enemy (Rabe 1988: 29). (Hence, of course, the academic vogue for the concept—or filter—of totalitarianism during the 1950s). Containment came to Latin America—in the shape of the Rio Pact and the Organization of American States—and Latin American elites began to exploit the potential of expedient anticommunism (Rabe 1988: 13, 15). Mexico, however, escaped relatively lightly from the United States' promiscuous use of what we might term the "red filter." As already suggested, Mexico was relatively sound; if its foreign policy veered toward the pink, its domestic treatment of "reds" over the years—Lombardo, Campa, Castillo—was reassuring. (And I do not think we need assume that Mexican repression of the Left implied simple deference to U.S. wishes: López Mateos surely broke the railroad strike without having to consult the "book on the dangers of communism" that Ike had considerately given the incoming Mexican president [Rabe 1988: 114]). Hence, as Cuba, the Dominican Republic, Chile, and Grenada absorbed American attention and suffered American intervention, Mexico was left to its own domestic devices.

Now, of course, we have entered a new era, in which—even if Cuba constitutes both an actual problem and a potential crisis—anticommunism can no longer serve as the touchstone of U.S. policy. To what extent this constitutes a genuine liberation remains to be seen: we should recall that anticommunism was capable of various interpretations and applications, some of them quite imaginative; hence its simple imperative could in fact cover—and justify—a wide range of policies (Blasier 1986: 553–554). Several alternative filters (none of them entirely new) now count for more in the selection of friends and enemies, policies, and priorities: democracy, human rights, trade liberalization, migration, drug trafficking. These, too, are capable of casuistical or imaginative application. Demonizing drug villains or scare mongering about the loss of border control may not reflect a rational appraisal of U.S.–Mexican relations. In the case of drugs, as Jorge Chabat shows, the perceived severity of the problem reflects U.S. priorities as much as any objective evaluation; the shrill concern expressed during 1985–1987 was muted less by any diminution in drug traffic than by an upturn in U.S.–Mexican relations (Chabat 1993). Furthermore, the replacement of one dominant (red) filter by several, while it may allow for greater discrimination, ergo realism, may also tend to confuse analysts and policy makers who, over the years, have grown lazy, one-eyed, and prone to seeing the world through a red mist. It would be neat and helpful if Latin American democrats also espoused human rights, neoliberal economics, and a tough line on drugs, but such convenient symmetry is not apparent. Nor is it easy for the United States to liquidate its cold war liaisons overnight (take the case of Manuel Noriega). The PRI of Carlos Salinas—a cold war ally obligingly transforming itself along neoliberal and, perhaps, democratic lines—looked a good bet and there was no lack of American experts who plunged accordingly. But now the neoliberalism looks fragile, and the democracy—never perfect—is compromised by drug money and related political violence. It will not be easy for the United States to reimpose a monochrome filter on Mexico; for the time being, expedient muddling through, strongly conditioned by the U.S. electoral cycle, is likely to be the order of the day. It seems pretty certain, however, that—global crises permitting—Mexico's renewed salience in U.S. politics will remain, and a key question, therefore, will be which filters will prove most eye-catching to the U.S. public, media, and policy makers.

Actors

Attitudes and filters are associated with, though not reducible to, U.S. institutions and lobbies. Several have played a part in the formulation of policy toward Mexico. Within the U.S. government, the executive and legislative branches engaged in their familiar tussles; the executive itself was sometimes divided. Wilson and Bryan were distinctly more dovish than, say, Secretary of War Garrison, or later, Secretary of State Lansing. Yet, in a curious anticipation of recent events, the military was sometimes less hawkish than its civilian masters: the Navy regarded a naval assault up the treacherous Pánuco River with alarm; hence Veracruz eventually suffered for Tampico's alleged insult to the American flag in 1914 (Knight 1986: 152). Within the diplomatic branch of the executive, career officials tended to regard the armed revolution with concern and hostility; President Wilson therefore introduced his own special agents, who shared his sympathy with Mexican democratic aspirations (Hill 1973). Twenty years later, Roosevelt's New Dealers were similarly more sympathetic than some career officials (hence their progressive disillusionment with cold war diplomacy in the later 1940s, which drove Laurence Duggan to suicide [Niblo 1995: 250–251]). Yet it was a distinguished career official— whose career, significantly, included recent postings in fascist Austria and Germany—who proved the chief architect of U.S.–Mexican collaboration during World War II: George Messersmith. By the 1940s, of course, the revolution was an institutional fact of life with which foreign representatives, European as well as American, had to deal, hence doctrinaire antipathy could hardly be sustained.

Within Washington, the growth of big government added to the players' roster. During the armed revolution the border was monitored by the military, the Department of Justice, and the Customs Service. By the 1940s the FBI had become a significant player, even if its efforts were, in the worst American tradition, amateurish and sensationalist. (J. Edgar Hoover was a notorious alarmist and racist, who saw nefarious Japanese everywhere, attributed Cárdenas' alleged antiforeign disposition to the president's "Indian antecedents," and anticipated a Mexican attack on British Honduras "synchronized with the [German] attack on Scandinavia." Not surprisingly, State Department experts declined to take him seriously [Niblo 1995: 46, 66–67]). During the 1950s, as economic questions supplanted security and foreign policy concerns, the

Treasury increased its role at the expense of the State Department (Niblo 1995: 243). More recently a host of new bureaucratic actors have come to play a part: the Drug Enforcement Administration, the Environmental Protection Agency, and the Immigration and Naturalization Service. Particularly since the 1980s, as Mexican questions have become more pressing, so institutional jockeying has increased, and policy has emerged—if it has emerged at all—from a complex contest of interests and agencies.

Beyond Washington, the border states were important, particularly prior to the establishment of a stable government during the 1920s. Migrants, refugees, smugglers, and arms dealers made the border a hive of activity during the 1910s, the first decade of mass migration from Mexico to the United States. The presence of U.S. troops—and the prospect, alluring or alarming, of U.S. armed intervention—added to the equation; recurrent Mexican raids—of which Villa's attack on Columbus was simply the biggest—engendered anxiety and provoked an Anglo backlash against hapless Mexican victims that turned the lower Rio Grande Valley into "a virtual war zone" (Montejano 1987: 117–125). Border state governors were therefore key players in U.S. policy: hawkish and aggressive in the 1910s, they were more often forces for détente and stability in the early 1920s, when, for example, Governor Hobby of Texas argued forcefully for the recognition of the shaky Obregón government (Smith 1972: 214–215). As the revolutionary government stabilized, basic questions of regime survival receded; day-to-day problems of border relationships (trade, customs controls, contraband, migration) came to the fore. Cross-border economic interdependence, a matter of frequent comment in the 1980s, was in fact much older: in the 1930s, Mexican fiscal and tariff policy could have an immediate effect on the prosperity of U.S. border ports; even drug-related political assassinations in border towns had their 1930s precedents (Wormuth 1938). More recently, as the cold war consensus has fractured and economic integration with Mexico has advanced, regional actors have again come to the fore; but, once more, the messages are mixed. Southern conservatism, combining ideological anticommunism, Christian fundamentalism, and economic self-interest, underpinned Republican policy in the 1980s. If the Sandinistas were the chief target, a corrupt, statist, drug-peddling PRI figured as a minor villain (Kurth 1986: 80–82). The prospect of economic integration—hence enhanced markets, competition, and immigration—also elicited strong but inconsistent opinions from the southern and southwestern states. The cast of political actors interested in Mexico has grown, and there is no controlling cold war script; the outcome may be episodic dramas with loose plots and a good deal of individual improvisation.

As we broaden the perspective to include civil society as well as government, the complexity of the picture is further enhanced. Business may have shared a preference for a stable, congenial, capitalist Mexico, but this was a lowest common denominator that permitted wide variations in business opinion. Big companies, capable of riding out the revolution, tended to be less keen on U.S. intervention, more prepared to rely on their political and economic resources in Mexico or on threats of intervention that would never be realized (Knight 1987: 117). (In this they were helped their greater capacity for bribery, their central role in regional economies, and the fact that they usually offered better paying jobs.) But big business was not a monolith. Exporters benefited from revolutionary inflation (though not revolutionary disruption of communications); public utilities whose income accrued in paper pesos were hard hit. The oil companies, realizing hefty profits during and despite the revolution, were a special case, since unstable, insolvent governments coveted hard currency, while fearing the oil companies' political machinations, both within Mexico and overseas. Through the 1920s and 1930s U.S.–Mexican relations often danced to the tune of petroleum, even though oil earnings were less than those of the older mining industry. Oil became a symbol: of capitalist and managerial prerogatives on the one hand, of revolutionary aspirations and national sovereignty on the other (Knight 1992: 96–103). The 1938 expropriation, though crucially important, was a unique aberrant case. Meanwhile, oil company intransigence contrasted with the cautious diplomacy of the bankers. The latter wanted a revived, prosperous Mexico that could pay its debts; the oilmen were prepared to take chances with political stability: had not their Gulf Coast enclaves continued to churn out oil at the height of revolutionary upheaval? The oil companies also feared a demonstration effect elsewhere (e.g., in Venezuela), if Mexico was allowed to flout property rights; therefore, they felt they had to "win a victory over the Mexicans" (Smith 1972: 255). Over time, the bankers, adroitly marshaled by Dwight Morrow, won the day, chiefly because their accommodationist approach suited not only Mexican interests but also those of the U.S. government. In 1938, FDR resolutely declined to back the oil companies' demands for sanctions against Mexico. Though the company boycott hurt Mexico, the U.S. government placed geopolitical security above the sanctity of petroleum property and declined to "nationalize" the conflict.

An important consideration was public opinion. Since Teapot Dome, if not before, the U.S. oil companies had enjoyed a low reputation in many U.S. circles. There were few votes in rescuing Standard Oil, especially for an administration like Roosevelt's, which was spurned by big business and supported by organized labor. Congruence thus had an impact north of the border. Furthermore, throughout the first half of our period, organized labor—relatively stronger then than now—played an important role in U.S.–Mexican relations. During the 1910s, labor and other leftist, socialist, and pacifist groups actively espoused a progressive policy in Mexico, broadly supporting President Wilson in his resistance to pro-Huerta or pro-intervention policies. The AFL allied with the infant Confederación Regional de Obreros Mexicanos (CROM); Gompers and Morones were mutually supportive; and, in times of U.S.–

Mexican crisis (1916, 1919, 1927) American organized labor pressed hard for dialogue and détente (Smith 1972: 53–54, 127–128; Levenstein 1971). Left-wing groups—recall that the 1910–1940 period was the brief heyday of American syndicalism and socialism—also raised their voice, while leftist intellectuals—Steffens, Beals, Tannenbaum—played an important part as interlocutors between Mexico and the United States, countering conservative propaganda, painting an enticing picture of a progressive revolution and a culturally rich society (Delpar 1992). Progressive Protestant leaders chimed in: they applauded the Protestant presence in the revolution, and the latter's efforts to extirpate a feudal and reactionary Catholicism. The familiar *leyenda negra,* which had uniformly blackened old Mexico, could now be invoked to justify the new, liberal, reformist Mexico of Calles and Cárdenas. Like their opponents, of course, Mexico's boosters saw reality through distorted filters and produced some travesties of the truth. But they had a distinct impact on U.S. policy, generating some bizarre alliances. In 1926–1927, for example, the intervention scare was headed off, in part, by a pro-Mexico, anti-intervention coalition that included the AFL, Morgans Bank, and the Ku Klux Klan (Smith 1972: 238).

This case was illustrative of the dynamics of lobbying, to which we might apply a kind of Newtonian mechanics, roughly based on the principle "action and reaction are equal and opposite." The salience of Mexico in U.S. politics has, as I argued earlier, varied over time. There have been long fallow periods, notably, the period of the cold war and the heyday of the PRI, but both before and after (i.e., roughly 1910–1940 and post-1982) the absence of both U.S. consensus and Mexican stability placed Mexico squarely on the U.S. political agenda. However, even during these periods the U.S. attention span has been brief. Attention, focused by specific crises (e.g., 1914, 1916, 1927, 1988, 1994), has soon wandered, although one might expect that recent economic integration will focus the collective mind and counteract such wandering during the 1990s.

One important reason for this short attention span has been the perceived absence of a major security threat to the United States (Mexico is not Cuba, Mexico is "safe," in cold war terms). Another, however, has been the inner dynamics of U.S. politics and the role played by public opinion in foreign policy questions. In the absence of a clear cold war consensus, Mexico has been kicked around by diverse competing lobbies and Mexican policy has emerged, often messily, as a result of this unpredictable contact sport. The most obvious recent case was NAFTA, whose outcome hung in the balance until the last minute. But during the 1920s, too, the political actors just mentioned (business, unions, churches, intellectuals, the Klan) all jostled for position and the U.S. government—weighing whether to recognize Obregón in 1923 or to coerce Calles in 1926–1927—reacted to their lobbying in a relatively pragmatic, ad hoc fashion. Ultimately, we might note, mainstream public opinion tended to favor peace over belligerence—an indication, perhaps, that lack of real expertise did not rule out a certain commonsensical caution. "The public," Hunt observes, "belittled as ignorant and fickle, deserves recognition and respect as a brake against some of the excesses of reigning American foreign-policy ideology" (1987: 181).

The Newtonian principle meant that strong pressure in one direction—prointervention in the 1920s, pro-NAFTA in the 1990s—often resulted in countervailing pressure from the other side. The more the Catholic Church protested Callista anticlericalism, the more the Protestant Churches—some but not all of progressive inclination—rushed to the defense of Mexico.[8] The louder the pro-NAFTA lobby spoke, the more labor, ecologists, and critics of the PRI raised their collective voices. I am not asserting that these rival ad hoc coalitions possessed equal clout, but rather suggesting that pressure in one direction tends to elicit countervailing pressure in another: action and reaction, if not "equal," do tend to be "opposite," and somewhat proportional. While this might be true of major issues in any polity, the American system, with its checks and balances, active lobbyists, moralistic rhetoric, and deference to public opinion, is particularly vulnerable to this syndrome; not surprisingly, foreign policy experts of the elitist/realist school have habitually deplored the American tendency to drop delicate diplomatic questions into the mire of populist politics. As Dean Acheson put it, "If you truly had a democracy and did what the people wanted, you'd go wrong every time" (Hunt 1987: 180).

But the Newtonian model also offered opportunities for Mexican lobbying. The scale of the latter became notorious during the run-up to the NAFTA vote. But the Mexican government—and its opponents—were only doing what most governments and powerful interests do; furthermore, they were following an old, if somewhat forgotten, Mexican tradition. For the NAFTA campaign was only the latest in a long line of Mexican interventions in U.S. domestic politics, several of which have been notably successful. As one would expect, these interventions have followed the pattern of salience mentioned above: they were significant during periods of flux and "pluralism" (1910–1940, post-1982) when the stakes were high; they atrophied at the height of the cold war and Pax PRIista when the stakes shrank and both sides could take mutual stability for granted.[9] During the Revolution, Carrancista lobbying was unusually successful and probably quite cheap. Carranza retained professional U.S. lobbyists but more importantly, he dispatched the adroit company lawyer and ideologue, Luis Cabrera, to Washington in 1913–1914 where, it is clear, Cabrera did a good job of presenting the Constitutionalist case against Huerta. Cabrera not only vilified Huerta and pledged the Constitutionalists' commitment to democracy, which Wilson and Bryan wanted to hear, he also persuaded Wilson of the essential social goals of the revolution to such an extent that when the skeptical British representative Thomas Hohler met Wilson in early 1914 he was appalled to find the president spouting derivative social-reformist "bosh" (Knight 1986: 139–140). The revolutionary leadership also took pains to welcome and enlighten sympathetic visitors to Mexico: Villa ran an effective public relations campaign along the border and the Carrancistas massaged the opinions—and egos?—of gringo visitors like Lincoln Steffens. While this lobbying did not determine the result of the revolution, since that result did not hinge upon U.S. actions, it may have hastened the fall of Huerta.

Furthermore, the precedents set during the 1910s were continued through the turbulent 1920s and 1930s, when the revolutionary government—including labor allies like Morones—took steps to influence U.S. opinion, both official and public. Key spokespeople were again warmly welcomed and subtly briefed (Britton 1988). Gruening defended Calles, Tannenbaum wrote up Cárdenas. The Obregón government mounted a sophisticated press campaign to sway U.S. opinion; the Confederation of Mexican Workers (CTM), in the 1930s, produced *Labor News*, a detailed English-language weekly appealing to a progressive, labor audience in the United States. (We may note, by way of contrast, the relatively ineffective lobbying of Cristero spokesmen in the United States: while their failure no doubt obeyed several causes, the most important was probably the ingrained suspicion of many Americans—in and out of government—toward the Catholic Church, otherwise known, in many American homes, as the Whore of Babylon; this made not only government representatives but even members of the Catholic hierarchy reticent in their support [Bailey 1974: 100–105].) In more discrete diplomatic exchanges, too, the Mexican spokesmen (and they were all men) put the case for the revolutionary regime. Ramón Beteta, representing Cárdenas in Washington during the late 1930s, updated the role Cabrera had played twenty-five years earlier; in Mexico City, meanwhile, the Cárdenas administration appealed to the progressive sentiments—and residual guilt feelings?[10]—of Ambassador Josephus Daniels, who played an important role in cushioning the impact of the oil expropriation (Blasier 1976: 85).

Mexican lobbying did not, of course, stop during the long period of "low salience" from the 1940s to the 1980s: questions of tariffs, trade, and migration persisted. But these were low key, quotidian questions whose outcome was hardly critical. By the 1980s, the picture had changed: the debt crisis and NAFTA negotiations greatly augmented the stakes; the rise of the PAN and the Frente Democrático Nacional (FDN) and the Partido Revolucionario Democrático (PRD)—trends that affected Chicano opinion in particular and southwestern/border opinion more broadly—encouraged the embattled PRI to increase its political lobbying north of the border. The Mexican embassy in Washington burgeoned; its personnel and output of glossy brochures greatly increased; U.S. politicians, journalists, and academics found themselves courted as never before. While, again, it is desperately difficult to establish causal links, it seems very likely that the effusions of support—verging on eulogy—that the Salinas administration received from opinion makers and mongers in the United States were not entirely unconnected to this sustained, costly, but quite effective public relations campaign.

Conclusion

Drawing contemporary conclusions from history is a difficult business; furthermore, the recent history of Mexico—with its ups and downs, acclaimed triumphs, and unexpected disasters—serves as a cautionary tale, warning against the hubris of prediction. My conclusions are, therefore, brief and tentative.

First, the Mexican factor within U.S. politics has obviously not been a constant. Its importance has varied considerably: there have been short-term oscillations and, more significantly, two or two-and-a-half long waves. Between the 1910s and the 1940s, the United States came to terms with the revolution— violent and institutional—and the revolution came to terms with the United States. Recurrent conflicts, some of a serious nature, gave Mexico greater salience in U.S. politics; however, that salience was affected by countervailing global events, particularly the two world wars, which tended to alleviate U.S. pressure on Mexico. During the pivotal decade of the 1940s U.S.–Mexican relations stabilized, as the United States entered on its imperial heyday; like much, though not all, of Latin America, Mexico lost salience; arguably, the United States now took Mexico for granted. Since the 1980s we appear to have entered a third long wave as the cold war thawed and U.S.–Mexican relations entered a more intimate, but also more contentious phase, characterized by increased interdependence and a weakening of the traditional hegemony of the PRI.

Second, although the United States and Mexico have had no shortage of quarrels (particularly in the 1910–1930 period), these have been limited in scope and impact: following the Calles-Morrow détente the threat of intervention receded; following the outbreak of World War II relations became remarkably collaborative. Given the contiguity of two unequal states, sharing a long land border, the potential for conflict was always greater than the actuality (compare, say, Poland and Russia). It is the "limits of conflict," as well as the "limits of friendship," that demand attention and explanation. One explanation relates to congruence: the fact that the United States and Mexico, for all their historic and cultural differences, share certain political ideas and experiences (note the roughly parallel presidencies); and, specifically, that the Mexican Revolution—which supplied much of the dynamism in the bilateral relationship—was, at the end of the day, a "bourgeois" revolution that the Americans could understand, endorse, and even massage: hence the recurrent phases of "constructive engagement," most recently under the aegis of the Washington consensus. However, the revolution also fortified the Mexican nation-state, facilitating nationalist resistance, deterring both Mexican kowtowing and gringo interventionism. For most of this century, therefore, U.S.–Mexican relations have revolved around the contrary poles of U.S. pressure (usually more successful when it is discreet and economic) and Mexican resistance (usually least successful in times of economic intimacy, such as the 1940s and 1990s).

While these conditions have structured the relationship, leaving both sides with limited scope for autonomous decision making, there has also been flux, change, and opportunity. U.S. attitudes toward Mexico varied greatly over time and place. However, we may note greater variation, pluralism, and competition in the early period (1910s–1940s), giving way to a broad consensus, linked to the "low salience" of the cold war era of the 1940s to 1980s. Now, as the cold war concludes and Mexico's capitalist, civilian, and democratic stability looks less unusual and attractive in American eyes, so consensus has again eroded and a variety of filters has replaced the old monochrome filter of the cold war. As in the 1920s and 1930s, different attitudes and different lobbies compete for attention; given the relatively democratic, even "populist," character of U.S. foreign policy making, this may make for instability and expedience. It may also reproduce the Newtonian dynamics of the 1920s, whereby contentious issues (oil or anticlericalism in the 1920s; trade, drugs, or migration in the 1990s) tend to generate "equal and opposite reactions," i.e., rival coalitions which, to a degree, cancel each other out. In such a situation, Mexican lobbying in the United States becomes more feasible and perhaps more attractive: as the cold war stasis shifts, U.S. decisions increasingly affect Mexico, and in a context of Newtonian dynamics, U.S. decisions are amenable to a degree of Mexican pressure. Perhaps the central theme of this volume—"dealing with the American political system"—is less arcane and academic, more practical and even profitable, than that of most such volumes.

Notes

1. These observations are based on a review of the *New York Times* index for the period 1910–1940, the (very cautious) findings of which I presented in Knight 1987 (16). A follow-up review of the index for the period 1940–1991 again tends to confirm expectations: coverage is crisis driven, and crises depend a good deal on cold war configurations. Mexico therefore figures consistently below, for example, Cuba and China, although Mexico begins to creep up during the 1980s, overtaking Cuba in the process.

2. "Its own advantage" tends to suggest a clearly defined national interest, shared by all Mexicans. In fact, Mexico, like the United States, is a complex, divided society, whose collective foreign policy may not reflect a consensus (certainly none is sought), and may not even serve the broad interest of the majority of Mexicans. To put it more polemically: foreign policy may reflect narrow, sectional interests— private and/or public. Hence, while the "advantage" in question *may* be broad, collective, and national, it may also be narrow and sectional. This is another way of saying that Mexico is not a (realist) billiard ball, careening around the geopolitical table, powered by its own momentum and interests. Rather, it is a (nonrealist) black box, whose inner workings need to be disassembled if we are to understand its foreign policy.

3. By which, I mean the old American habit of preaching high morals while practicing low politics, thus establishing some remarkable double standards. As Rafael Braun has pointed out, North Americans would not take too kindly to Latin Americans, for example, questioning "the FBI's methods of detecting corruption among [U.S.] legislators;" nor is it clear how, "if the United States has the right to intervene in other countries in order to impose democracy, one can deny Nicaragua the right to promote the 'liberation' of El Salvador, or Argentina the right to promote 'national security' in Bolivia" (Braun 1986: 400–401).

4. Is this a possible lesson for Cuba?

5. According to Arthur Schlesinger, the goal of the Alliance for Progress was to persuade developing countries "to base their revolutions on Locke rather than Marx" (Coker 1989: 113).

6. However, a residual nationalism and fear of nationalist reaction may still inhibit the outright privatization of PEI-PEMEX.

7. However, a viable alternative to neoliberalism cannot be based on a return to economic nationalism or autarky and will have to involve greater international collaboration, designed to constrain the mercurial movement of capital, to protect human and environmental resources, and to counter the modern equivalent of the beggar-your-neighbor policies of the 1930s. Of course, this is easier said than done.

8. It is interesting to compare how in the 1920s the Catholic Church in the United States adopted, roughly, conservative (antirevolutionary) policies vis-à-vis Latin America (especially Mexico), while in the 1980s and 1990s it has been a voice for more progressive causes; conversely, the Protestant Church has tended to move in the opposite direction. This clearly has something to do with the changes initiated (from without) by Vatican II, and with the leftward drift to Catholicism in Latin America. But it no doubt also reflects shifts within U.S. Catholicism, as the old sectarianism of the 1920s faded (enabling Kennedy to secure election in 1960), and the Catholic constituency in the United States became less European and northeastern, more Latino and southwestern.

9. Of course, Mexico continued to lobby for benefits (e.g., sugar quotas) through the cold war period; perhaps, in view of its low profile, the scale of such lobbying is underestimated. However, there seems little doubt that the NAFTA campaign broke all records.

10. Daniels was secretary of the Navy at the time of the 1914 Veracruz landing; FDR was his assistant secretary of state.

References

Aron, Raymond. 1974. *The Imperial Republic; The United States and the World. 1945–1973*. London: Weidenfeld and Nicolson.

Bailey, David C. 1974. *Viva Cristo Rey! The Cristero Rebellion and the Church-State Conflict in Mexico*. Austin: University of Texas Press.

Blasier, Cole. 1976. *The Hovering Giant. U.S. Responses to Revolutionary Change in Latin America*. Pittsburgh: University of Pittsburgh Press.

————. 1986. "Security: The Extracontinental Dimension." In Kevin J. Middlebrook and Carlos Rico, eds., *The United States and Latin America in the 1980s.* Pittsburgh: University of Pittsburgh Press.

————. 1987. *The Giant's Rival. The USSR and Latin America.* Pittsburgh: University of Pittsburgh Press.

Braun, Rafael. 1986. "The Human Rights Question in U.S.–Latin American Relations." In Kevin J. Middlebrook and Carlos Rico, eds., *The United States and Latin America in the 1980s.* Pittsburgh: University of Pittsburgh Press.

Britton, John A. 1988. "Propaganda, Property, and the Images of Stability: The Mexican Government and the U.S. Print Media, 1921–1929." *SECOLAS Annals,* 19: 5–28.

Centeno, Miguel Angel. 1994. *Democracy within reason: technocratic revolution in Mexico.* University Park, Pa.: Pennsylvania State University Press.

Chabat, Jorge. 1993. "El Narcotráfico en la Relación México–Estados Unidos: Lo que Se Ve Es Lo que Hay?" *Estados Unidos Informe Trimestral,* III, 3: 5–14.

Cline, Howard F. 1965. *The United States and Mexico.* New York: Athenaeum.

Coker, Christopher. 1989. *Reflections on American Foreign Policy Since 1945.* London: Pinter Publications.

Crahan, Margaret E. 1986. "Human Rights and U.S. Foreign Policy: Realism Versus Stereotypes." In Kevin J. Middlebrook and Carlos Rico, eds., *The United States and Latin America in the 1980s.* Pittsburgh: University of Pittsburgh Press.

Craig, Ann L. 1983. *The First Agraristas. An Oral History of a Mexican Agrarian Reform Movement.* Berkeley: University of California Press.

Delpar, Helen. 1992. *The Amazing Vogue for All Things Mexican.* Tuscaloosa: University of Alabama Press.

Diskin, Martin. 1983. "Introduction." In Martin Diskin, ed., *Trouble in Our Backyard. Central America and the United States in the Eighties.* New York: Pantheon Books.

Fein, Seth. 1995. "Everyday Forms of Transnational Collaboration: Distribution and Reception of U.S. Film Propaganda in Post–World War II Mexico." Paper presented at the conference "Rethinking the Post-Colonial Encounter. Transnational Perspectives on the Foreign Presence in Latin America." Yale University, New Haven, Conn., October.

Francis, Michael J. 1988. "United States Policy toward Latin America during the Kissinger Years." In John D. Martz, ed., *United States Policy in Latin America. A Quarter Century of Crisis and Challenge. 1961–1986.* Lincoln: University of Nebraska Press.

Gilderhus, Mark. 1986. *Panamerican Visions: Woodrow Wilson and the Western Hemisphere.* Tucson: University of Arizona Press.

Hamilton, Nora. 1982. *The Limits of State Autonomy: Post-Revolutionary Mexico.* Princeton, N.J.: Princeton University Press.

Hill, Larry D. 1973. *Emissaries to a Revolution.* Baton Rouge: University of Louisiana Press.

Hofstadter, Richard. 1955. *The Age of Reform: From Bryan to F.D.R.* New York: Knopf.

Hunt, Michael. 1987. *Ideology and U.S. Foreign Policy*. New Haven, Conn.: Yale University Press.

Ikenberry, G. John, and Charles A. Kupchan. 1990. "Socialization and Hegemonic Power." *International Organization* 44 (3): 283–315.

Kennan, George F. 1967. *Memoirs 1925–1950*. New York: Pantheon Books.

Kissinger, Henry. 1994. *Diplomacy*. London: Simon and Schuster.

Knight, Alan. 1985. "The Mexican Revolution: Bourgeois? Nationalist? Or Just A 'Great Rebellion'?" *Bulletin of Latin American Research* 4 (2): 1–37.

———. 1986. *The Mexican Revolution. Vol. 2. Counter-revolution and Reconstruction*. Cambridge: Cambridge University Press.

———. 1987. *U.S.–Mexican Relations 1910–40. An Interpretation*. San Diego: Center for U.S.–Mexican Studies, University of California at San Diego.

———. 1992. "The Politics of the Expropriation." In Jonathan C. Brown and Alan Knight, eds., *The Mexican Petroleum Industry in the Twentieth Century*. Austin: University of Texas Press.

Kolko, Gabriel. 1988. *Confronting the Third World. United States Foreign Policy 1945–1980*. New York: Pantheon Books.

Kurth, James R. 1986. "The United States, Latin America, and the World: The Changing International Context of U.S.–Latin American Relations." In Kevin J. Middlebrook and Carlos Rico, eds., *The United States and Latin America in the 1980s*. Pittsburgh: University of Pittsburgh Press.

Levenstein, Harvey. 1971. *Labor Organization in the United States and Mexico: A History of Their Relations*. Westport, Conn.: Greenwood.

Lowenthal, Abraham F. 1992. "Changing U.S. Interests and Policies in a New World." In Jonathan Hartlyn, Lars Schoultz, and Augusto Varas, eds., *The United States and Latin America in the 1990s*. Chapel Hill: University of North Carolina Press.

Lundestad, Geir. 1990. *The American "Empire" and Other Studies of U.S. Foreign Policy in Comparative Perspective*. Oslo and Oxford: Norwegian University Press and Oxford University Press.

Mallon, Florencia E. 1995. *Peasant and Nation. The Making of Postcolonial Mexico and Peru*. Berkeley: University of California Press.

Meyer, Jean. 1973. *La Cristiada, v. 2, El conflicto entre la iglesia y el estado. 1926–1929*. Mexico: Siglo Veintiuno.

———. 1979. *El Sinarquismo. Un fascismo mexicano?* Mexico: Joaquin Mortiz.

Meyer, Lorenzo. 1972. *Mexico y los Estados Unidos en el conflicto petrolero*. Mexico: El Colegio de Mexico

Meyer, Lorenzo, and Josefina Zoraida Vásquez. 1982. *Mexico frente a los Estados Unidos: un ensayo histórico. 1776–1980*. Mexico: El Colegio de Mexico.

Middlebrook, Kevin J., and Carlos Rico. 1986. "The United States and Latin America in the 1980s: Change, Complexity, and Contending Perspectives." In Kevin J. Middlebrook and Carlos Rico, eds., *The United States and Latin America in the 1980s*. Pittsburgh: University of Pittsburgh Press.

Montejano, David. 1987. *Anglos and Mexicanos in the Making of Texas, 1836–1986*. Austin: University of Texas Press.

Niblo, Stephen R. 1995. *War, Diplomacy, and Development. The United States and Mexico, 1938–1954*. Wilmington, Del.: Scholarly Resources.

O'Donnell, Guillermo. 1986. "The United States, Latin America, Democracy: Variations on a Very Old Theme." In Kevin J. Middlebrook and Carlos Rico, eds., *The United States and Latin America in the 1980s.* Pittsburgh: University of Pittsburgh Press.

Pastor, Manuel, and Carol Wise. 1994. "The Origins and Sustainability of Mexico's Free Trade Policy." *International Organization,* 48 (2): 459–489.

Pastor, Robert A., and Jorge G. Castañeda. 1988. *Limits to Friendship. The United States and Mexico.* New York: Knopf.

Petras, James, and Morris Morley. 1990. *U.S. Hegemony Under Siege. Class, Politics, and Development In Latin America.* London: Verso.

Poitras, Guy. 1990. *The Ordeal of Hegemony. The United States and Latin America.* Boulder, Colo.: Westview Press.

Rabe, Stephen G. 1988. *Eisenhower and Latin America. The Foreign Policy of Anticommunism.* Chapel Hill: University of North Carolina Press.

Rippy, J. Fred. 1958. *Globe and Hemisphere. Latin America's Place in the Postwar Foreign Relations of the United States.* Chicago: Henry Regnery Co.

Schmitt, Karl. 1974. *Mexico and the United States 1821–1973. Conflict and Coexistence.* New York: John Wiley & Sons.

Schoultz, Lars. 1987. *National Security and United States Policy toward Latin America.* Princeton, N.J.: Princeton University Press.

Smith, Joseph. 1979. *Illusions of Conflict. Anglo-American Diplomacy toward Latin America 1865–1896.* Pittsburgh: University of Pittsburgh Press.

Smith, Robert Freeman. 1972. *The United States and Revolutionary Nationalism in Mexico 1916–1932.* Chicago: University of Chicago Press.

Whitehead, Laurence. 1986. "Debt, Diversification and Dependency: Latin America's International Political Relations." In Kevin J. Middlebrook and Carlos Rico, eds., *The United States and Latin America in the 1980s.* Pittsburgh: University of Pittsburgh Press.

Wiarda, Howard J. 1986. "Can Democracy Be Exported? The Quest for Democracy in U.S.–Latin American Policy." In Kevin J. Middlebrook and Carlos Rico, eds., *The United States and Latin America in the 1980s.* Pittsburgh: University of Pittsburgh Press.

Wormuth, Romeyn. 1938. Report of U.S. Consul, Nuevo Laredo, to State Department. 29 March. State Department Records, 812.00-Tamaulipas/340.

Chapter 2

Mexico's Foreign Policy after NAFTA: The Tools of Interdependence

Jorge Chabat

The United States uses various instruments to carry out its international relations. These instruments, or tools, range from the more traditional ones, like war, to more cooperative ones, such as diplomacy and propaganda (Palmer and Perkins 1969; Holsti 1995: chap. 6–10). According to the Realist school, the type of instrument used depends on the state's structural capabilities, i.e., its power. This allows the superpowers to resort to war more often because war gives them a greater guarantee that their interests will be achieved. Weak states, on the other hand, have to resort more often to negotiation and diplomacy (with fewer guarantees of success) because these are more in keeping with their positions of power. There are other reasons that explain interstate warfare, such as territorial conflicts or other interests that compel the state to solve its conflicts through the use of military force. Nevertheless, the course of military conflicts in the twentieth century suggests that while in the past they occurred mainly among the superpowers, they have tended to move to the periphery (Holsti 1995: chap. 14). This suggests that the use of war as an instrument of foreign policy is not always a function of state power, but of other elements as well.

Some scholars have suggested that war and violence are used to resolve conflicts in peripheral countries (that is, weak countries or Third World countries) because—unlike industrialized countries—they are not interdependent (Goldgeier and McFaul 1992: 467–491). This perspective holds that it is the presence of interdependent links, rather than power, that makes a military solution costly and thus makes negotiation the preferred option (Keohane and Nye 1989: 25). The tendency toward negotiation stems from the presence of mutual vulnerabilities between two countries in an interdependent relationship. This theory posits that an act of State A that harms State B will also have negative repercussions for State A. This situation does not mean that all or the majority of State A's relations have to be concentrated on State B, with which there are links of interdependence. For mutual vulnerability to exist, it is sufficient only that a primary nexus of interdependence exist. Consequently, an interdependent relationship will develop and will eventually lead to secondary linkages of interdependence. In other words, vulnerability is not derived from a state's concentration of links with another state, but from the type of links established with that state. In fact, there are some issues that alone generate vulnerability with the other state and that eventually lead to the development of interdependent linkages.[1]

Thus, the instruments a state uses to achieve its goals depend on the type of relationship it has with a country or group of countries. In a world of independent countries, clearly connected but lacking mutual vulnerability, a state may use instruments without worrying about the repercussions from the other side. Therefore, conflicts between states tend to be resolved through violent means rather than through negotiation. The main reason for this is that interstate relations—in a noninterdependent world—are carried out in an "anarchic" world that functions on a self-help basis, in which states are only looking after their own interests, and in which the use of force prevails because hurting another state has no negative repercussions on the attacking state. Under these conditions, a weak state (a state with fewer military capabilities than the superpowers) will seek alliances to protect itself from attacks of other states. Further, a weak state will isolate itself and interact as little as possible with this anarchic world, a world in which it is at a great disadvantage.

However, there is no guarantee that this approach will avoid superpower confrontation. In other words, although a state may lean toward negotiation and cooperation over military confrontation, this approach does not ensure that the state will not itself be on the receiving end of states with military or confrontational instruments, such as an economic embargo. In order to resist this type of external pressure, it is necessary that a state: 1. possess the traditional requisites of power, such as an abundance of natural resources or a large military machinery (instruments clearly lacking in most developing countries); or 2. is able to generate vulnerabilities in other countries by developing interdependence.

The policies followed by Mexico after World War II reflected its structural weaknesses and emphasized negotiation rather than military confrontation. With limited military power to compete in an anarchic world, a geographic reality that predetermined its international alliances, and lacking national interests abroad,

Mexico's foreign policy was defensive and reactive. The instruments used by Mexico in its international relations were confined to a reticent diplomacy that sought only the minimum contacts necessary to survive as a political unit. Not only were military instruments set aside, but so were other instruments that might signal the country's willingness to compete internationally for power. Neither economic pressure nor covert or intelligence operations were employed abroad. Along with this lack of power (and lack of external interests) was an official discourse that reaffirmed state sovereignty and nonintervention in the affairs of other countries. Within this understanding of foreign policy, the mere expression of opinion was regarded as an act of meddling.[2]

Nevertheless, the effectiveness of a foreign policy based on isolationism and legalism cannot be ignored. The last military intervention on Mexican territory occurred in the heat of the Mexican Revolution in 1914 with the invasion of Veracruz and the Punitive Expedition of General Pershing in 1916. In fact, the threat of a subsequent intervention by the United States (and the outside world in general) disappeared with the recognition of the government of Alvaro Obregón in 1923. Since then, the governments that emerged out of the revolution have not faced any threats that endangered their existence or the nation's territorial integrity. Furthermore, Mexico showed unusual autonomy in its foreign policy when it opposed Cuba's expulsion from the Organization of American States in 1962 and opposed the diplomatic and commercial blockade against the island in 1964, both of which were sponsored by the United States within the context of the cold war. The official interpretation of this success of Mexican diplomacy is emphasized in the coherency of the discourse of nonintervention and in the adherence to the principles of international law. Nonetheless, it is likely that the real reason for Mexico's actions was that, despite its structural weaknesses, its border with the United States had already allowed primary linkages of interdependence and consequently some bargaining power to emerge, which was demonstrated with the nationalization of oil in 1938.[3]

During this period, which was characterized by passive interdependence and which lasted until the mid-1980s, the instruments the Mexican government used were a function of not just its structural weaknesses (or of the incipient bargaining power offered by primary linkages of interdependence with the United States) but of the type of interests that it tried to defend. Mexico's interests were clearly limited to internal matters: a closed economic development and internal political stability. The incipient bargaining capability with the United States was a function of its domestic stability. This period did not demand the use of active instruments abroad, and Mexican policy thus became accustomed to this passivity, which coincided with a successful maintenance of traditional sovereignty.

However, this framework started to break down during the 1970s. In fact, the anchor of this model of foreign policy, the import substitution development model, precipitated a crisis during President Echeverría's administration. Thus, in an embryonic manner, the Mexican government began to employ instruments characteristic of a state with interests outside its national territory. Mexico thus entered a new era of foreign policy activism that was a reflection of the development and consolidation of interdependent links with the United States.

Yet the use of these new instruments was not always planned or systematic. Both President Echeverría and President López Portillo carried out foreign policy in a poorly articulated fashion, but in a way that announced Mexico's need to diversify its foreign relations in an environment in which isolationism was increasingly difficult. Both Echeverría and López Portillo abandoned silent diplomacy and began to speak out on international events. López Portillo even supported the Sandinista uprising with words as well as arms and money, a step that constituted a point of departure for the country's foreign policy. But the economic crisis in 1982 crumbled the possibility of foreign involvement using classic instruments of power[4] although it did not force a return to the isolationism of the 1950s and 1960s. Contrary to the post–World War II period, in the 1980s Mexico's interests began to include foreign affairs, which meant that Mexican foreign policy was redesigned not only according to the country's ends but also its means. Thus, despite the limitations imposed by the economic crisis on the traditional uses of foreign policy, President De la Madrid's government had to energize its diplomacy abroad—this time more systematically than the two previous governments had, though not as efficiently—and even had to resort to using instruments previously viewed as interventionist, like hiring lobbyists in the United States (Chabat 1990: 398–418). However the effectiveness of some of these instruments was limited by an imbalance in the government's official discourse, which was still fashioned after the old foreign policy, a policy designed within the context of noninterdependent foreign relations. These imbalances persisted during President Salinas de Gortari's administration, despite an intensified use of instruments characteristic of an interdependent foreign policy that reached unprecedented levels.

The Foreign Policy of Salinas de Gortari: New (and Old) Instruments, Old Rhetoric

The New Instruments: Negotiating NAFTA

President Salinas de Gortari's official foreign policy had the following objectives: 1. strengthening national sovereignty; 2. promoting economic development; 3. protecting Mexicans living abroad; 4. promoting national culture; 5. promoting a positive image of Mexico abroad; and 6. encouraging international economic development (Solana 1994a: 3–4). Several of these objectives involve the use of foreign policy instruments characteristic of a country with interdependent relationships in the world. Clearly, not all of the objectives are attainable in the same way, and the evaluation of their results can be a difficult task. However, it is important to highlight that the combination of these objectives and their gradual attainment involve a redefinition of traditional foreign policy, and consequently, a redefinition of the first objective: national sovereignty. In particular, the second objective, promoting economic development through external relations, constitutes a radical redefinition of Mexico's traditional understanding of national sovereignty, which has traditionally had only a domestic axis.

This radical departure started at the beginning of President Salinas de Gortari's administration when the government's interest in mitigating the political impact of the country's economic opening, particularly toward the United States, became evident. The administration's concern over the erosion of the traditional notion of sovereignty was evident when Salinas, in order to expand foreign investment in Mexico, made modifications to the foreign investment law in May 1989, just six months after taking office. However, the president did not dare rewrite the law, no doubt concerned over the reaction of the Chamber of Deputies, where the PRI had a narrow majority. This sensibility was also apparent during the initial negotiations of the North American Free Trade Agreement (NAFTA) with the United States. These negotiations started in secret, apparently in February 1990, after Salinas de Gortari's trip to Europe a month earlier (where he met with little success on the economic front) (Truell 1990). It is worth recalling that these negotiations took place despite objections by both De la Madrid and Salinas de Gortari to forming a commercial trading block with the United States.[5] Once the free trade negotiations became public knowledge, the Mexican government tried to rationalize its actions in order to assuage domestic concerns about national sovereignty. The Mexican Senate convened a national forum to discuss Mexico's trade relations with the rest of the world.

As an outcome of this forum, which occurred a week before Salinas traveled to the United States to announce the start of trade negotiations, the Mexican Senate recommended negotiations towards a free trade agreement with the United States (*La Jornada* 1990). It is interesting to note that, in its recommendations, the Senate echoed the concern of the Mexican government about the impact that this agreement could have on the concept of sovereignty. Thus, the Senate warned: "This agreement—contrary to a common market—would preserve the political and economic sovereignty of the country and would leave Mexico completely free to design its trade policy with the rest of the world" (*La Jornada* 1990).

By the end of 1990 NAFTA included Canada, a development that actually helped the Mexican government downplay the political impact of reaching a trade agreement with just the United States. The negotiating process that led to

NAFTA featured a wide range of foreign policy instruments used by the Mexican government to achieve its objectives and included four of the six aforementioned foreign policy goals: promoting economic development, promoting national culture, promoting a positive image of Mexico abroad, and encouraging international economic development.

The NAFTA negotiations involved the intensive use of diplomacy involving the Secretariat of Commerce and Industrial Development as well as the Coordinator of Advisors to the President while neglecting the Ministry of Foreign Relations.[6] From 1990 to 1993, numerous meetings to draft the NAFTA document and its side agreements consumed considerable attention and energy from the Salinas de Gortari administration. Parallel to this process, the Mexican government resorted to the use of an instrument previously employed very little: advertising and lobbying.

The Mexican government's campaign for NAFTA had four main targets: a) American public opinion, particularly that of the Mexican American population; b) potential investors in the United States; c) the White House and members of the Bush and Clinton administrations; and d) U.S. members of Congress and their staff. The first objective, to sway Mexican American public opinion, was carried out through advertisements in the mass media, particularly on Spanish-language television. These advertisements urged Mexican American voters to pressure their representatives to approve the fast-track strategy in 1991. The second objective, to attract North American capital within the framework of NAFTA (and thus win the support of investors), was carried out in the mainstream media.[7] In addition, the Mexican government tried to promote foreign investment by buying small manufacturing companies and then moving them to the state of Yucatán. This program was made possible by an investment fund called AmeriMex Maquiladora Fund L.P. (Fondo Maquiladora AmeriMex). After word of this project was leaked to the press in February 1993, the government abandoned this fund, although Nacional Financiera, Mexico's national development bank, continued supporting similar projects.[8]

The third objective, to obtain the support of the White House and the secretary of state, was relatively easy for the Salinas administration. The reasons for Bush's initial support of NAFTA are probably related to his roots in Texas, which familiarized him with Mexico's problems, and to his Republican Party affiliation. A structural factor that may perhaps explain Clinton's decision to support NAFTA, even in the face of the Democratic Party's opposition, was the U.S. government's perception of its interdependence with Mexico.[9] The fourth objective, lobbying members of Congress and their staff, was mainly done by the Mexican embassy in Washington. This effort greatly surpassed any lobbying previously carried out by the Mexican government. According to the Center for Public Integrity, a non-governmental organization in Washington, D.C., supported by foundations, unions, and private citizens, "Mexico has set up the most expensive and elaborate campaign ever conducted by a foreign government in the United States" (Lewis et al. 1993; Eisenstadt 1993: 10–15). According to this organization, Mexico's lobbying expenses for NAFTA exceeded the cost of the three largest lobbying campaigns carried out in Washington over the last twenty-five years: the South Korean operation known as Koreagate; the Japanese lobbying for Toshiba sales to the Soviet Union; and Kuwait's campaign to persuade the American public to support U.S. intervention in the Persian Gulf (Eisenstadt 1993: 1, 17–18). Mexico's NAFTA lobby included all-expenses-paid trips for at least forty-eight key congressional staff members as well as the hiring of at least thirty-three former government officials with contacts in various offices of the executive branch and Congress (Lewis et al. 1993: 26; Lewis and Ebrahin 1993: 835). These trips were sponsored by the Coordinadora de Organismos Empresariales de Comercio Exterior (COECE) (the Association of Exporting Companies), whose members are major Mexican companies and which receives funding from the Consejo Coordinador Empresarial (CCE) (Entrepreneurial Coordinating Council). Their participation confirmed the trend toward the private sector's greater involvement in Mexico's foreign policy, which was clearly visible during President De la Madrid's presidency (Chabat 1989: 73–112). The Center for Public Integrity points out that from 1989 to mid-1993 the Mexican government and business sectors spent at least $25 million to promote NAFTA. It is likely that this figure increased to about $30 million by the end of 1993.

The Effects of the New Instruments: The Rhetoric of Diversification

As we have seen, the use of instruments of interdependence during the Salinas de Gortari administration changed the concept of nonintervention, and thus, of sovereignty (Heiberg 1994: 9–17). Further, because the main target of these new instruments was the United States, a redefinition of Mexico's foreign policy was required. In other words, as John D. Negroponte, the U.S. Ambassador to Mexico from 1989 to 1993, pointed out, the negotiations over NAFTA would finally stop the camouflaging of the real focus of Mexico's foreign policy: the United States.[10] While this recognition highlights a fundamental aspect of Mexican foreign policy after NAFTA, it does not tell the whole story because the NAFTA negotiations encouraged an alternative cover-up of the importance of the United States to President Salinas de Gortari's foreign policy. Thus, parallel to the announcement of negotiations with the United States and Canada, the Mexican government not only began a discourse focused on national sovereignty, but also hinted at a greater geographic diversification of its foreign policy. While the NAFTA talks were progressing with the United States, President Salinas de Gortari participated regularly in the meetings of the Group of Eight; he sponsored the creation of an intercontinental forum called the Inter-American Summit; he created the Group of Three, made up of Colombia,

Mexico, and Venezuela; he participated in the Group of Fifteen meetings (a pro–Third-World forum); he signed trade agreements with Chile, Central America, Colombia, and Venezuela; and he became a member of the Asian Pacific Economic Council (APEC), and the Organization for Economic Cooperation and Development (OECD) (Solana 1994b: 561–565).

There are two possible interpretations of these efforts at diversification. The official interpretation is that this strategy fundamentally tried to: a) "balance and serve as a counterbalance to our links with the United States" (Solana 1994b: 561); and b) "reduce the risk of falling into a position of vulnerability with another country or group of countries when links are excessively concentrated with them" (Solana 1994b: 562). The evaluation of the first interpretation depends on the statistic one uses. If one uses foreign trade as the criterion, the figures clearly show that Mexican trade was mainly concentrated with its northern neighbor, even though its volume and trade agreements increased with Latin America and the rest of the world during Salinas' six years in office. Trade with the United States increased from 66.3 percent of total trade in 1988 to 74.9 percent in 1994. On the other hand, trade with the rest of the continent (except Cuba) decreased from 5.94 percent to 4.15 percent during that same period (see Table 2.1).

Using alternative criteria—such as the number of diplomatic meetings held—the government's participation in regional forums and the creation of new forums (such as the Inter-American Summit) was much greater than the number of meetings at the presidential level, although they hardly have the same qualitative weight. The amount of energy consumed by the NAFTA negotiations was so high that the secretary of foreign relations himself grumbled: "Unfortunately, I think there were some issues that absorbed too much attention

Table 2.1 Mexico: Exports and Imports, 1988–1994
(in millions of dollars)

Year	Exports			Imports		
	U.S.	Latin America	Total	U.S.	Latin America	Total
1988	13,454	1,531	20,409	13,043	842	19,557
1989	16,163	1,645	23,046	15,554	1,064	22,792
1990	18,837	1,791	27,167	19,848	1,400	30,014
1991	18,729	1,968	26,939	24,682	1,900	38,072
1992	18,657	2,545	27,166	30,129	2,574	47,945
1993	37,041	2,503	47,123	41,635	2,377	60,240
1994	45,778	2,614	56,951	50,840	2,742	72,039

Source: International Monetary Fund 1995: 307–308.

of the decision makers. In fact, I think that there came a time when NAFTA became an end in itself, and that distracted us" (Riva Palacio and Gómez Leyva 1994: 10A).

With respect to the concern about avoiding concentrating one's foreign relations on a single country (ironically, the emphasis on the United States has been present for several decades and has only recently increased), it is important to mention two points. On the one hand, in an interdependent relationship vulnerability is not a function of the concentration of ties, but rather a function of the specific issues that link the two countries, some of which generate vulnerability on their own. On the other hand, in an interdependent relationship, the way to counteract a situation of vulnerability (which is inherently structural and intensifies over time) is to generate vulnerabilities in the other country. These vulnerabilities are produced through an issue that creates primary linkages of interdependence or by developing a policy that creates secondary linkages of interdependence (Chabat 1996). Within this context, the diversification of foreign policy is not always the best way to create countervulnerabilities. Moreover, it is likely that some linkages such as foreign trade need to be temporarily concentrated on one country (as occurred with trade with the United States) in order to generate vulnerabilities.

An alternative interpretation of the diversification rhetoric has to do with the different paces of economic and political change in Mexico. This became apparent during the second half of President de la Madrid's administration when the economic opening began. The consequences of these economic changes were felt at about the time the government announced its decision to negotiate NAFTA. Moreover, President Salinas de Gortari himself consciously delayed implementing political changes, arguing that carrying out economic and political reforms simultaneously would be highly destabilizing to the country.[11]

The lack of synchronization in the implementation of both political and economic reforms forced the Mexican government to carefully control how the repercussions of the economic opening would affect its traditional bases of political stability. Given that this stability was based largely on a strong anti-American nationalism, a likely consequence of rapid reforms would have been a rapid erosion of the government's legitimacy. Thus, it was reasonable for the government to try to mitigate the domestic impact of changes in its foreign policy. A simple and inexpensive method of doing so was through the diversification rhetoric. In fact, there is sufficient evidence that, despite such rhetoric, the Salinas de Gortari government did not really diversify its foreign relations. Moreover, the NAFTA negotiations were an explicit recognition that that strategy does not function within the context of interdependency. The use of all the aforementioned instruments to promote NAFTA leads one to conclude that the Mexican government indeed knew the rules of the game of interdependency. In addition, parallel to the development of the alternative cover-up strategy, the Salinas de Gortari administration tried to change the traditionally held nationalist discourse (Chabat 1993: 47–62). However, during much of his administration this rhetoric had a very solid foundation in one of the least developed aspects of political reform: the electoral context.

The Old Instruments: Resorting to Sovereignty and Pretense

Along with the intensive use of new foreign policy instruments that an active interdependent relationship with the United States required, the Salinas de Gortari administration also responded in two different ways to the international situation. It openly rejected the logic of interdependence within the domestic electoral context but pretended to accept this logic with regard to drug trafficking.

Regarding the electoral context, it is important to mention two fundamental expressions of the "sovereign democracy" discourse. On the one hand, in international forums, the government rejected any conditions on democratization in order to belong to international organizations. This policy clearly isolated Mexico from the rest of Latin America in December 1992 when Mexico was the only country to oppose the suspension of a member country of the OAS when a democratic government was overthrown (Bloomfield 1994). On the other hand, for five and a half years the Salinas government rejected allowing international observers for Mexican elections (Chabat 1991: 1–25). In fact, this policy was in place until March 1994 when the PRI presidential candidate, Luis Donaldo Colosio (murdered that month for as yet unclear reasons), suggested that "international visitors" could observe the August 1994 elections. Denying access to foreign electoral observers seemed to have more to do with an electoral process that lacked sufficient "cleanliness" to withstand foreign scrutiny than with the fear of nationalist reactions to the surrendering of sovereignty. From this perspective, the persistence of the traditional discourse on sovereignty and nationalism, which coexisted with instruments appropriate to situations of interdependence, was due more to Salinas de Gortari's conscious maintenance of practices typical of an authoritarian regime than to nationalist pressures from the Mexican citizenry, who in fact supported the president's proposals of economic integration with the United States.[12]

It is probably the permanence of traditional Mexican political dynamics that led the Salinas de Gortari administration to try another way of answering to the demands of an interdependent relationship. In the case of the war on drugs, there were internal factors that prevented a policy of "total war." The persistence of widespread illegal drug production and transportation in Mexico suggests the government's ineffectiveness in combating this problem, especially because signs of complicity between drug dealers and high-level functionaries of Salinas de Gortari's government indicate that the war against drugs has not been fully engaged.

However, it is important to point out that with the war on drugs, unlike the election observer issue, the government's noncompliance with internationally accepted norms was not justified on the basis of national sovereignty (though it is not an absent element). Rather, superficial efforts were made to combat drug trafficking in order to satisfy international public opinion, mainly in the United States. In fact, during Salinas de Gortari's term, the statistics measuring the campaign against drug trafficking substantially improved: budget, seizures, drug eradication, arrests, legal and institutional reforms, signing of international agreements, and cooperation with the United States (Chabat 1995). However, despite such actions, neither drug volume nor trafficking significantly decreased, nor has the percentage of drugs entering the United States declined. Although my objective is not to evaluate the success of Mexico's war on drugs, it is important to highlight the interest of Salinas de Gortari's government in improving its image regarding this issue, a regard that stems from Mexico's attempt to insert itself into worldwide networks of interdependence. In fact, the NAFTA negotiations significantly contributed to the improvement of Mexico's image. Further, it is likely that both the Bush and Clinton administrations exaggerated Mexico's successes in fighting drug trafficking in order to preserve its reputation and to negotiate NAFTA (Golden 1995: A1). If this interpretation is true, in the future it would be worth paying attention to the image factor in the use of foreign policy instruments.

Toward a Discourse of Interdependence?

Despite Salinas de Gortari's aforementioned reticence to adapt the foreign policy discourse to the rules of the game of interdependence, by the end of his term he began to modify these practices. Allowing international observers for the August 1994 elections—explained in large part by the government's decision to carry out clean elections—marked the beginning of the end of the discourse of "sovereign democracy." However, it must be said that the same cosmetic answer that appeared in the fight against drug trafficking is also evident to some degree with the issue of democracy, at least while the old practices of the Mexican political system persist. Yet the reality of active interdependence that Mexico must face increasingly limits the success of the old nationalist discourse as well as the success of the cover-up strategies such as the rhetoric on diversification. It is now more difficult to maintain such strategies, as the media reports on Clinton's economic aid to Mexico in 1995 or the press leaks on drug trafficking to the U.S. media in 1994 and 1995 seem to suggest.

At the same time, domestic pressures for democracy and for the rule of law are making Mexico's political reality more compatible with the rules of interdependence. The old discourse and concealed practices in essence stemmed from the persistence of Mexican authoritarianism. As the transition to democracy reaches its end, the discourse and instruments of the Mexican government will end up adapting to the new international reality. In the short term, the "error of December 1994" and the economic crisis the country went through in 1995 and 1996 have discredited the economic model of liberalization followed by Salinas de Gortari. This could spark a temporary revival of nationalist tendencies and a delay in adapting the foreign policy discourse to the realities of interdependence. However, it is likely that, in the medium term, the logic of interdependence will end up modifying what remains of Mexico's second postwar foreign policy.

Notes

1. Regarding specific issues that generate vulnerability, and thus, primary and secondary links of interdependence, see Chabat (1996).
2. This was how the Estrada Doctrine stated the issue. The doctrine was written in 1930 by Mexico's secretary of foreign relations, Genaro Estrada, who said that "Mexico is not inclined to express recognition because it considers this a denigrating practice which, besides hurting the sovereignty of other nations, places them in a position in which their internal matters can lead to remarks by other governments, who have already assumed a critical attitude as they decided, favorably or unfavorably, to judge the legal status of foreign governments." See Secretaría de Relaciones Exteriores (1978).
3. Lázaro Cárdenas himself was clear about Mexico's bargaining power in carrying out the expropriation of oil: "Several administrations of the Revolutionary Regime have attempted to intervene in the concession over the subsoil, awarded to foreign companies, but the circumstances have not been appropriate due to international pressure and domestic problems. But today conditions are different, the country no longer experiences armed struggles, and is at the door steps of a new world war in which England and the United States often speak in favor of democracy and respect for the sovereignty of the states. Thus now it is appropriate to see whether those governments that speak of democracy and sovereignty deliver what they preach as Mexico prepares to make use of its sovereign rights" (Meyer 1972: 338).
4. In fact, beginning with Lopez Portillo's activism, Mexico is allegedly referred to as a "middle power" or "regional power." See González G. (1983: 15–81) and Bagley (1981: 353–356, 386, 393–394).
5. In 1987 President De la Madrid declared to *The Economist* that a free trade zone between Mexico and the United States was not possible because Mexicans were not prepared to surrender their economy and society to United States hegemony (*CQ Researcher* 1991: 500). In mid-1989 President Carlos Salinas de Gortari, responding to an initiative on a common market between Mexico, the United States, and Canada presented by a business leader, said that Mexico did not belong nor did it want to join "any economic zone or political block" (Valderrama and Jiménez 1989: 1-A).
6. Fernando Solana, who was secretary of foreign relations during the first five years of Salinas de Gortari's administration, complained about how the ministry was neglected (Riva Palacio and Gómez Leyva 1994: 10-A).

7. One of the most well-known advertisements featured a businessman who asserted that he could not find "good and loyal workers to work for one dollar an hour within one thousand miles." The ad continued: "Yes, you can. Yucatán." These ads ended with the tag line: "When the United States is very expensive and the Far East is too far. Yes, you can in Yucatan" (The Center for Public Integrity 1993: 105–106).

8. During the summer of 1992 it was announced that Nacional Financiera and the Mexican Hispanic Board, which belongs to the Hispanic-American Business Affairs, administered a $20 million fund to finance small and mid-size Hispanic American business projects in Mexico. Early in 1993, Nacional Financiera lent $35 million to the Hispanic Capital Fund, based in Los Angeles, for the purpose of financing road and railroad construction projects, as well as water treatment plants in Mexico (*Mexico & NAFTA Report* 1993: 4).

9. This was evident when President Clinton granted an emergency credit to Mexico in February 1995 to help contain the economic crisis resulting from the "December error" of 1994. Clinton's own reason was that this aid was in the interest of the United States.

10. This opinion was expressed by Negroponte in a confidential memo later leaked during a Mexican conference (Puig 1991: 6–11).

11. President Salinas de Gortari himself declared at an interview in 1991 that "when you are introducing an economic reform that is very strong, you must be certain to build a political consensus around it. If, at the same time, you are introducing a drastic political reform, in addition to the economic one, you can end up with neither. And what we want is reform not disintegration" (Gardels 1991: 8).

12. According to a government poll taken in October 1992, 64.3 percent of the Mexican population supported NAFTA. In September 1993, the percentage was 53.7%. The decline in support for the agreement can be explained in terms of the problems that NAFTA faced in 1993 (Golden 1993: 1A).

References

Bagley, Bruce Michael. 1981. "Mexico in the 1980s: A New Regional Power." *Current History*, Vol. 80, No. 469, November.

Bloomfield, Richard J. 1994. "Making the Western Hemisphere Safe for Democracy? The OAS Defense-of-Democracy Regime." *The Washington Quarterly*, Vol. 17, No. 2, Spring.

CQ Researcher. 1991. Vol. 1, No. 1, 19 July.

Chabat, Jorge. 1989. "The Making of Mexican Policy toward the United States." In Rosario Green and Peter Smith, et al., *Foreign Policy in U.S.–Mexican Relations*. San Diego: Center for U.S.–Mexican Studies, University of California, San Diego.

————. 1990. "Los Instrumentos de la Política Exterior de Miguel De la Madrid," *Foro Internacional*, 119, Mexico: El Colegio de Mexico, Vol. XXX, No. 3, January–March.

————. 1991. "Mexico's Foreign Policy in 1990: Electoral Sovereignty and

Integration with the United States." *Journal of Interamerican Studies and World Affairs*, Vol. 33, No. 4, Winter.

———. 1993."Mexico en 1991: Diversificando la Interdependencia." In Jorge Heine, ed., *Enfrentando los Cambios Globales. Anuario de Políticas Exteriores Latinoamericanas 1991–1992.* Santiago, Chile: Ediciones Dolmen/PROSPEL.

———. 1995. "The Combat of Drug Trafficking in Mexico under Salinas: The Limits of Tolerance." Mexico: Centro de Investigación y Docencia Económicas (CIDE).

———. 1996. "La Integración de México al Mundo de la Post-Guerra Fria: del Nacionalismo a la Interdependencia Imperfecta." In Arturo Borja, Guadalupe González, and Brian J. R. Stevenson, eds., *Regionalismo y Poder en América: Los Límites del Neorrealismo.* México: Centro de Investigación y Docencia Económicas (CIDE).

Eisenstadt, Todd. 1993. "El TLC o los Límites del Cabildeo." *Este País*, No. 30, September.

Gardels, Nathan. 1991. "North American Free Trade: Mexico's Route to Upward Mobility." *New Perspectives Quarterly*, Vol. 8, No. 1, Winter.

Golden, Tim. 1993. "As U.S. Vote on Trade Pact Nears, Mexicans Are Expressing Doubts." *New York Times,* 8 November.

———. 1995. "To Help Keep Mexico Stable U.S. Soft-Pedaled Drug War." *New York Times*, 31 July.

Goldgeier, James M., and Michael McFaul. 1992. "A Tale of Two Worlds: Core and Periphery in the Post–Cold War Era." *International Organization*, Vol. 46, No. 2, Spring.

González G., Guadalupe. 1983. "Incertidumbres de una Potencia Media Regional: las Nuevas Dimensiones de la Política Exterior Mexicana." In Olga Pellicer, ed., *La Política Exterior de México: Desafios en los Ochenta.* Mexico: Centro de Investigación y Docencia Económicas (CIDE).

Heiberg, Marianne. 1994. "Introduction." In Marianne Heiberg, ed., *Subduing Sovereignty: Sovereignty and the Right to Intervene.* London: Pinter Publishers.

Holsti, K. J. 1995. *International Politics: A Framework for Analysis.* Englewood Cliffs, N.J.: Prentice Hall.

International Monetary Fund. 1995. *Direction of Trade Statistics Yearbook.* Washington, D.C.: International Monetary Fund.

Keohane, Robert O., and Joseph S. Nye. 1989. *Power and Interdependence.* Glenview, Ill.: Scott, Foresman, and Company.

La Jornada. 1990. "México y el Mundo, por un Comercio Más Intenso y Más Benéfico." Conclusions from the *Foro de Consulta sobre las Relaciones Comerciales de México con el Mundo.* 27 May.

Lewis, Charles, et al. 1993. *The Trading Game—Inside Lobbying for the North American Free Trade Agreement.* Washington, D.C.: Center for Public Integrity.

Lewis, Charles, and Margaret Ebrahin. 1993. "Can Mexico and Big Business USA Buy NAFTA?" *The Nation,* 14 June.

Meyer, Lorenzo. 1972. "Diario Personal del General Cárdenas." In *Mexico y los Estados Unidos en el Conflicto Petrolero (1917–1942).* Mexico: El Colegio de Mexico.

Mexico & NAFTA Report. 1993. "Divisa in Partes Tres." London: Latin American Newsletters. 23 September.

Palmer, Norman, and Howard C. Perkins. 1969. *International Relations*. Boston: Houghton Mifflin Company.

Puig, Carlos. 1991. "Conclusión de Negroponte: con el Tratado de Libre Comercio, México Quedará a Disposición de Washington." *Proceso*, No. 758, 13 May.

Riva Palacio, Raymundo, and Ciro Gómez Leyva. 1994. "No Me Arrancaron la Cancillería." Interview with Fernando Solana, *Reforma*, 27 June.

Secretaría de Relaciones Exteriores. 1978. "Doctrina Mexico." In *Genaro Estrada: Diplomático y Escritor*, Mexico: Secretaría de Relaciones Exteriores, Colección del Archivo Histórico Diplomático Mexicano.

Solana, Fernando. 1994a. *Cinco Años de Política Exterior*, México: Editorial Porrua.

————. 1994b. "Balance y Perspectivas del decenio 1981–1991." In César Sepúlveda, ed., *La Política Internacional de Mexico en el Decenio de los Ochenta*. Mexico: Fondo de Cultura Económica.

Truell, Peter. 1990. "U.S. and Mexico Agree to Seek Free-Trade Pact." *Wall Street Journal*. 27 March.

Valderrama, José, and Edith Jiménez. 1989. "México no Pertenece ni Quiere Asimilarse a Bloques: CSG." *Excelsior*, 27 June.

Chapter 3

Decentralized Diplomacy: The Role of Consular Offices in Mexico's Relations with its Diaspora

Carlos González Gutiérrez

In an article published in 1987, Mexican analyst Jorge Castañeda wondered why the Mexican government had not abandoned its ancient diplomatic practices in order to make full use of the consular offices in the United States to openly promote its interests. This approach would allow the consulates to lobby for and promote the Mexican government's positions. At that time a common response was that the consulates were devoted full time to processing travel documents and to protecting their nationals in the United States; that is, they were involved in traditional consular activities, leaving political matters to the embassy in Washington. Why then did the Mexican government fail to take advantage of an existing consular infrastructure located in a country whose political system (characterized by its openness and decentralized decision-making process) allowed for this type of participation (Castañeda 1987)?

Seen in retrospect, the role of Mexican consulates in the United States seems to have changed substantially. The forty consular offices in the United States have abandoned their traditional profile.[1] New functions have been given to the consulates, partly as a consequence of the evolution of bilateral relations, and partly because the Mexican government decided to deliberately use them as channels to promote its interests. This change became evident during President Carlos Salinas de Gortari's administration, when the consulates were institutionally strengthened. The offices no longer constituted the semiexclusive space of the foreign service, specialized in technical consular matters. Instead new staff were added, including people with extensive records in public service such as career diplomats, as well as former governors and secretaries and undersecretaries of state.[2]

Parallel to this process, staff resources were strengthened in most consular offices, not only in number, but by appointing specialized and better trained officers. Press offices were added to the most important consulates, in addition to representatives of the attorney general's office and the Social Security Institute. Further, the distinction between diplomatic and consular branches was eliminated, a decision that was justified on the basis that it created unnecessary difficulties in designating suitable candidates for the consular offices.

Finally, while the bureaucratic paperwork burden of the consulates was being eliminated or reduced, more resources were committed to the protection of Mexicans living in the United States. The Program for Mexican Communities Living in Foreign Countries (PMCLFC) was created as an adjunct to the Ministry of Foreign Relations, enabling the consulates to foster a long-term relationship between these communities and Mexican American as well as Mexican leaders. This program increased the consulates' ability to promote Mexico's educational and cultural programs among Mexican communities living in the United States. Under the sponsorship of this program, eighteen Mexican cultural institutes were created in the United States.

This chapter attempts to answer why these changes occurred as well as analyze the causes that led the Mexican government to modify the traditional role of consular offices in the United States. Additionally, this chapter will examine the problems that Mexican consulates are facing today, their progress and limits, as well as the expectations that these changes have created.

The crux of the problem for the consulates was the issue of nonintervention. As the relationship between the two nations has strengthened, it is becoming more difficult to clearly distinguish the boundaries between domestic and foreign policies. The new functions of Mexican consular offices are not a cause but rather a reflection of this change. As will be shown, the foreign policy role performed by Mexican consulates is a function of three things. The first is related to Mexico's redefining its relations with the world that occurred in the early 1980s. The second is a function of pure bilateral matters: the pluralization of contacts and the compartmentalization of governmental relations between the United States and Mexico. The third refers to changes in the consulates' primary clientele: the Mexican diaspora in the United States.

Mexican consulates have been forced to redefine their role within the context of their country's foreign policy toward the United States in order to justify their existence. This chapter will show that given the explosive increase of first-generation Mexican immigrants, the growing political power of Mexican Americans, and the growing interest of Mexican political parties and public opinion in the consular offices, the consulates had no choice but to redefine their role. This chapter will also show how, parallel to this experience, this redefinition required them to surrender their simplistic and preestablished definitions of the principle of nonintervention. With their new duties Mexican consulates have explored the limits that separate the boundary between foreign and domestic policy but have also discovered, perhaps paradoxically, that their room for maneuver has been narrowed due to the anti-immigration climate and the multicultural crisis in the United States.

Rethinking Foreign Relations

The transformation of the role of Mexican consulates in the design of foreign policy can be explained, first of all, as an unavoidable consequence of Mexico's overall rethinking of its foreign relations, which occurred after the economic crisis of the 1980s. As the Mexican economy opened up to the world over the last decade and exports became the leading engine of economic growth, the country's foreign policy was used as just one more pillar of support for the country's development plans, particularly because they depended on Mexico's exterior ties. Within a short time, the Mexican economy became one of the most open economies in the world. This circumstance compelled the use of embassies and consulates to promote the country's image, inform the principal financial, political, and academic centers abroad about the country's internal changes and, in general, take full advantage of the opening and thus attract more foreign capital, technology, and trade.

In 1990, Mexico's decision to negotiate a free trade agreement with the United States and Canada represented a critical step in the process of globalization that was swamping the international economy. Given the importance of NAFTA to the Mexican government, President Salinas's administration did not skimp on resources to promote its passage. In so doing, Salinas challenged the antiquated practices governing Mexico's reluctance to openly lobby in the United States. Although the Ministry of Foreign Relations did not intervene directly in the NAFTA negotiations—even as other agencies like the Department of Commerce and Industrial Development (SECOFI) hired consulting firms to lobby the U.S. Congress—the Mexican consulates played an active role in promoting the agreement among local leaders and the media. The contrast with the old days could not have been greater: the consulates that did *not* follow the Ministry of Foreign Relations' instructions were the ones that avoided the media and not the ones who used it.

As the experience with NAFTA showed, the success of a country's efforts to influence the decision-making process in the United States is contingent on the current political conditions of the day and on the ability to find American political allies who have the legitimacy to pressure decision makers and the ability to link their cause to the national interest (Franco Hijuelos 1995: 27). Because of their position as diplomats, consuls can not and should not substitute for professional lobbyists when seeking local allies for their causes, not just because of their status as diplomats, but perhaps more importantly because unlike lobbyists they lack the contacts and other relationships that accompany the privileged position of an insider. However, the NAFTA negotiations also showed the double-edged nature of the consulates' position. Precisely because consulates are official representatives of the Mexican government (unlike lobbyists), they were sought out by the media and by political leaders. From the Mexican point of view, this was a healthy step: the NAFTA negotiations encouraged consular officers in the United States to abandon their self-imposed and exaggerated cautiousness, which was based on a rigid interpretation of nonintervention and which failed to take advantage of the opportunities offered by the American political process.

Diversifying Contacts

In addition to the structural reasons that motivated Mexican authorities to search for a free trade agreement, it is important to mention the framework used by both governments to manage their bilateral relations at the beginning of the 1990s when it became clear that relations between the two nations had entered an era of reduced tension. A new framework emerged from a recognition on both sides that in order to maximize the benefits of proximity, they needed to ensure that whatever differences might emerge in their dealings over one issue would not contaminate relations in other spheres. Increased common interests between the two societies compelled them to pursue a more mature and pragmatic relationship that, while acknowledging their differences, could produce a political understanding that would question old-fashioned resentments with the goal of benefiting both economies, especially in the wake of Mexico's new economic opening.

In the words of a former Mexican secretary of state, one of the main assumptions of the new model of intergovernmental relations was that it would not consume the two countries' relations as a whole. It was recognized that the two governments, or rather, the bureaucracies in Washington and Mexico City, were saturated in their common perceptions and respective modus operandi due to the extensive contact between them (Rozental 1993: 72).

The pluralization of contacts, the dispersion of conflict, and the proliferation of interest groups trying to influence policy in both countries all multiplied as a result of the silent integration between the two economies and the gradual disappearance of the border. These processes were the most important challenges for decision makers. As contacts became pluralized, good intergovernmental relations were no longer enough; it became imperative to move from relations at the federal level to relations with non-governmental organizations as well as with state and municipal agencies (Thorup 1990: 60).

From Mexico's perspective, the consulates in the United States are useful tools for confronting the growing proliferation of actors and conflicts. The consulates contribute to the compartmentalization of relations in the sense that they will not contaminate other spheres of relations in the event of a minor conflict. In fact, in a large and diverse country like the United States it is difficult for the embassy in Washington to cover all the issues. Most contacts and exchanges that take place between both societies do not go through Washington or Mexico City, which is another reason why it was better for consulates to handle matters in a decentralized fashion.

With regard to federal activities, decentralized decision making in the United States encourages contacts with local and state authorities. Consuls are the immediate and permanent federal representatives in these types of contacts. In practice, however, Mexico views U.S. federalism as cumbersome because it is often difficult to identify one's counterparts, given Washington's reluctance to get involved in matters that fall within the jurisdiction of local or state authorities (Rico Ferrat 1995: 56). A concrete example illustrates this. Among the programs that Mexico offers to Mexican American communities in the United States, educational programs have the highest priority. It is in this area where Mexico has a clear advantage because economies of scale derive from the size of the national educational system. In addition, Mexican communities in the United States urgently require assistance from their country of origin because of their low educational levels and because of immigrants' need to learn their mother tongue in addition to English. The priority that both governments give to cooperation in educational matters was evident from bilateral meetings between both ministers of education. However, on a day-to-day basis these types of federal-level meetings are insufficient because education in the United States is the domain of state and local governments, not Washington. For example, when the Mexican government (through the Ministry of Foreign Relations and the Ministry of Public Education) offered to train bilingual teachers, the content of the training had to meet the guidelines of every state in the United States. Once these programs were approved, they would need to be "sold" to each school district because money and school teachers are allocated at that level. There are hundreds of school districts in California and Texas alone, so consular support is essential for negotiating with superintendents, school boards, and overseeing the implementation of the educational cooperation agreement.

On the other hand, as consular offices become more effective channels for handling regional conflict, there will be greater opportunities for coping with differences, within manageable limits. The best example of this is the "Mechanisms of Federal Linkage over Boundary Incidents." These are bilateral forums organized periodically by Mexican and U.S. consuls who review incidents that occur in their respective areas. The purpose of these forums is to exchange information and find in situ solutions to border conflicts "so as not to magnify their importance and not afford them the opportunity to produce other consequences" (Loaeza Tovar 1995).

Relationships with the Diaspora

A third group of explanations of the new role of consulates deals with the growing significance of Mexicans in the United States due to their importance as an ethnic minority in the United States as well as their burgeoning influence in Mexico.

Mexican migration to the United States is not a new experience. Since the beginning of this century, and with the construction of the railroad in the Southwest, Mexican labor has been in demand in the United States. However, it is important to note the dimensions of this immigration since the 1970s. According to the U.S. Bureau of the Census, in 1994 there were 6.2 million people living in the United States who were born in Mexico. This number includes undocumented aliens, permanent residents, and citizens. Of that number, 1.3 million arrived between 1990 and 1994, 2.7 million arrived in the 1980s, 1.5 million arrived in the 1970s, and 700,000 arrived before 1970 (Hansen and Bachu 1995). In other words, during the 1970s the number of Mexican immigrants to the United States doubled from the previous decade; in the 1980s their number doubled again from the previous decade. Unless the United States is successful in its efforts to stop the flow of Mexican immigrants, and assuming that the second half of the 1990s will repeat the same migratory trend of the first half, the 1990s figures will reach the same levels as the 1980s.[3]

The simple numerical growth of the Mexican population in the United States would be reason enough to build up the Mexican consulates. It is also important to mention the effects of the Immigration Reform and Control Act of 1986 (IRCA), which legalized 2.3 million undocumented Mexicans. As legal residents, the so-called "rodinos" were able to freely cross the border, change jobs, receive public services and, in general, live their everyday life without fear of being detained or deported.[4] These newly legalized immigrants went to their local consulates to request the necessary travel documents in order to enjoy the acquired privilege of traveling to Mexico at their leisure.[5] Consequently, the rodinos (as well as those who benefited from IRCA's family reunification provisions) increased the demand for consular services, such as information about a bureaucratic task, consular protection for a relative or friend in trouble, or assistance in preparing paperwork for making donations to their hometowns in Mexico. In general, the new freedoms and rights of these millions of newly legalized Mexicans translated into a greater appetite to participate in community-based issues in both their host and home countries. That is how first-generation Mexican-immigrant organizations (such as those sponsored by the Catholic Church and local community centers) started out and then grew, such that by the end of the 1980s and throughout the 1990s they multiplied in Latino barrios in Los Angeles, Chicago, New York, and Dallas (González Gutiérrez 1993).

Mexican political parties, particularly the Party of the Democratic Revolution (PRD) and to a lesser extent the Institutionalized Revolutionary Party (PRI), also took advantage of the outcome of IRCA. Growing competition among parties in the Mexican political system, as well as the postelectoral conflict that followed the 1988 elections, catalyzed the internationalization of the Mexican parties' disputes in some major U.S. cities. These parties identified sympathizers and resources in the United States and built international coalitions that contributed to the erosion of the longstanding exclusivity of the Mexican government as the sole interlocutor of national leaders and Mexican American organizations (Dresser 1993: 82–112). Even when these organizations did not have a base of support or the standing of community-based organizations (immigrants are not just distrustful of the government in their country of origin; they are also reluctant to get involved in party politics), the attention afforded by the Mexican media gave political activists an audience for staging public demonstrations, most of which took place in front of consular offices. Under these circumstances, the seizure of consulates by various groups for twelve to twenty-four hours became a frequent style of protest.

Inevitably, the consulates' function became politicized. Through the U.S. and Mexican media, the political parties called for greater monitoring of the consulates' role. Consulates in the United States became a channel for public opinion regarding events in Mexico. Mexican candidates for municipal, state, and federal office campaigned for support in the United States. Opposition candidates invariably accused the Mexican consul of representing the interests of the ruling party, not of Mexico.

In due course, it became difficult for consular representatives to maintain their formerly low public profile. Contrary to the situation in other countries where the legislature and the general public pay scant attention to the activities of the consular offices and consider them apolitical (Walentynowicz 1982), in Mexico the national media frequently monitors the consulates, follows U.S. immigration policy, and is keen to denounce human rights violations against immigrants. As the demonstrations against Proposition 187 in California showed, the fate of Mexicans living abroad has become an issue of national unity in Mexico, a reality that the consulates have not ignored. Proof of this is the frequency of interviews with Mexican consuls in the Mexican media. With a few exceptions, these consular officers appear on Mexican television more often than do Mexican ambassadors.[6]

Finally, to explain this new consular activism another segment of the Mexican diaspora in the United States must be considered: the leaders of

Mexican American organizations. It is calculated that by the year 2010 Latinos will surpass African Americans as the largest ethnic minority in the United States. Their importance to investor and commercial relations between the two countries will grow concomitantly. By virtue of their high birth rates, their youth, and increased rates of citizenship, the disparity between the numbers of Mexican Americans and their political power could be reduced over time. The NAFTA experience suggests that, like some other ethnic groups, Mexican Americans may begin to have a privileged role in policy making affecting their "homeland."

Owing to the diaspora's growing influence in matters concerning Mexico, the expanding network of Mexican nongovernmental actors on both sides of the border, and the need to strengthen the job of protecting Mexicans through close links with local community organizations, the Mexican government acquiesced to a longstanding demand of Latino leaders and in February 1990 created the Program for Mexican Communities Living in Foreign Countries (PMCLFC). By then it was evident that the more time went on, the greater the political cost without such a program. The program was housed within the Ministry of Foreign Relations and was given the exclusive responsibility for coordinating Mexico's relationship with its diaspora (García Acevedo 1996: 28; González Gutiérrez 1993: 234).

From the beginning it was decided that the PMCLFC would be managed by the consular network in the United States (Secretaría de Relaciones Exteriores 1990: 6). Upon the creation of the PMCLFC, the consulates received a clear mandate: although their fundamental obligation was to protect the human rights of Mexican immigrants and their families living in the United States, it was now important to foster a long-term relationship with the heterogeneous Mexican diaspora in the United States through educational, cultural, sports, health, business, and community programs. In the end, this mandate did not conflict with the consulates' primary objective of protecting the rights of first-generation Mexicans in the United States. On the contrary, the PMCLFC strengthened the capacity of Mexican consulates to provide protection to its nationals as it promoted contact with immigrant organizations and other Latino advocacy groups.

Parallel to this, the PMCLFC expanded the horizons of the consulates as it opened the door for greater contact with U.S. citizens of Mexican origin. Although these citizens do not come under consular protection by Mexico, the PMCLFC adopted an open and pluralist definition that was more political than legal of the links that unite Americans of Mexican origin with their ancestors. Strictly speaking, consulates are supposed to assist and protect the nationals of Mexico, but why limit the sense of belonging of second- and third-generation Mexican Americans only to juridical links of nationality? Of course, a U.S. citizen cannot seek protection from his or her parent's country of origin when confronted with a legal matter, but why not respect and cultivate the yearning of many of these citizens who want to be close to Mexican traditions and culture? Why not recognize their legitimate right to feel like an inheritor of a common origin and feel part of a nation that crosses political boundaries? Why treat these citizens in the same way foreigners are treated?

The creation of PMCLFC reshaped Mexico's foreign policy to resemble that of other countries with large diasporas scattered throughout the world. Both in the immediate context of consular action, as well as in the broader context of public opinion, the PMCLFC raised the significance of U.S. citizens of Mexican origin. The PMCLFC gave consulates the authority to encourage, along with Mexican and Mexican American leaders, the participation of diverse communities in the international cooperation programs that were offered to the diaspora. In the national debate, the creation of the PMCLFC spurred, among other things, a serious debate about the wisdom of making Mexican citizenship nonrenounceable. Mexicans lose their citizenship when they acquire a new citizenship.[7]

The Dilemma of Mexican Consulates

As with their counterparts in other countries, Mexican consuls are sent to the United States to help their conationals. They expedite travel documents like visas and passports; exercise notary and civic registry functions; deliver legal documents; obtain testimonies and carry out orders by Mexican judges; inform their government about the political situation in the region where they are assigned; and in general, promote the image of the country and defend the interests of their nationals living abroad.

However, the consuls' job is distinct in various respects. The peculiarities of the Mexican consuls in the United States stem from the size of their most immediate clientele which, according to the U.S. census, totals six million. Because many of these people were socialized in Mexico, they will continue considering themselves Mexicans until the day they die, even if they have acquired U.S. citizenship. In that sense, first-generation immigrants are a "captive audience" of Mexican consuls. Moreover, because most of them have retained Mexican citizenship, they are the consuls' fundamental obligation. Further, one must also add the secondary population of the approximately 14 million American citizens of Mexican origin who can not be expected to feel the same degree of ancestral attachment.[8]

Another characteristic that distinguishes Mexican consuls in the United States (much like their Turkish counterparts in Germany or their Algerian counterparts in France) relates to the socioeconomic situation of their nationals: people of Mexican origin are not only becoming the largest ethnic minority in the United States, but the majority of them hold the least remunerated and least prestigious jobs in the labor market: they work as janitors, gardeners, laborers, and domestic help. Mexicans are overrepresented in manual labor activities and, compared to other immigrant groups, have one of the lowest indices of self-employment (Portes and Rimbaud 1990: 75–78). In the agricultural sector, 85 percent of migrant workers in the United States were born abroad, the majority of them in Mexico (Gabbard, Mines, and Boccalandro 1994: 19).

In sum, the problems of Mexican immigrants in the United States are those of a young unskilled population with poverty levels above the national average. It was revealing that during the Los Angeles riots in May 1992 (the most violent urban revolt in the modern history of the United States), of the ten thousand people arrested by the police and the National Guard, 40 percent were Mexican and Central American immigrants, mostly monolingual and recently arrived (Miles 1992: 41). Few of these immigrants knew the precise reasons for the riots, which were started by African American youths demonstrating against the acquittal of four policemen accused of beating black motorist Rodney King. To the Latin American immigrants, there was no ideological justification behind their participation, other than to loot businesses for goods that were normally out of their reach.

The marginalization of the Mexican-origin immigrant population sets the working agenda of Mexican consuls. Thus, some of the factors that explain the priority of consular offices are the low educational levels of immigrants and their families, the universal correlation between poverty and criminal behavior, as well as a feeling of a lack of empowerment among immigrants. To mention only the most dramatic cases, between January 1993 and May 1995, Mexican consulates in the United States counted 24 cases of violent deaths and 29 injuries among Mexican-born citizens at the hands of the police. During this same period, there were 22 cases of Mexicans who received compensation of more than $3 million as victims of police brutality (Aponte 1996).

The socioeconomic characteristics of the Mexican immigrant community also explain the nature of the international cooperation projects offered by the consular offices. A brief review of the current projects carried out by the PMCLFC shows that education is the priority: adult education (literacy programs and primary and secondary school instruction in Spanish); bilingual education (distribution of Spanish textbooks, training for U.S. teachers); and migrant education (programs to accredit the education of children of migrant workers). Given the natural virtue of sports as a social integration tool among immigrant communities, sports promotion via local and international soccer tournaments is an important initiative of the PMCLFC. In the area of health, AIDS-prevention campaigns have received special attention due to the rural mobility of epidemics in Mexico and that the spread of AIDS is closely related to the migratory experience.[9]

Another priority of the PMCLFC is the community-organizing programs that aim to identify Mexican communities in the United States by hometown. The PMCLFC supports the organizational efforts of clubs consisting of people from the same hometown and, in general, promotes long-term relationships with officials in these localities in Mexico. More than an end in itself, community organizing by the Mexican consuls is a way to achieve other objectives. Due to the vast number of Mexican immigrants,[10] consuls require the support of these community organizations in order to efficiently accomplish their duties. Thus, the success of these consular offices depends on their capacity to be grounded in the very communities they serve.

The most frequent way in which first-generation immigrants organize is by place of origin. The family and friendship networks that facilitate migration reproduce themselves in the settling community. Place-of-origin clubs are the formal expression of these networks. They are organized around sports or around fund-raising to finance a construction project in their hometowns in Mexico. Their function is to promote and strengthen social networks. While these clubs are "bottom-up" groups led by community leaders, consuls work with them to establish channels of communication and access to their hometowns in Mexico (González Gutiérrez 1995: 88).

Once the relationship between these groups and the consulates is established, it confers upon the group a highly respected form of recognition. They seek recognition for their right to belong to both their communities and the country they abandoned—not because they wanted to, but because they were forced to for economic reasons. The benefit in the short term to the Mexican government is that this relationship helps strengthen the immigrants' ability to defend themselves, which in turns makes it easier for the government to protect them. In the long term, community work facilitates the instrumentalization of international cooperation projects in health, education, and sports. More importantly and looking to the future, the work with immigrant organizations will nurture the links upon which the relationship of Mexico with its diaspora will rest.

The Nonintervention Boundary

The uniqueness of the dilemma of Mexican consuls in the United States is also a function of the context in which they operate. In addition to the aforementioned point that the U.S. political system is characterized by its open and decentralized decision-making process, it is important to mention the recognition that the United States gives ethnicity as a basis for political organization. This legitimizes the ethnic mobilization of Mexican communities (Nagel c1986, 1991: 76).

As a result of the Civil Rights movement, since the 1960s the U.S. government has tried to remedy the damages caused by longstanding practices that discriminated against African Americans as well as other ethnic, religious, and racial groups. The government designed policies granting explicit preference to members of diverse social groups. This legacy has given people of Mexican descent the necessary motivation to mobilize politically toward a common ethnic identity, which in a broad sense is defined as "Hispanic" or "Latino," and in a stricter sense may be defined as Chicano, Mexican, or Mexican American. To Mexican Americans, it is not difficult to maintain a common identity in light of the ongoing flow of new Mexican immigrants, of their concentration in a few regions (especially in the Southwest), and of the open or tacit discrimination by majority groups. This latter point ironically has served to reinforce the ethnic identity of Mexicans (Arce 1981: 177).

The political organization of Latino minorities along ethnic lines has challenged the consulates but it has also offered opportunities. As ethnicity becomes politicized, almost any effort by Mexican diplomats to promote the Mexican-ness of the communities they serve assumes political connotations. Whatever the diplomats do (or don't do) takes place in the context of interethnic competition that occurs inside and outside the diaspora.

Inside the diaspora, Mexican American leaders have their own agenda that differs greatly from that of the Mexican government. There is no doubt that there are points of agreement, as in their repudiation of Mexico-bashing by American politicians who have blamed Mexico and Mexicans for problems that have nothing to do with them. An example of this was the debate surrounding Proposition 187. Both Mexican Americans and the Mexican government maintained close communications in their efforts to repudiate the initiative, which both sides saw as not only threatening the fundamental human rights of immigrants, but also as a cover for discrimination and interethnic hostility toward Latinos in California.[11]

However, Proposition 187 also showed that it was not because they were Latinos that Mexican Americans agreed with Mexico on immigration matters. Had it not been for the discriminatory fervor of the initiative's sympathizers, Mexican American voters would have approved Proposition 187 by an ample margin (Burgess and González Gutiérrez [forthcoming]). Clearer still is the example of the debate over NAFTA. Bowing to labor union demands, Mexican American members of Congress would have voted against NAFTA (which probably would have jeopardized NAFTA's passage due to their influence among their colleagues) had it not been for the last-minute acceptance by Mexico and the United States to their demands: the creation of the North American Bank for Development (Franco Hijuelos 1995: 20). The debate around NAFTA showed that the heterogeneity of the Mexican diaspora causes class differences to prevail over solidarity with their country of origin.

Outside the diaspora, majority–minority relations in the United States serve as a framework for Mexico's efforts to protect its citizens and to foster Mexican-ness among its absent children. Today, the United States is experiencing one of its cyclical revivals of nativism and xenophobia. Fear of and hatred toward the foreign-born have flourished partly due to the growth of this population. From

1980 to 1994, the Hispanic population grew by 82.4 percent while the non-Hispanic population grew by only 10 percent.[12] However, this is not the only cause of the anti-immigration climate.

In 1964 the U.S. Congress ended its immigration policy based on national origin quotas and instead made family unification criteria the central feature of its policy. This opened the door to an explosive growth of Third World immigration. Thirty years later the demographic, cultural, and linguistic consequences of this policy shift are being felt. Economic stagnation in California, greater disparities in income distribution, concerns about crime and the moral crisis of the postindustrial society, anti-intellectual populism, and heightened racial tensions have contributed to doubts about the ideal of the multicultural society as well as about the usefulness of programs that emerged out of the 1960s Civil Rights movement.

Because the Latino population, which is primarily Mexican American, will soon replace African Americans as the largest ethnic minority in the United States, attacks against multiculturalism have turned into a frontal attack on this population's growth. The movement against bilingualism became one of the first campaigns by those who sought to stop the "Third World-ization" of the American social fabric. To date, the English-only movement, which emerged in the 1980s to force immigrant assimilation through the proscription of English as the official language of the United States, has been replaced by a more generalized concern (no longer just the province of conservative groups) to stop the flow of immigrants from Latin American and the Caribbean. This public anxiety is manifest in the restrictionist proposals of the Clinton administration, as well as in Congress, where both Democrats and Republicans rail against undocumented immigrants.

Within this context, the Mexican consulates' room for maneuver has been considerably reduced. The revival in the United States of nationalist theses and cultural prejudices, increasingly articulated with greater precision by the ideologues of modern nativism, has painted cultural diversity as a weakness rather than a strength. Challenging the classic liberal notion of the United States as the land of immigrants—a land in which citizens' loyalty to the Constitution and the Declaration of Independence is what unites the nation, not a single ethnicity and a common culture—conservatives have presented a simpler, less abstract vision in which the national identity of the country lies in its Anglo-Saxon culture and values. There is no space for plurality: multiculturalism is a virus that erodes the inner fabric of American society by weakening the Anglo-Saxon cultural base.

Hence, Mexico's efforts to foster a relationship with Mexican Americans are viewed as harmful to the country's national security. Large-scale immigration is a threat to the slow and gradual process of the construction of an American identity partly because it has encouraged a surge of subcultures foreign to the Anglo-Saxon culture and heightened the awareness of ethnic differences among

Anglo Americans. Mexico's relationship with its diaspora is perceived to be a utilitarian attempt to use the Mexican-born for its own interest, in a zero-sum game that, taken to its extreme, would Balkanize the United States (Brimelow 1995; O'Sullivan 1994).

One of the most widely read authors of the anti-immigration movement, Peter Brimelow, summarizes the Mexican government's position in this way:

> [A] development that already appears well under way: the Mexican government's claim to what amounts to extraterritorial rights over Mexican immigrants in the territory of the (former?) United States. Recently, Mexico has opened "cultural institutes" and sponsored programs to teach Spanish to illiterate Hispanics from New York to California. It has, for example, reportedly donated textbooks and bilingual teachers to the Los Angeles school system. It has announced that it is "monitoring" death penalty cases involving Mexican citizens and is lobbying for abolition of capital punishment in the states where they are held. . . . The plain fact is that this is a rational strategy for the Mexican elite. They can dump their poor in the United States *and* become the tail that wags the geopolitical dog. (Brimelow 1995: 194)

Conclusion

Once Mexico made the decision to redesign its foreign relations, the fate of Mexican consulates was defined. In part, the new activism of consulates began when Mexico shifted its strategy during a period of reduced tensions at the beginning of the 1990s. However, it might be more useful to view these changes as an outcome of the need for Mexican consulates to remain effective in times of change.

The consistent growth of immigration during the past two decades, the Immigration Reform and Control Act of 1986, the gradual integration of the U.S. and Mexican economies, the virtual disappearance of the borders that separate internal and external matters in bilateral relations, the pluralization of contacts between both societies, and the internationalization of Mexican policy are some of the reasons that explain the changing role of Mexican consulates in the United States. A strategic reason must also be added: Mexico's need to foster a long-term relationship with the people of Mexican origin living north of the Mexican border. Hypothetically, even if these communities were uninterested in Mexico, and even if the overlap between Mexico's agenda and the diaspora's were practically nil, and even if a prominent Mexican American viewed relations with Mexico as a source of weakness rather than strength—in any of those circumstances, it would still be in Mexico's national interest to promote affinity with these communities, whose economic and political power is expected to grow in the near future. Aside from the merits of the Program for Mexican Communities Living in Foreign Countries, the truth is that the longer Mexico delayed creating a coherent and long-term policy toward Mexicans living in the United States, the greater the price.

Mexican consuls are the last resort of Mexico's strategy vis-à-vis its diaspora. Their success is contingent on the priority the Mexican government attaches to this strategy, as well as on the consistency and coherence with which it is applied. Hence, much of this work takes place in Mexico rather than in the United States. Nothing erodes the consuls' work more than when Mexican nationals fall prey to corruption and abuses of authority when they return temporarily or permanently to Mexico. Mexico's policy toward Mexicans living abroad will lack coherence if it is not accompanied by a domestic policy to fight abuses against repatriated immigrants. This policy must also raise the importance of Mexicans living abroad in the minds of state governments and federal agencies like the Ministry of Public Education or the Ministry of Tourism.

In addition to being coherent, Mexico's approach toward its diaspora in the United States also needs to be consistent in the long term. Contrary to Israel's relationship with its Jewish diaspora in the United States—where pro-Israeli organizations were a pressure group even before the creation of the State of Israel—in the case of Mexico's relations with its "absent children," the efficacy of Mexican Americans as an ethnic lobby in the United States is relatively limited. Besides, it is difficult to argue that there is a convergence of interests between Mexico and its heterogeneous diaspora. For Mexican American leaders, interethnic solidarity is a very weak link when it comes to conflicts between its own immediate economic interests and Mexico's.

Also unlike Israel, Mexico is confronted with the challenge of building channels of communication that will allow it to maintain a continuous dialogue with its diaspora.[13] This is a significant task whose results will not be seen until the next generation. As a point of departure, it is important to recognize that Mexico's objective is not to use its diaspora as a device for pressuring the United States nor to achieve a communion of interests between the two sides. What Mexico is attempting is to be an interlocutor in a dialogue that until recently did not exist in any organized fashion.

The dilemma of immigrant communities—characterized by their marginal levels of income and education—as well as the politicization of ethnicity in U.S. society, have compelled Mexican consuls to redefine the concept of non-intervention in the internal affairs of the United States. With the backdrop of controversy over multiculturalism, it is likely that the very forces that compelled the Mexican consulates to base their work in the communities they serve simultaneously narrowed their room for maneuver.

The mandate of Mexican consulates is limited by the need to respect the internal jurisdiction of the United States. A sine qua non of the consulates' activities is to ensure that nothing they do constitutes interference in the domestic matters of the host country. Pluralism and tolerance are crucial ingredients of the Mexican government's relationship with its diaspora. It is understood that most immigrants' loyalty toward their country of origin does not contradict their desire to be loyal and honest citizens of their adoptive country.

From this perspective, Mexico's approach toward its "absent children" in the United States must be understood as an effort of neighborly cooperation, though in this case cooperation blows from a poor country to a rich country. Mexico's pursuits of Mexicans abroad must not be detrimental to U.S. national interests, but rather must enhance them. After all, neither country prospers if Mexican immigrants maintain low educational levels, are threats to public health, or are incapable of organizing to protect their rights and interests.

Notes

I would like to thank the following people for their support and comments on this chapter: Roger Díaz de Cossío, Rodulfo Figueroa, Remedios Gómez-Arnau, Enrique Loaeza, Jaime Paz y Puente, Enrique Rojo, as well as the co-authors of this volume. The opinions expressed here, however, are the exclusive responsibility of the author.

1. In addition to the embassy in Washington and the general consulate in Puerto Rico, Mexico has consular offices in the following thirty-nine U.S. cities: Austin, Texas; Atlanta; Boston; Brownsville, Texas; Calexico, California; Chicago; Corpus Christi, Texas; Dallas; Del Rio, Texas; Denver; Detroit; Eagle Pass, Texas; El Paso; Fresno; Houston; Laredo, Texas; Los Angeles; McAllen, Texas; Miami; Midland, Texas; New Orleans; New York; Nogales, Arizona; Orlando; Oxnard, California; Philadelphia; Phoenix; San Antonio; San Bernardino, California; San Diego; San Jose; St. Louis; San Francisco; Santa Ana, California; Sacramento; Salt Lake City; Seattle; and Tucson.

2. A parallel process that undoubtedly favored the transfer of politicians to consular offices was the shrinking of the state: as privatization of state-owned companies took place, the number of high-ranking officials decreased.

3. Two related phenomena make the above-mentioned inflows (whose growth has been remarkable) seem larger than what they really are: one, high fertility rates among first-generation Mexicans (which are higher than those of the native population); two, Mexican immigrants tend to be concentrated in a few states, and in a few regions in those states.

4. For a detailed analysis of the effects of IRCA on the relations of Mexico with its diaspora, see González Gutiérrez (1993: 224).

5. The demand for travel documents that resulted from IRCA occurred mainly in 1988, 1989, and 1990. For example, in 1987 the largest Mexican consulate (located in Los Angeles) granted "consular registration" to 65,000 Mexicans; in 1988 that number increased to 150,000; in 1989, to 120,000; and in 1990, to 90,000. It was not until 1991 that the issuance of consular registration returned to its normal annual level of 60,000. The consular registration (*matrícula consular*) is the travel document most often used by Mexicans living in the United States when traveling to Mexico. This document is cheaper and easier to acquire than a passport (Mexican Consulate in Los Angeles 1993: 24).

6. Another way to measure this is by analyzing the questions asked of the secretary of foreign relations during hearings before the Mexican Congress: one of the two or three most frequent topics of legislators' questions is the status of Mexicans in the United States and the activities of the secretary (Secretaría de Relaciones Exteriores 1995).

7. During the presentation of the National Development Plan, President Ernesto Zedillo proposed making Mexican nationality nonrenounceable. In recognizing that "the Mexican nation goes beyond the territory that is contained by the outlined borders," the president assured that his government would try to "promote legal and constitutional reforms so that Mexicans can preserve their nationality, independent of the citizenship or residence they had adopted" (Presidencia de la República 1995).

8. The balance between these two groups of the diaspora is exceptional. Relatively speaking, from the beginning of the century there were not as many foreigners in the United States as there are now due to the intensity of migratory flows over the past two and a half decades. In 1910 the U.S. population was 14.7 percent foreign born; in 1970 it was 4.8 percent, and since then has continually increased to 8.7 percent in 1994. The 6.2 million Mexicans are the largest foreign-born group in the United States (which totals 22.5 million), followed by Filipinos with 1.03 million, Cubans with 0.8 million, and Salvadorans with 0.7 million (Hansen and Bachu 1995: 2).

9. The PMCLFC also has organized programs in cultural, business, and leadership areas. However, these programs have been directed mostly at Mexican American communities.

10. To cite one example, in the Los Angeles area there are more people of Mexican origin than any other city in the world after Mexico City and Guadalajara.

11. One way of interpreting President Ernesto Zedillo's decision to promote the nonrenounceability of Mexican citizenship is as a product of Proposition 187. Zedillo's action can be seen as a way for Mexico to support the Latino leadership's efforts to increase citizenship rates of Mexican legal residents. As citizens, they would be better poised to exercise their electoral rights, thereby raising the political stakes of those who would promote anti-Mexican campaigns.

12. Today, 85 percent of immigrants to the United States are non-European. Historically, however, 85 percent of immigrants arrived from the European continent (Castro 1995).

13. This does not mean that Mexico's relations with its diaspora are new. Perhaps its novelty lies in Mexico's effort to develop a policy with long-term objectives. For a history of these relations, see García Acevedo 1996 and Gómez Quiñonez 1976.

References

Aponte, David. 1996. "En Dos Años Fueron Ultimados en E.U. 24 Mexicanos en Incidentes Violentos." *La Jornada*, 2 January.

Arce, Carlos H. 1981. "A Reconsideration of Chicano Culture and Identity." *Daedalus*, Spring.

Brimelow, Peter. 1995. *Alien Nation: Common Sense about America's Immigration Disaster.* New York: Random House.

Burgess, Katrina and Carlos González Gutiérrez. Forthcoming, 1997. "Reluctant Partner: California in U.S.–Mexico Relations." In Sidney Weintraub, Mónica Verea, and Rafael Fernández de Castro, eds., *U.S.–Mexico: The New Agenda.* Washington, D.C.: Center for Strategic and International Studies.

Castañeda, Jorge G. 1987. "Más Allá de los Principios." *Nexos,* Vol. 10, No. 110, February.

Castro, Max J. 1995. "Ideología, Ciencias Sociales y Política: el Debate sobre la Política de Inmigración en Estados Unidos." Paper presented at the XXth Congress of the Asociación Latinoamericana de Sociología, Mexico City, 2–6 October.

Dresser, Denise. 1993. "Exporting Conflict: Transboundary Consequences of Mexican Politics." In Abraham F. Lowenthal and Katrina Burgess et al., eds., *The California-Mexico Connection.* Stanford: Stanford University Press.

Franco Hijuelos, Claudia. 1995. "El Cabildeo como Instrumento de Política Exterior: el Caso del Tratado de Libre Comercio." *Revista Mexicana de Política Exterior,* 46, Spring.

Gabbard, Susan, Rick Mines, and Beatriz Boccalandro. 1994. *Migrant Farmworkers: Pursuing Security in an Unstable Labor Market.* Research Report #5. Washington, D.C.: U.S. Department of Labor.

García Acevedo, Maria Rosa. 1996. "Contemporary Mexico's Policy Toward the Mexican Diaspora in the United States." Ph.D. Dissertation. University of Arizona.

Gómez Quiñonez, Juan. 1976 "Piedras Contra la Luna: México en Aztlán y Aztlán en México. Chicano-Mexican Relations and the Mexican Consulates, 1900–1920." In James Wilkie, Michael C. Meyer, and Edna Monzón de Wilkie et al., eds., *Contemporary Mexico.* Los Angeles: University of California Press.

González Gutiérrez, Carlos. 1993 "The Mexican Diaspora in California: Limits and Possibilities for the Mexican Government." In Abraham F. Lowenthal and Katrina Burgess, eds., *The California-Mexico Connection.* Stanford: Stanford University Press.

———. 1995. "La Organización de los Inmigrantes Mexicanos en Los Angeles: la Lealtad de los Oriundos." *Política Exterior,* 46, Spring.

Hansen, Kristin, and Amara Bachu. 1995. "The Foreign Born Population: 1994." *Current Population Reports P20-486.* Washington, D.C.: U.S. Department of Commerce, Census Bureau. August.

Loaeza Tovar, Enrique. 1995. Presentation by the General Director for Protection and Consular Affairs of the Department of Foreign Relations during the Public Hearing "La Política Migratoria en México." Senate Commission on Boundary Affairs of the Republic. 28 March.

Mexican Consulate of Los Angeles. 1993. *Anuario 1992.* Los Angeles.

Miles, Jack. 1992. "Blacks vs. Browns: the Struggle for the Bottom Rung." *The Atlantic Monthly.* October.

Nagel, Joane. c1986, 1991. "The Political Construction of Ethnicity." In Norman R. Yetman, ed., *The Dynamics of Race and Ethnicity in American Life.* Boston: Allyn and Bacon.

O'Sullivan, John. 1994. "America's Identity Crisis: Why Kemp and Bennett Are Wrong." *National Review*. Vol. 46, No. 22, 21 November.

Portes, Alejandro, and Rubén G. Rumbaut. 1990. *Immigrant America, a Portrait*. Berkeley: University of California Press.

Presidencia de la República. 1995. *Plan Nacional de Desarrollo 1994–2000*. México: Presidencia de la República.

Rico Ferrat, Carlos. 1995. "La Frontera México-EEUU: sus Particularidades y Efectos en la Relación Bilateral." *Revista Mexicana*, 46, Spring.

Rozental, Andrés. 1993. *La Política Exterior de México en la Era de la Modernidad*. México: Fondo de Cultura Económica.

Secretaría de Relaciones Exteriores. 1990. *Programa para las Comunidades Mexicanas en el Extranjero: Objetivos, Políticas y Campos de Acción*. México: Secretaría de Relaciones Exteriores.

———. 1995. "Versión Estenográfica de la Comparecencia del Secretario de Relaciones Exteriores, Angel Gurría, al Comparecer ante las Comisiones Unidas de Relaciones Exteriores del Senado de la República y de la Cámara de Diputados." 12 September.

Thorup, Cathryn L. 1990 "Más Allá del Romance Bilateral." *Nexos*, 146, February.

Walentynowicz, Leonard F. 1982. "Needed: More Imagination and Flexibility." In Martin F. Herz, ed., *The Consular Dimension of Diplomacy*. Lanham, Md.: University Press of America.

Chapter 4

Foreign Policy Comes Home: The Domestic Consequences of the Program for Mexican Communities Living in Foreign Countries

Rodolfo O. de la Garza

In 1990 the Mexican government established the Program for Mexican Communities Living in Foreign Countries (PMCLFC), a comprehensive initiative involving a wide range of federal, state, and nongovernmental actors aimed at expanding and regularizing relations with the Mexican-origin population in the United States. To date, analysts have viewed PMCLFC as an extension of the relatively recent and marginally important foreign policy initiative that began in the 1970s (Edmonds 1994; García 1995; González Gutiérrez 1993). This chapter disagrees with that perspective and argues instead that PMCLFC is a unique development illustrating that the distinction between foreign and domestic policy is blurry, and that PMCLFC may have more significance for Mexican domestic politics than for Mexican foreign policy. Specifically, this chapter will: 1) describe the factors that gave rise to this program; 2) evaluate its significance for Mexican domestic politics; and 3) assess its impact on U.S.–Mexico relations.

Central to this analysis is a clear definition of the two groups that PMCLFC targets. These include Mexican immigrants and U.S–born citizens of Mexican origin. The former include legal and undocumented immigrants and will be referred to as Mexicans. The latter will be referred to as Mexican

Americans. Together, they constitute the Mexican-origin population of the United States and will be referred to as the Mexican diaspora.

The Origins of PMCLFC

PMCLFC came into being because of changes affecting the Mexican political system and the U.S. foreign policy-making processes. Historically, each of these functioned quite independently. Today, while each maintains its own distinct dynamics, at times the two are so linked that changes in one may directly and immediately affect the other. This is why President Salinas so ardently courted the U.S. press even as he was rarely available to Mexican journalists (Dresser 1993: 92). PMCLFC's establishment and trajectory have been affected by the interaction of these arenas as well as by each arena independently. To understand PMCLFC's evolution, therefore, it is necessary to link it to these changes and the new relationship they have produced.

The Mexican polity has experienced tumultuous transformations during the past decade. As recently as 1985, the state dominated a highly protectionist and inefficient economy. Today the state has little control over either the nation's productive capacity, its markets, or its own fiscal and monetary policy. The contested presidential and congressional victories in 1988, the Chiapas uprising, electoral triumphs by opposition parties in major cities and states, political assassinations, increasing evidence that drug cartels have penetrated the highest levels of government, public internecine battles among leaders of the Partido Revolucionario Institucional (PRI), and a sitting president with limited authority and declining legitimacy also suggest that the *ancien régime* is changing and may be on the brink of radical restructuring if not collapse.

Together, these changes have resulted in expanding the issues and actors that define Mexico's politics. As has been well-established, historically the president and the revolutionary family's inner circle determined both who would participate in politics and who would influence the nation's political agenda. This is no longer the case, as evidenced by the rise of organizations such as El Barzón and by the inability or unwillingness of the state to impose a PRI candidate on a triumphant Partido de Acción Nacional (PAN) in Mexican locales such as Baja California (1989 and 1995) or Guanajuato (1995), or to prevent recalcitrant PRI-istas from imposing themselves in Tabasco (1995) and Yucatan (1995).

At least as significant as these transformations, and in some ways contributing to them, has been the virtual reversal of Mexico's relationship with the United States (Dresser 1993: 4). Modern Mexican political identity is to a substantial degree defined in opposition to the United States. Many if not most of the battles revolutionary leaders waged to create the Mexican nation involved the United States. The U.S. government was a staunch supporter of the Porfirio

Díaz regime that the revolution overthrew; Henry Lane Wilson, the U.S. ambassador in 1910, was implicated in the assassination of Francisco Madero. President Woodrow Wilson's intervention during the revolution resulted in American troops killing Mexican soldiers in Veracruz and rallying warring factions to the common defense of the nation. Mexican oil was nationalized in 1938 after American oil companies refused to abide by a Mexican Supreme Court decree regarding property rights and turned to U.S. authorities to intervene in their behalf. Mexico's major foreign policy principle, the Estrada Doctrine, was developed to protect Mexico from American intervention. Combined with the memory of the bitter defeat in the U.S.–Mexico war, these events and the all-too-frequent heavy-handed manner in which U.S. officials have dealt with Mexico until the late 1980s remind Mexicans that the United States is the only enemy that modern Mexico has had. The centrality of this lesson to Mexican nationalism is revealed in one aspect of how cadets at the national military academy are socialized. After the cadets pass in review and are called to order, the reviewing officer and the cadets perform the following ritual: the officer calls out the names of each of the *niños héroes* (cadets who died defending Mexico's military academy during the U.S.–Mexico war) and of the soldiers killed at Veracruz, all of whom died fighting U.S. troops. After each name, the cadet corps bellows back "murió por la patria" ("he died for his country").

Mexico's posture vis-à-vis the United States changed profoundly under the Salinas regime. By the early 1990s, nationalism and sovereignty were redefined so that the United States became an ally rather than the enemy. Mexican officials would no longer invoke the Estrada Doctrine to justify keeping foreigners (i.e., Americans) out of Mexican affairs and Mexicans out of domestic politics abroad (i.e., the United States). Instead, Mexican economic and political concerns would be protected and advanced through consultation and negotiation with American state and nonstate actors in Mexico and the United States. The Mexican state, in other words, would now broaden its spheres of activity from official diplomatic contacts to include the full spectrum of American domestic political arenas in order to defend its national interests.

This new approach has been greatly facilitated by major transformations in American foreign policy that began during the Vietnam War and culminated with the end of the cold war (Clough 1994). First, U.S. foreign policy is no longer held hostage to a national interest defined by anti-Soviet and anticommunist objectives. Second, there no longer exists a consensus regarding the national interest that governs foreign policy as had existed since the end of World War II. Third, American elites now define the major issues in foreign policy to include issues such as trade, drugs, and immigration (Rielley 1995). Fourth, the U.S. political agenda is so dominated by domestic concerns that, with notable exceptions such as the Persian Gulf War, foreign policy becomes salient only to the extent that it is linked to domestic issues. Finally, all of these changes enable a wide range of new actors who are primarily concerned with domestic issues to directly and indirectly shape the nation's foreign policy agenda. Directly, they do so through engaging issues such as the North American Free Trade Agreement (NAFTA), policy toward South Africa, and granting China most-favored-nation status, even though their involvement is often triggered by domestic rather than foreign policy concerns. Indirectly, their influence has been felt through the mushrooming economic, social, and political networks that nongovernmental actors and state and local governments have established with counterparts throughout the world (Nye and Keohane 1977). Not only do these networks help shape the context within which bilateral and multilateral relations are conducted, but, as the side agreements to NAFTA on the environment and labor issues illustrate, they also are able to influence the content of formal agreements and treaties (Southwest Voter Research Institute 1994: 6).

These changes have greatly affected the new U.S.–Mexico relationship and have helped make Mexico a first-tier concern for American foreign policy makers. U.S.–Mexico relations have long been colored by U.S. anticommunist policy, as was especially evident during the Reagan administration when Mexico pursued policies toward Central America that were at odds with U.S. preferences (Loeza 1994: 118). With the advent of the Salinas administration in 1988, Mexico's foreign policy began to "'bandwagon' the United States on virtually all issues" (Domínguez 1995: 5). Consequently, the major issues affecting the relationship, such as immigration, drugs, and trade, are now limited to those inherent to the relationship. Moreover, these issues are central both to the relationship and to the current U.S. national security and foreign policy agenda, thus adding to Mexico's importance. Also, because these issues are central to current U.S. domestic politics, they are vitally important to a wide range of domestic actors who would not normally be involved with foreign policy and who engage these issues as they would any other domestic issue. Consequently, these actors marshall whatever resources they can to press their case, and in the post–cold-war environment, these may be drawn from both sides of the border. Thus, rather than constitute a distinct foreign policy arena guided by the national interest, official U.S. policies toward Mexico reflect the outcome of a wide range of political battles waged among foreign policy decision makers and in a variety of domestic arenas involving many actors who are primarily motivated by domestic concerns. These federal policies coexist with an expanding array of arrangements and agreements between U.S. state and local agencies and nongovernmental actors on the one hand, and Mexican federal and, to a much lesser extent, state and local governmental agencies and nongovernmental actors on the other hand.

The viability of Mexico's new approach to its policy vis-à-vis the United States, thus, has been enhanced by the transformations that the American foreign policy process was simultaneously experiencing. Within this new environment, Mexican policy makers are no longer constrained from crossing the border to influence policy decisions that might affect Mexico. To the contrary, their new foreign policy requires that they do so. In 1978, for example, Mexican officials refused to respond to the suggestion that they work with Mexican Americans to oppose proposed immigration reforms because they feared how U.S. officials would react to such a collaboration (Edmonds 1994: 11–12). They reacted similarly to a proposal to contract with a group of Mexican Americans to serve as brokers for PEMEX. The profits that would result from this arrangement would cancel a debt owed by the Mexican government to these Mexican Americans and would be used to fund community development projects in South Texas. Among the principal concerns raised in response to this proposal by the senior presidential adviser with whom it was discussed was whether the U.S. State Department approved of the proposal. Additionally, he expressed concern that American officials could consider the contract to be an intervention in domestic politics (de la Garza and Schmitt 1986: 133–134). These examples suggest that, absent a new and amorphous foreign policy-making environment within the United States, official American responses to such behaviors may have been sufficiently blunt to have forced Mexico to abandon them.

The rise of PMCLFC is an example of how Mexican foreign policy has evolved within this new environment. Although the Mexican government has intermittently reached out to Mexican Americans since 1849, it was not until the 1970s that such contacts approximated coherence. Nonetheless, PMCLFC constitutes a distinctly new policy that builds on but differs fundamentally from the several initiatives that began in the administration of Luis Echeverría Alvarez (1970–1976) and continued through the de la Madrid presidency (1982–1988) (de la Garza and Vargas 1991). Those activities established PMCLFC's foundation even though they were unclear in their objectives and reflected little understanding of the target population. This changed in 1990 when the Salinas administration established the PMCLFC as an institutionalized program within the Ministry of Foreign Relations (SRE). Evidence that PMCLFC reflects a new foreign policy is best illustrated by the contrast in the temerity that characterized the government's outreach prior to 1988 and the boldness with which PMCLFC is now being implemented. Prior to Salinas' term, Mexican officials were constrained by the Estrada Doctrine and the fears that gave rise to it, such as the likelihood that U.S. officials would retaliate against such initiatives. President López Portillo, for example, rejected a proposal from Chicano leaders in 1978 to work together against proposed immigration reforms after learning that the U.S. government disapproved of such an alliance (Edmonds 1994: 11–12). President de la Madrid was so committed to not alienating the United States around this issue that Jorge Bustamante, scholar-turned-government-spokesman on Chicano relations, declared that there was no concrete possibility of Chicanos or their organizations exerting any real political influence on Mexico's behalf and that relations with Mexican Americans would be limited to cultural relations (Bustamante 1986: 17). The SRE's efforts to mobilize Mexican Americans for NAFTA and against California's Proposition 187 illustrate a complete reversal of that policy. Indeed, during a private meeting with Mexican American leaders in Dallas in 1995, President Zedillo announced that his objective was to "develop a close relationship between his government and Mexican Americans, one in which they could be called upon to lobby U.S. policy makers on economic and political issues involving the United States and Mexico" (Corchado 1995).

It should be noted, nonetheless, that Mexican officials remain attentive to possible criticisms of their intervening in American politics. This would explain why Foreign Minister José Angel Gurría denies that PMCLFC is designed to "turn Mexican-Americans [sic] into political allies . . . (or) 'to influence Mexico's relationship with the United States'" (Dillon 1995). It is also likely that concerns about U.S. reactions explain why Mexican officials deny they are pursuing an ethnic lobby when they address non–Hispanic American audiences, but indicate that they seek such a relationship in meetings limited to or dominated by Mexican Americans. For example, President Zedillo advocated for a Mexican American lobby in a private meeting in Dallas, and Foreign Minister Gurría called on Latino leaders to play a role in combating the discriminatory and anti-immigrant attitudes that dominate the current immigration policy debate in his speech at the 1995 conference of the National Association of Latino Elected and Appointed Officials (NALEO) (Gurría 1995).

Thus, not only does PMCLFC illustrate Mexico's new approach to dealing with the United States, but at least one senior SRE official argues that the Mexican government's interests in the Mexican diaspora in the United States have become so salient so as to become the engine of Mexico's new foreign policy. In terms reminiscent of Mario Ojeda's classic analysis (Ojeda 1976), this official argues that Mexico's foreign policy had always been limited, ad hoc, and reactive. With PMCLFC, however, the federal government for the first time established a clear, long-term objective, and then designed a strategy, developed tactics, and committed resources to realize its goal. Supporting this view is President Zedillo's *1995–2000 Plan Nacional de Desarrollo* in which he declares that improving relations with the Mexican and Latino populations of the United States has the "very highest political priority." According to Foreign Minister Gurría, "this is the first time that official policy emphasizes that the relationship with our countrymen abroad is of particular significance" (Gurría 1995).

PMCLFC, thus, is a key component if not the cornerstone of Mexico's new foreign policy. It also appears to have become increasingly significant in domestic politics. Indeed, there is evidence suggesting that PMCLFC may now be driven as much by domestic considerations as by foreign policy objectives.

PMCLFC and Mexican Domestic Politics

Since their inception in the 1970s, Mexican governmental efforts to develop relations with the Mexican diaspora have had domestic political consequences.

Beginning in 1976, meetings with Mexican American leaders became a regular part of PRI presidential campaigns. Prior to establishing PMCLFC within SRE, there were bureaucratic turf battles over the program's objectives and over what ministry should house it (Edmonds 1994: 9–12). By 1987, outreach to the Mexican diaspora had become so significant that the campaign for the 1988 PRI presidential nomination saw presidential aspirants include as part of their platform how they would deal with the Mexican communities in the United States (de la Garza and Vargas 1991: 194–197).

Creating an institution to coordinate and expand these efforts has, predictably, resulted in more significant domestic consequences. Most noteworthy has been the response to PMCLFC's dual nationality proposal. SRE officials proudly introduced the proposal in mid-1995, expecting it to be approved quickly by the traditionally quiescent Congress. Instead, the proposal generated such intense controversy that no action was taken before the legislature adjourned in December 1995 and it is unclear when it will be reconsidered.

The dual nationality proposal has three objectives, all of which reinforce PMCLFC's overall mission. First, it is intended to maintain and strengthen relations with Mexican emigrants. This would be achieved by allowing emigrants who become U.S. citizens to retain their Mexican citizenship. With that, they would retain property rights in Mexico and additional privileges unavailable to foreigners. For example, it would be easier for them to take cars and other goods into Mexico. Government officials expect that enhancing cultural ties would strengthen and expand economic links between émigrés and home-country counterparts. This is significant because as of 1993, the remittances of Mexican emigrants totaled between $2 and $3.2 billion (Lozano Ascencio 1993). Additionally, the Mexican diaspora, after adjusting for income levels, constitutes a market that is equal to Mexico's internal market and is vital to the well-being of Mexican industries (Millman 1996). Close cultural and economic ties with the diaspora are, thus, essential to Mexico's economic health.

Second, offering dual nationality would demonstrate to the diaspora, and in particular to recent emigrants, that the Mexican government and society are concerned with their well-being. Government officials hope that by making such concerns explicit they will avoid protests such as those that began erupting in the 1980s. In 1985, for example, the PAN carried its protests against electoral fraud to several U.S. forums, including the U.S. Congress (Dresser 1993: 95). In 1986, an emigrant organization boycotted a Christmas ceremony in El Paso because the mayor of Juárez, a PRI member, had been invited. The group declared that the PRI "represents an illegitimate government . . . and we want to inform Juárez officials that they are not welcome in El Paso" (de la Garza and Vargas 1991: 200). Similar rallies were held in Chicago to protest a visit by President de la Madrid (de la Garza and Vargas 1991: 200). Most significantly, supporters of Cuahtemoc Cárdenas held large demonstrations in front of the

Mexican consulate to protest the fraudulent elections that resulted in Carlos Salinas de Gortari's victory in the 1988 presidential election (Dresser 1993: 97–99).

Third, by reducing the costs of naturalizing, the dual nationality proposal would encourage naturalization, and this in turn would empower the diaspora to defend its interests within the United States. This is necessary because, even under the parameters of Mexico's new foreign policy, the Mexican government lacks the resources to protect Mexicans from all of the attacks and discrimination they encounter. Additionally, Mexican officials assume that as U.S. citizens, Mexicans would also mobilize in support of Mexican state interests. They believe, in other words, that dual nationality would stimulate the development of an ethnic lobby.

Opponents of dual nationality raise two types of criticisms, one reflecting domestic perspectives and the other concerning foreign policy. Those concerned with domestic issues see the proposal as but one more example of cynical rhetoric rather than as evidence of increased governmental concern for emigrants. They correctly note that dual nationality is of no benefit to undocumented immigrants, who are the most vulnerable of the emigrants. Some activists also argue that if the Mexican government genuinely wanted to maintain ties with the emigrants, it would offer them the right to vote in absentia because that is what emigrants want, and to offer less is an insult (Robles 1995: 3A).

Those concerned with the foreign policy aspects of the proposal argue that rather than create an ethnic lobby it will create an ethnic Trojan horse (Rodríguez 1995). According to this view, Mexicans who naturalize with dual nationality rights would be perceived as less patriotic than other Americans. That is, believing that the primary loyalty of these new citizens will remain with Mexico, "real" Americans would discriminate against them. That California's Republican Party passed a resolution asking Mexico not to implement dual nationality offers some credence to this argument (Migrant News 1995). Mexican opponents of dual nationality fear that in order to overcome such discrimination and prove their loyalty, these new citizens will become superpatriots and use the advantages of their dual nationality to mobilize against Mexico.

A less controversial but very significant policy initiative that has resulted from PMCLFC has been the widely acclaimed Paisano program. Established by President Salinas in response to emigrant demands, it provides a variety of services that assist Mexicans in the United States, and most significantly, has eliminated much of the abuse they experienced at the hands of corrupt customs officials when they returned home (Smith 1995b). Given the limited success that the Mexican state has had in reducing corruption and given that the customs agency is an important agency with a long and notorious history of corruption, Paisano's success must be considered a significant bureaucratic and political accomplishment.

PMCLFC's most explicit and direct impact on Mexican politics is evident at the local level. A clear example of this is in Ticuani, Puebla, in Mexico (Smith 1995b). Ticuani emigrants in New York City play an active and major role in the political and economic life of their home village. They and their families in Mexico have created the Comité Solidaridad Ticuani de Nueva York (the New York Committee) so that they may work together to improve living conditions in Ticuani; the New York Committee provides funds, and Ticuanis provide the labor. The projects have included purchasing bricks for the main plaza, building two schools, church repairs, and an ongoing potable water project that will cost over $100,000. Local PRI officials lack the funds to provide these services. Moreover they can not raise them by taxing the emigrants who reside in New York. Furthermore, the New York Committee perceives local officials to be corrupt and therefore will not respond to government requests for contributions. Local government, therefore, is dependent on the New York Committee for the funds it needs to provide basic services to its constituents.

The New York Committee's role in local politics evolved to the point that it ran a candidate for mayor of Ticuani in 1989. Although he won little support and dropped out of the race, his candidacy led to a formal agreement between the committee and the *municipio*. This agreement means, in effect, that, a local PRI-dominated government recognized a specific segment of the Mexican diaspora as one of its major constituents and in effect agreed to negotiate future local decisions with that community's representatives. Ironically, this is a privilege few autonomously organized community-based groups within Mexico enjoy.

PMCLFC has also worked with other émigré communities to assist with community development programs in their home pueblos. Program officials not only provide technical assistance and help with bureaucratic obstacles, they also have secured federal funds for projects coordinated through PMCLFC. "With the program talking for the U.S.-residing Mexicans, the Mexican bureaucracy listens" (Smith 1995a: 235).

PMCLFC also is situated to impact state-level politics, and in so doing may contribute to further changes in Mexican domestic politics. As part of its national strategy, program directors have worked with the governors of high-emigration states to establish Offices of Emigrant Affairs (Smith 1995a: 18). In states with large emigrant outflows, such as Guanajuato and Jalisco, that are controlled by the PAN, these offices may be used to pursue objectives that support the original intent of the program but conflict with the political objectives of the national government. This is already the case in Guanajuato where the governor is working closely with the private sector to develop investment opportunities that will attract investors from the Mexican diaspora whether or not they are from his state (Szekely and de la Garza 1995). This initiative is in keeping with PMCLFC's objectives, but to the extent that it is successful it may further entrench PAN in that state and, potentially, strengthen it elsewhere in the country. This is clearly contrary to the initial partisan objectives of the program, given that the PRI was totally dominant when PMCLFC was developed and that the program was designed to benefit the PRI.

State Offices of Emigrant Affairs may also be used to develop policies that contradict PMCLFC's objectives and, if they are successful, these, too, will undermine the PRI and the federal government. In Guanajuato, policy makers are attempting to devise a mechanism that would have the state rather than the national government process the remittances that Guanajuatences send home. One proposal under consideration involves establishing a relationship between a bank in Guanajuato and one in North Texas, where many emigrants from Guanajuato reside, which would enable emigrants to deposit funds in Texas that their relatives could access in Guanajuato. This program would make transactions safer and cheaper for the individual. It would also increase the dollars circulating within the state while reducing the dollars under the control of the federal government (Szekely and de la Garza 1995). If effected, this innovation would provide an independent revenue source for the state thereby increasing its autonomy vis-à-vis the federal government. If all PAN-controlled states followed suit, the political and economic implications for the PRI would be substantial. It should also be noted that, given their history of malfeasance, PRI officials would have difficulty persuading émigrés to participate in such a program. The PAN, however, has made clean government central to its platform and therefore is much more likely to succeed in such an effort.

Clearly, PMCLFC has already had important domestic consequences that may become even greater in the future. Indeed, when compared to its likely effect on U.S.–Mexico relations, it becomes evident that PMCLFC's importance will reflect its impact on domestic economic and political issues rather than on Mexico's foreign policy. An examination of the program's objectives and impact to date illustrates why this is so.

PMCLFC and Mexico–U.S. Relations

Established by executive decree in 1990, PMCLFC has as its objectives the following:

- Promoting and facilitating joint projects, and serving as a link between Mexican and Mexican-origin communities residing in foreign countries and public and private institutions in Mexico.
- Improving the perception that Mexicans have of Mexican Americans, of their struggles and achievements, and promoting greater knowledge and respect of their culture.
- Enhancing the prospect of a dignified treatment of these communities by Mexicans themselves and a better understanding by such communities of Mexico's national reality (Szekely and de la Garza 1995).

Such broad goals encompass a wide variety of activities ranging from trying to establish an ethnic lobby, as President Zedillo has indicated, to nothing more than strengthening cultural and economic ties, as Foreign Minister Gurría asserts. Examining PMCLFC's programs and the populations they target will suggest the program's potential impact on Mexico–U.S. relations relative to its effect on Mexican domestic politics.

PMCLFC's activities emphasize cultural, educational, and economic ties. Although in principle the cultural and economic initiatives are designed to serve the Mexican diaspora in its entirety, Mexican immigrants are much more likely than Mexican Americans to participate in these. For example, the educational initiatives focus on schools with large numbers of immigrant children. One of their achievements has been to establish relations between U.S. schools with large numbers of immigrant children and Mexican schools in communities of origin so that these children are given credit for their studies in the United States when they return to their local schools. Similarly, PMCLFC provides educational materials and other types of support for bilingual programs in schools with large numbers of immigrant children. PMCLFC also actively promotes soccer leagues and other types of athletic events. The program in New York, in collaboration with the Mexican consulate, has federated eighteen independent sports leagues into the Mexican Sports League of the Northeastern United States (Figueroa 1995).

Although Mexican Americans may benefit from these programs, there is no doubt that immigrants are PMCLFC's primary target. This is even more the case with the Paisano program and the support that PMCLFC officials provide to emigrants engaged in community development projects in their pueblos of origin. Taken together these examples typify PMCLFC's emphasis and indicate that its objectives are to establish and maintain positive relationships with emigrants. This is not surprising given that it is emigrants, especially those who emigrated more recently, who are most likely to remit funds to their families and to be concerned about Mexican political events. By successfully courting them, PMCLFC helps maintain that flow of funds and reduces the likelihood of protests such as occurred following the 1988 elections. In other words, in these cases PMCLFC's objectives have much more relevance for domestic issues than for Mexico–U.S. relations.

PMCLFC's economic initiatives more explicitly target Mexican Americans, as Foreign Minister Gurría emphasized in his address to NALEO. This began when PMCLFC and other Mexican agencies collaborated to mobilize Mexican American leaders to support NAFTA. Mexican officials claimed that the agreement would greatly benefit the Mexican American community because Mexican American entrepreneurs were uniquely qualified to benefit from the new opportunities NAFTA would produce, an argument that Mexican American leaders accepted (Chavarria n.d.). Indeed, the Latino Summit, an event that brought together major Hispanic leaders in the United

States, defended NAFTA against Hispanic critics by emphasizing the profits it would bring to Latino businesses: ". . . NAFTA can foster greater economic growth, job creation, and ownership opportunities in the Latino community . . . NAFTA offers an obvious potential for Latino business formation and growth and greater involvement and participation, including joint ventures, with the mainstream economy" (Spener n.d.: 10).

During the NAFTA debate, Mexican Americans representing virtually every type and level of organization met with Mexican officials in Mexico and the United States to discuss the forthcoming opportunities. Organizations such as the National Council of La Raza and the National Hispanic Chamber of Commerce, with the support of PMCLFC, organized numerous junkets to Mexico. Additionally, prominent Mexican Americans such as Eduardo Hidalgo, former secretary of the Navy; Jerry Apodaca and Toney Anaya, former governors of New Mexico; and former ambassador Abelardo Delgado were hired by the Mexican government to lobby for the agreement.

To further strengthen its links with the Mexican American business community, the Mexican government established the Mexican Council for Hispanic Business within PMCLFC. The council includes the National Association of Importers and Exporters of the Mexican Republic, the National Bank for Foreign Trade, the National Chamber of Commerce, the National Chamber of Manufacturing Industry, the Mexican Investment Board (MIB), the Mexican National Development Bank (NAFIN), the Ministry of Trade and Industry, the Ministry of Foreign Relations, the Treasury, and the Ministry of Tourism. The expectation is that the council will work with Mexican American communities to further their own interests and those of the Mexican government itself.

The Council's most significant accomplishment is the creation of the NAFIN-MIB Hispanic Reserve that consists of a $20 million commitment from NAFIN's annual budget. NAFIN sets this sum aside annually, and if it is not used, the money is returned to the general fund to support the agency's regular activities. Mexican American investors are encouraged to apply for these funds, with preference given to those working with partners in Mexico. The applications require well-developed business plans which, if accepted, award funds to the applicants under preferential conditions. It must be noted that there is no affirmative action component to this program. Thus, Mexican American applicants compete with Mexican applicants on an equal basis. The same Hispanic organizations that were mobilized to generate Latino support for NAFTA have endorsed the Hispanic Reserve and are in effect its cosponsors.

Despite its potential, this initiative has had no substantive impact. The program is not well-known and efforts to promote it have diminished since its inception. Few Mexican American (or Hispanic) businesses have applied, and PMCLFC claims notwithstanding, none have been accepted into the program (Szekely and de la Garza 1995).

Furthermore, PMCLFC's general effort to promote economic ties between

Mexican American and Mexican businesses has had minimal success. This is because of the faulty assumption that cultural similarities would facilitate Mexican American–Mexican business relations. Ironically, ties of this nature were more likely prior to NAFTA when the obstacles to trading with Mexico were so substantial that those Mexican Americans who knew Mexico well were ideally situated to serve as middlemen between American and Mexican businesses. As the barriers to trade with Mexico were dismantled, the need for middlemen declined and Mexican and American businesses were more likely to work directly with one another. Additionally, few Mexican American businesses were in those sectors that could benefit from the increased trade opportunities (Spener n.d.), and even if they were in those sectors, few had the resources to engage in international commerce (Fajardo 1995).

Further impeding the development of Mexican American–Mexican business relations is the attitude of many Mexican entrepreneurs. A common complaint of Mexican American businessmen is that their Mexican counterparts view them with disdain, as typified by the following statement: *"Ni sabemos qué son, si son mexicanos, o americanos, u otra cosa, como les decimos: pochos"* ("We don't even know what they are. Are they Mexicans? Americans? Or something else, like 'pochos'?") (Spener n.d. 17). Consequently, Mexican entrepreneurs prefer dealing with Anglos. According to a representative of a California Latino chamber of commerce, Mexicans hold these views in part because they think Mexican American firms lack clout: "If they want accounting services, they will go to Peat, Marwick, & Co., not Vargas and Associates. If they want legal services, they will seek Arnold and Porter, not Barbosa and García" (Fajardo 1995: 21). Second, the cultural capital that Mexican Americans bring to the relationship is of little value to Mexicans. For Mexican businessmen the fact that Anglos are culturally different is of little consequence because they want "to do business, not to make friends." Some Mexican Americans recognize this: "[Y]es, we've got the language, and we've capitalized on that—but I think they are always looking for good business. . . . [O]f course it helps that we speak Spanish. But if we didn't speak Spanish, he'd still save money and he'd still do it. . . . They can speak English, or find people who speak English for them" (Spener n.d.: 17–18).

Another obstacle to developing business connections is that few Mexican Americans know how to do business in Mexico. Interviews with businesspeople and Latino chamber of commerce representatives indicate that most Mexican Americans who have tried to work in Mexico have had little success. In some cases their ignorance of Mexican business practices has made them vulnerable to fraudulent business schemes. More frequently it has resulted in frustration and resentment stemming from licensing and other bureaucratic encounters, such as *mordidas* (bribes).

The very limited success of business links between Mexican Americans and Mexicans notwithstanding, it may be argued that even if they were successful such initiatives have little direct relevance for Mexico–U.S. relations. NAFTA has made the U.S. and Mexican economies accessible to Mexican and American businesses alike without the assistance of Mexican Americans. Furthermore, even Mexico's mobilization of Mexican American elites may have been of marginal significance to NAFTA's enactment. Mexico spent at least $30 million promoting NAFTA, and only a small portion of this went to Mexican American lobbyists or to win Mexican American support. Only five of the thirty major lobbyists involved with NAFTA were Hispanic, and only two of these with contracts totaling $520,000 reported that their mission was to promote NAFTA among Hispanics (Lewis et al. 1993). Although all but one Mexican American member of Congress voted for NAFTA, they did so only after the side agreements were modified to address Mexican American domestic concerns, such as the establishment of the North American Development Bank in order to fund community development and environmental projects along the border. Had these provisions not been included, it is reasonable to conclude that Mexican American legislators would have opposed and thus prevented NAFTA's enactment. There is no evidence, in other words, that Mexican American members of Congress voted for NAFTA because of Mexican lobbying or because they supported Mexican interests.

Similarly, there is no evidence that PMCLFC's efforts have rallied Mexican Americans to support Mexican government preferences regarding U.S. immigration policies, the issue that most intimately links Mexicans and Mexican Americans. Rhetoric aside, the Mexican government's preferences are clear: it favors increased legal immigration, opposes crackdowns on illegal immigration, considers the construction of physical barriers such as walls and fences to be an egregious affront to Mexican dignity, and supports the full participation of Mexican immigrants, regardless of their status, in American social welfare programs.

Mexican Americans disagree with the Mexican government on three of these four positions. They agree on allowing legal and undocumented immigrants to participate in social services (The Tomás Rivera Center 1996: 9–10). On the other hand, in 1990 the majority of Mexican Americans favored a reduction in the number of legal immigrants entering the United States (de la Garza, et al. 1992: 100–102). In 1995, five years after PMCLFC's inauguration, a survey in Texas produced similar results and found that over 40 percent of Mexican Americans support building walls and fences along the border to prevent illegal immigration (The Tomás Rivera Center 1996: 10). More significantly, the great majority of Mexican Americans in El Paso support Operation Hold the Line, the intensified efforts of the Immigration and Naturalization Service to control undocumented immigration by stationing border patrol officers in visible positions along the river (Bean et al. 1994: 93–94).

Relatedly, Mexican Americans in California have been silent regarding similar recent U.S. Immigration and Naturalization Service (INS) efforts in the San Diego–Tijuana area, suggesting that they, too, support such initiatives.

This is especially significant in light of Mexican American responses to Proposition 187. During the early stages of the "Prop 187" debate, opinion polls indicated that Latinos, most of whom were Mexican Americans, were divided on the issue. As the debate evolved, it took on an increasingly anti-Mexican tone and it became clear that the bill would indiscriminately target anyone of Mexican origin. Mexican Americans, therefore, not only became ardent opponents of the bill, but they turned out in huge numbers to vote against it (The Tomás Rivera Center 1995: 23). INS began its San Diego initiative during this same period, and yet an already mobilized Mexican American community did not rally against it.

This pattern is consistent with well-established patterns of Mexican American responses to immigration control (de la Garza 1985). That is, Mexican Americans distinguish between immigrants who are already here, regardless of their legal status, and those who will come in the future. They also support the right of the nation to defend its borders and policies to control undocumented immigration so long as these do not target them (Pride Coalition 1993). Border control efforts such as Operation Hold the Line focus on those not yet in the country by protecting the nation's border, an approach that protects Mexican Americans from INS abuses. Thus, Mexican American members of Congress and the leaders of the major Mexican American civil rights organizations have publicly declared that "the United States is entitled to control and regulate its borders" (Pride Coalition 1993). Proposition 187 would have affected everyone within the Mexican diaspora, and Mexican Americans therefore opposed it out of self-interest and concern for those Mexicans already in California.

Clearly, Mexican Americans do not rally around the positions of the Mexican government regarding U.S. immigration policies. When Mexican Americans and the Mexican government agree on a policy, as was the case with Proposition 187, it is coincidental rather than because Mexican Americans are being mobilized in behalf of Mexico's preferences. In other words, Mexican Americans would have opposed Proposition 187 regardless of Mexico's position, and their opposition can not be interpreted as an indication of PMCLFC's success.

If Mexican Americans do not rally to support Mexico around policies such as NAFTA and immigration even after PMCLFC officials invested substantial resources to woo them, it is unlikely they will do so on issues that do not directly affect them or are on behalf of the Mexican government per se. Less than 15 percent say they follow Mexican politics, and almost 90 percent indicated that Mexico's economic crisis was the result of governmental corruption and incompetence (de la Garza et al. 1992: 103–104).

Despite this widespread disinterest and negativism, PMCLFC may have laid the foundation for an ethnic lobby through the relationships it has established with Mexican American elites, especially the leaders of organizations such as Hispanic chambers of commerce, the National Council of La Raza, and the Southwest Voter Registration and Education Project. PMCLFC has courted and worked with these groups to organize and host a variety of activities including junkets to Mexico. It has also bestowed the Aztec Eagle, Mexico's highest civilian award, to the heads of several of these organizations. These accolades and support help explain why dissidents were effectively shut out of the Latino Summit on NAFTA. They also may explain why the leaders of these organizations (who are staunch defenders of civil liberties and democratic reform in the United States) remained silent regarding human rights abuses and the lack of political reforms during the Salinas administration and why they maintain their silence even now.

This is a tenuous foundation, however. There is no doubt that the heads of these organizations are the most visible spokespersons for Mexican Americans. Nonetheless, these organizations are not widely recognized or supported by the Mexican American community (de la Garza et al. 1992: 114–115), and there is no evidence that they have the capacity to influence Mexican American opinion or mobilize them to action. For example, these organizations have historically and strongly opposed creating national identity cards, a policy that has much more support among Mexican Americans (The Tomás Rivera Center 1996: 10). Also, despite a decade of efforts aimed at increasing voter turnout, Mexican American voting rates relative to Anglo voting rates remain unchanged (The Tomás Rivera Center 1995: 9–11).

Even if these organizations accurately articulated Mexican American policy preferences, the significance this would have for Mexican foreign policy goals is tenuous. These organizations make their influence felt primarily through Hispanic elected and appointed officials. Although the number of such officials has increased greatly in recent years, especially at local levels, Mexican American political influence has grown much more slowly and may now be declining because of the nation's changing political climate. There is no doubt, for example, that Mexican Americans are less influential in Texas under Governor George Bush Jr. than they were in 1992 when Ann Richards was governor. Doubtless their influence in California was greater under Governor Jerry Brown than it is under Governor Pete Wilson. Similarly, the Republican takeover of Congress in 1994 greatly debilitated the congressional Hispanic Political Caucus. In national elections, despite an important role in the 1988 presidential primaries (de la Garza 1992a) and in at least one state in the 1992 presidential election (de la Garza and DeSipio 1996: 29–34), Mexican American voters have not affected the overall results of any presidential election since 1960. Stated differently, if no Mexican American had voted in any of those elections, the results would have essentially remained unchanged.

It should also be noted that it is a mistake to assume that an increase in Mexican American officeholders will further Mexican interests. Mexican American officials will first serve their U.S. constituencies and work within their respective institutional frameworks. While this may sometimes result in better relations that will benefit Mexico, that it will not necessarily be so is illustrated in the recent controversy regarding NAFTA's provisions governing cross-border trucking. NAFTA would have permitted Mexican trucks to transport goods beyond the border beginning 17 December 1995. Under the leadership of Texas Attorney General Dan Morales, this provision was postponed because many Mexican trucks could not meet Texas Department of Highway safety standards. That decision was made by Transportation Secretary Federico Peña over the protests of Mexican officials.

Finally, given the relationship that now exists between the Mexican and the U.S. governments, it is not evident that Mexico needs an ethnic lobby to defend its interests. As has been clear since the latter part of the Carter administration (Pastor and Castañeda 1989: 102–107), American policy makers now consider the U.S.–Mexico relationship and Mexico's well-being essential to America's national interest. This was the argument behind NAFTA, and it explains why the Clinton administration bailed out the Zedillo administration at the risk of its own viability. With friends like that, who needs the Hispanic Chamber of Commerce?

Conclusion

The PMCLFC represents a major change in Mexican foreign policy. It is the first example of a coherent and continuous effort conducted within the United States designed to have American political actors influence U.S. policies to make them compatible with the preference of the Mexican government. Additionally, it represents the institutionalization of governmental efforts to establish, expand, and improve relations with the Mexican diaspora.

Ironically, the conditions that gave rise to PMCLFC have also contributed to its marginal importance as a foreign policy tool. PMCLFC came into being because Mexican officials abandoned their historically rooted defensive nationalism in favor of an approach that inextricably involved the United States in Mexican economic and political affairs. American foreign policy goals and decision-making processes were simultaneously undergoing equally significant changes, and these created the political space within the United States that has allowed the Mexican government to implement PMCLFC. However, the confluence of changes within Mexico and the United States has persuaded U.S. officials and major political actors that both a healthy Mexican economy and a stable—but not necessarily democratic—society are essential to American national interests. Consequently, Mexican officials have been able to establish relationships with a wide range of U.S. political actors, including Mexican Americans, that allow them to directly influence those American domestic and foreign policies that are especially relevant to them. Given this web and the relatively minor role that Mexican Americans play in national policy making, PMCLFC's success in establishing close linkages to Mexican American organizational leaders may contribute only marginally to the success that Mexican officials have had in their recent negotiations with U.S. policy makers.

The exception to this is PMCLFC's role in the NAFTA debate. By mobilizing major Mexican American organizations in support of NAFTA, PMCLFC helped create an environment that quieted NAFTA's Mexican American (and most Hispanic) critics. If Mexican American leaders who were ambivalent or opposed to NAFTA—and there were many, especially among labor leaders—had become vocal, it is possible to envision a scenario that would have resulted in NAFTA's defeat. PMCLFC, therefore, may not explain why Mexican American members of Congress voted for NAFTA, but it surely was an important factor in preventing Mexican American critics from joining other opponents to defeat it.

PMCLFC has been much more effective in dealing with Mexican emigrants. One reason for this is that most of its resources are invested in programs that target this population. However, these programs are not designed to meet foreign policy goals but are intended to influence the behavior of emigrant communities regarding political and economic developments in Mexico. The Mexican government, in other words, is using PMCLFC to maintain relations with emigrants so that remittances and other forms of direct financial investment in their pueblos will continue.

PMCLFC's successes with this aspect of its activities is having unintended consequences that may undermine the national government's objectives. Transnational communities such as the Ticuani are using the PMCLFC for their own purposes, and PAN-controlled states may soon follow suit. As these trends continue—and it is likely they will—PMCLFC's impact on domestic affairs may become quite significant.

PMCLFC, thus, illustrates the extent to which in Mexico, as in the United States, the distinction between foreign and domestic issues is continuously blurred. Although it is part of Mexico's foreign policy apparatus, PMCLFC has nonetheless become an important program because its significance for domestic policy has increased even while its relevance for U.S.–Mexico relations has declined or remained unchanged. It seems, then, that while PMCLFC is a key example of Mexico's new foreign policy, it may be an even better indicator of how Mexican domestic politics are changing.

References

Bean, Frank D., Roland Chanove, Robert G. Cushing, Rodolfo de la Garza, Gary P. Freeman, Charles W. Haynes, and David Spener. 1994. *Illegal Mexican Migration and the United States/Mexico Border: The Effects of Operation Hold the Line on El Paso/Juárez.* Washington, D.C.: U.S. Commission on Immigration Reform.

Bustamante, Jorge. 1986. "Chicano–Mexicano Relations: From Practice to Theory."

In Tatcho Mindiola and Max Martínez, eds., *Chicano-Mexicano Relations*. Monograph No. 4. Houston, Texas: Mexican American Studies Program, University of Houston.

Chavarria, Ernesto. n.d. *The North American Free Trade Agreement: Economic Opportunities for U.S. Latinos*. Austin: Texas Association of Mexican American Chambers of Commerce.

Clough, Michael. 1994. "Grassroots Policy Making: Say Goodbye to the 'Wisemen.'" *Foreign Affairs* 73 (1) (January–February).

Corchado, Alfredo. 1995. "Zedillo Vows to Vanquish Mexico Woes." *Dallas Morning News*. 8 April.

de la Garza, Rodolfo O. 1985. "Mexican Americans, Mexican Immigrants, and Immigration Reform." In Nathan Glazer, ed., *Clamor at the Gates*. San Francisco: Institute for Contemporary Studies.

——————. 1992. "From Rhetoric to Reality: Latinos and the 1988 Election in Review." In Rodolfo O. de la Garza and Louis DeSipio, eds. *From Rhetoric to Reality: Latinos in the 1988 Election*, 171–180. Boulder, Colo.: Westview Press.

—————— and Karl Schmitt. 1986. "Texas Land Grants and Chicano-Mexican Relations." *Latin American Research Review* 21 (1), 123–138.

—————— and Claudio A. Vargas. 1991. "Paisanos, Pochos, o Aliados Políticos." *Revista Mexicana de Sociología* 2 (April–June).

—————— and Louis DeSipio. 1996. *Ethnic Ironies: Latino Politics in the 1992 Elections*. Boulder, Colo.: Westview Press.

—————— and Louis DeSipio, F. Chris García, John García, and Angelo Falcón. 1992. *Latino Voices: Mexican, Puerto Rican, and Cuban Perspectives on American Politics*. Boulder, Colo.: Westview Press.

Dresser, Dennis. 1993. "Exporting Conflict: Transboundary Consequences of Mexican Politics." In Abraham F. Lowenthal and Katrina Burgess, eds., *The California-Mexico Connection*. Stanford: Stanford University Press.

Dillon, Sam. 1995. "Mexico Woos U.S. Mexicans, Proposing Dual Nationality." *The New York Times*. 10 December.

Domínguez, Jorge I. 1995. "Widening Scholarly Horizons: Theoretical Approaches for the Study of U.S.–Mexican Relations." Paper prepared for the seminar "La Nueva Agenda en la Relación Bilateral México-EUA." Instituto Tecnológico de México. 19–20 May.

Edmonds, Emily Doris. 1994. "Pochos No More: Mexican Americans and the New Mexican Foreign Policy." M.A. thesis, University of Texas at Austin.

Fajardo, Richard P. 1995. *Latino Business and NAFTA in Southern California*. Claremont, Calif.: The Tomás Rivera Center.

Figueroa, Rodulfo. 1995. Interview with the author. 17 October.

García, Maria Rosa. 1995. "Mexican Policy toward the Chicano Community: Rebirth, Flowering, and Limits." Unpublished manuscript. Department of Political Science, University of Arizona–Tucson.

González Gutiérrez, Carlos. 1993. "The Mexican Diaspora in California: Limits and Possibilities for the Mexican Government." In Abraham F. Lowenthal and Katrina Burgess, eds., *The California-Mexico Connection*. Stanford: Stanford University Press.

Gurría, José Angel. 1995. "Palabras del Secretario de Relaciones Exteriores Angel Gurría, Durante la Conferencia Anual de la Asociación Nacional de Funcionarios Latinos Electos y Designados (NALEO)." Austin, Texas. 24 June.

Lewis, Charles, et al. 1993. *The Trading Game—Inside Lobbying for the North American Free Trade Agreement.* Washington, D.C.: Center for Public Integrity.

Loeza, Soledad. 1994. "Political Liberalization and Uncertainty in Mexico." In Maria Lorena Cook, Kevin J. Middlebrook, and Juan Molinar Horcasistas, eds., *The Politics of Economic Restructuring.* San Diego: Center for U.S.–Mexican Studies, University of California at San Diego.

Lozano Ascencio, Fernando. 1993. *Bringing It Back Home: Remittances to Mexico from Mexican Workers in the United States.* Monograph Series #37. San Diego: Center for U.S.–Mexico Studies, University of California at San Diego.

Migrant News PLM. 1995. University of California at Davis. December.

Millman, Joel. 1996. "Following the Immigrants." *Forbes.* 1 January.

Nye, Joseph D. and Robert O. Keohane. 1977. *Power and Interdependence: World Politics in Transition.* Boston: Little, Brown & Co.

Ojeda, Mario. 1976. *Alcances y Límites de la Política Exterior de México.* México: Colegio de México.

Pastor, Robert A., and Jorge G. Castañeda. 1989. *Limits to Friendship: The United States and Mexico.* New York: Vintage Books.

Pride Coalition. 1993. News Release. Los Angeles: Pride Coalition. 21 December.

Rielley, John, ed. 1995. *American Public Opinion and U.S. Foreign Policy.* Chicago: Chicago Council on Foreign Relations.

Robles, Francisco. 1995. "Propuesta de la Doble Nacionalidad Puede Ser Divisiva para Mexicanos." Los Angeles: La Opinión. 1 December.

Rodríguez, Primitivo. 1995. Interview with the author. 11 December.

Smith, Robert Courtney. 1995a. "Transnational Localities: Community, Technology and the Politics of Membership within the Context of Mexico–U.S. Migration." Paper prepared for the American Sociological Association Meetings, Washington, D.C., August.

———. 1995b. "Los Ausentes Presentes: The Imagining, Making, and Politics of a Transnational Migrant Community Between Ticuani, Puebla, Mexico and New York City." Ph.D. dissertation, Columbia University.

Southwest Voter Research Institute. 1994. *Southwest Voter Research Notes.* Montebello, Calif.: Southwest Voter Research Institute. June.

Spener, David. n.d. "Small Firms, Capital, and Global Commodity Chains: Some Lessons From The Tex-Mex Border in the Era of Free Trade." In Roberto Patricio Korzeniewicz and William Smith, eds., *Latin America in the World Economy.* Westport, Conn.: Greenwood Publishers.

Szekely, Gabriel, and Rodolfo O. de la Garza. 1995. *Mexican Government Programs to Promote Business Ties with Mexican-American Entrepreneurs: A Report to the Tomás Rivera Center.* Claremont, Calif.: The Tomás Rivera Center.

The Tomás Rivera Center. 1995. *The Latino Vote at Mid-Decade.* Claremont, Calif.: Tomás Rivera Center.

———. 1996. *U.S. Hispanic Perspectives.* Claremont, Calif.: Tomás Rivera Center.

Chapter 5

The Rise of the Mexico Lobby in Washington: Even Further from God, and Even Closer to the United States[1]

Todd A. Eisenstadt

The Mexican government's strategy for representing its political and economic interests in the United States has been completely restructured over the last decade. In one of the most drastic increases ever in lobbying and public relations expenditures by a foreign government in Washington, the Mexican government, previously known as one of Washington's most passive foreign players, became one of the most visible in the several years leading to passage of the North American Free Trade Agreement (NAFTA) in November 1993. But the Mexican change in diplomatic style precedes the NAFTA vote by several years. Indeed, between 1985 and 1991 the Mexican government's lobbying representation jumped from two minor contracts (totaling $67,229) to more than a dozen contracts worth at least $9 million and perhaps much more. Several circumstances prompted such a magnitude of change, and the Mexican government has found a new structure for its new effort.

This chapter will document the truth to Mexicans' claims that their presence in Washington grew dramatically in the early 1990s, as the "Mexico lobby" came into its own as a political force. Consistent with theorists who explain foreign policy outcomes as the result of interactions between domestic interest coalitions and national governments (such as Putnam 1988), I argue that the main achievements of the Mexico lobby have resulted from allying with domestic U.S. lobbying efforts, led by special interests such as big business and to a lesser extent by the U.S. Latino community. Mexico and its national interests have been presented from a weak position of "asymmetrical interdependence," which does not carry sufficient risks and payoffs so as to create a strong negotiating position in bilateral relations with the United States (see Chabat in this volume). Only powerful nations like Japan, capable of wreaking havoc across several commercial sectors by reneging on a single trade commitment, are really capable of commanding sufficiently credible threats so as to turn bilateral trade negotiations into genuine two-level games. Since the early 1980s, Mexico's biggest threat to the United States and the rest of the international financial community has been its potential for default on loan repayments. This threat has always carried a tremendous cost for Mexico that, with the exception of a brief and desperate moment in 1982, it has not been considered credible.

Since the mid-1980s, Mexico has increasingly followed a policy of seeking out U.S. allies through which it could pressure the U.S. Congress. Hedging their bets, the Mexicans also hired some of Washington's leading old-style "influence peddler" lobbyists, especially in the run-up to the NAFTA vote. The sum total of these dual strategies, unprecedented for a traditionally nationalistic country unwilling to intervene in domestic politics anywhere—particularly not in the United States—for fear of the reciprocal meddling in Mexican affairs this could provoke, has been the passage of the most important trade accord ever in the nations' bilateral relations. But how much NAFTA's passage may be attributed to the efforts of Mexico's lobby remains an open question. No definitive answer can be offered to the counterfactual question, "What if Mexico had not spent so much lobbying for NAFTA's passage?" Indeed, this chapter will not claim to undertake such an exercise, at least not directly. It will, however, scrutinize the efficacy of the different lobbying techniques undertaken by the Mexican government, as well as describe the transformation of Mexico's approach to stewarding its interests in Washington.

Doubts about the value of the Mexico lobby were dismissed in the months after the NAFTA vote. However, these doubts do persist, especially given Mexico's current economic crisis, and the recent criticism of the NAFTA agreement in both Mexico and the United States. In short, did Mexico's hyped-up new Washington image (surpassing even the visibility of Japan's lobby in 1993), create new spaces for Mexican politicking in the United States?[2] Or, to paraphrase one succinct critic, did the Mexicans "waste a lot of money to say the same thing over and over?"[3]

NAFTA did pass, but only after the executive intervened, garnering the last several dozen votes in the House of Representatives through multibillion-dollar promises of federal largesse for the districts of members of Congress who supported President Clinton (see Table 5.5). This close call raises questions about the value-added of foreign agent lobbyists, as does the subsequent irrelevance of legislative lobbying in Mexico's successful bid to secure a $40 billion loan bailout in February 1995. I will consider these demonstrations of the limits of lobbying in concluding that while lobbying is a necessary evil for nations with high stakes in Washington, the practice is wrought with political, economic, and ethical complications. Furthermore, regardless of how much governments pay for Washington representation, lobbyists have only a limited effect on a nation's representation in the United States.

Indeed, all of Mexico's lobbyists could not create a strong international bargaining position where one did not exist by making Mexico into a heavyweight economic or geopolitical power. Nor could they have created domestic pressures within the United States where such did not exist. They could only glom onto existing domestic interests, ride them as far as possible (to victory in the case of NAFTA), and take credit for the victory, albeit an expensive one. While not offering a definitive answer to the question "Are they worth it?" I do propose to reconsider the success attributed to Mexico's NAFTA lobby in light of case evidence. Finally this chapter will raise broader structural debates about the role of foreign lobbyists in Washington, and from a more normative perspective, raise questions about the role of big money lobbyists in a democratic society.

It may be impossible to isolate whether Mexico's new lobby has been a cause of the unprecedented cooperation between Mexico and the United States, or an effect of this new relationship. Certainly, the Mexico lobby is a measurable indicator of the change in the level of Mexico's commitment to a better understanding of U.S. policy making, which also portends heightened expectations for greater bilateral cooperation. It is still too early to measure the long-term merit of Mexico's investment in improved Washington representation, but in describing and analyzing the rise of the Mexico lobby, this chapter will strive to at least offer an empirical starting point for further study of this drastic change.

Quantifying the Mexico Lobby

While in the mid-1980s there scarcely existed a Mexico lobby, by the early 1990s the magnitude of the Mexico lobby (in terms of expenditures declared) was competitive with that of larger medium powers such as South Korea. Moreover, while other nations relied on their private sectors to finance lobbying in Washington, Mexico's public sector bore this responsibility directly. A breakdown of declared lobbying expenditures by five nations—Canada, Chile, Israel, South Korea, and Mexico—over three-year intervals starting in 1985 dramatically illustrates the rise of the Mexico lobby relative to those of the other countries. Canada and South Korea were selected as important U.S. allies each known for having a large lobbying presence in Washington. Chile was selected as another Latin country with a minimal lobbying presence until it commenced its own free trade campaign in the early 1990s. Israel was selected because of analysts' frequent assertions that Mexico was following the Israeli lobbying strategy based on the grass-roots strength of sympathetic ethnic U.S. nationals.

Measured in dollar terms, the Mexico lobby, which was approximately one-fifteenth the size of Canada's in 1985 and one-tenth the size of South Korea's, was more than half the size of the lobbies of either Canada or South Korea by 1991. Israel was included in the study because during the NAFTA run-up constant comparisons were made between Mexico's courtship of U.S. Latinos and Israel's use of U.S. Jews as an interest group (Golden 1991; Katz 1992).

As can be seen from Table 5.1, however, the Israeli government spent relatively little (discounting expenditures on the nongovernmental World Zionist Organization). The bulk of the lobbying in Israel's behalf was directly conducted by nongovernmental groups of the U.S. Jewish community (such as that community's flagship organization—the American Israeli Public Affairs Committee (AIPAC)—which spends millions annually lobbying Congress). Growth in the Chile lobby is not visible during the sample years. In 1985 the Chile lobby was approximately the same size as Mexico's but it remained constant through the last year of this cursory study, 1991. The Chile lobby was augmented in 1992 with stepped-up but unsuccessful pressuring for a U.S.–Chile free trade agreement, but complete data for the five countries, as published by the U.S. Attorney General, is only available through 1991.[4]

Based on my own calculations, Mexico's 1993 lobbying expenditures on major foreign agent representatives (see Tables 5.2 and 5.3) surpass South Korea's 1991 total (comprehensive 1993 South Korea figures are not available). This establishes Mexico as one of Washington's biggest hirers of foreign agent representatives, second only to Japan, the perennial champion lobbyer, which spent between $100 million and $400 million annually (much of this by Japanese companies rather than the government),[5] Canada, and perhaps a few other longtime Organization for Economic Cooperation and Development (OECD) powers like Great Britain and West Germany. Even more dramatic than Mexico's expenditures when compared with those of other important U.S. allies is the thirtyfold increase found in comparing the Mexico lobby in 1978 (the first year the U.S. Department of Justice's Foreign Agents Registry required lobbyists to report earnings) with preliminary 1993 figures (see Table 5.2).

While the NAFTA campaign had commenced in earnest by the June 1991 opening of bilateral talks, a slight increase in Mexican expenditures on U.S. lobbyists could be noted by the mid- to late 1980s. A brief qualitative discussion of the rise of the Mexico lobby will serve to demonstrate Mexico's transition from the "smoke-filled room" approach to contemporary grass-roots campaign approaches, and how the latter were deployed as Mexico piggybacked on the electorally oriented efforts of the pro-NAFTA U.S. business community and the nascent political power of U.S. Latinos.

Table 5.1 Lobbying Expenditures in the United States by Five Medium Powers (millions of dollars)

Country and Expense Source	1985	1988	1991
Canada			
Public sector	5.972	9.464	10.684
Private sector	5.052	8.858	7.362
Sub-total	11.024	18.322	18.046
Chile			
Public sector	0.116	0.056	0.007
Private sector	0.128	0.295	0.884
Sub-total	0.244	0.351	0.891
Israel			
Public sector	0.566	3.712	1.248
Private sector	11.089	11.651	11.391
Sub-total	11.655	15.363	12.639
South Korea			
Public sector	0.702	0.138	0.688
Private sector	7.047	11.244	14.203
Sub-total	7.749	11.382	14.891
Mexico			
Public sector	0.190	0.361	6.852
Private sector	0.598	0.694	1.242
Sub-total	0.788	1.055	8.094

Source: U.S. Department of Justice 1985, 1988, 1991.

Table 5.2 Mexico's FARA* Expenditures (millions of dollars)

Classification of Expenditure	1978	1980	1983	1985	1988	1991
Public sector legal and technical services	0.018	0.046	0.299	0.108	0.065	0.033
Private sector legal and technical services	0.133	0.206	0.338	0.369	0.105	0.154
Public sector public relations and lobbying	0.173	0.456	0.044	0.082	0.296	6.819
Private sector public relations and lobbying	0.193	0.330	0.272	0.229	0.589	1.088
Lobby-related subtotal	0.517	1.038	0.953	0.788	1.055	8.094
Tourism promotion	7.963	11.803	5.742	13.106	12.668	25.851
Total FARA-listed expenses	8.480	12.841	6.695	13.894	13.723	33.945

*U.S. Department of Justice Foreign Agent Registration Act.

Source: U.S. Department of Justice 1978, 1980, 1983, 1985, 1988, 1991.

**Table 5.3 Top Foreign Agents Retained by Mexican Interests:
Reported Earnings (millions of dollars)**

Foreign Agent	Mexican Principal	1991	1992	1993	Total Charges
Burson-Marsteller	SECOFI	3.821	4.155	3.191	11.167
Burson-Marsteller	CMHN	—	—	3.5	3.5
Burson-Marsteller	CEMEX	—	0.275	0.261	0.536
Burson-Marsteller	President	0.136	0.376	—	0.512
Shearman & Sterling	SECOFI	0.884	1.169	4.787	6.84
Cleary, Gottlieb, etc.	Finance	2.275	3.198	0.707	6.18
Walker & Associates	SECOFI	0.22	0.508	0.525	1.253
Public Strategies, Inc.	SECOFI	0.16	0.299	0.381	0.84
COECE	COECE	0.22	0.352	0.231	0.803
Brock and Company	SECOFI	0.24	0.189	0.33	0.759
Moya, Villaneuva	SECOFI	—	0.453	0.233	0.686
Gold & Leibengood	SECOFI	0.18	0.303	0.162	0.645
Toney Anaya	SECOFI	—	0.221	0.27	0.491
Abelardo Valdéz	SECOFI	—	0.199	0.253	0.452
Campos Communications	SECOFI	—	0.277	0.172	0.449
TKC International	SECOFI	0.263	0.126	—	0.389
Edward Hidalgo	SECOFI	0.05	0.17	0.132	0.352
Guerra & Associates	SECOFI	—	—	0.305	0.305
Solar & Ellis	SECOFI	—	0.081	0.219	0.3
SJS Advanced Strategies	COECE	—	0.223	—	0.223
Manchester Trade	SECOFI	0.08	0.113	0.023	0.216
Thomas Scanlon	ALFA	0.08	0.065	0.058	0.203
CHACMA	Arancia	0.175	—	—	0.175
Steptoe & Johnson	COECE	—	0.147	—	0.147
Apodaca and Sosa	SECOFI	—	0.045	0.074	0.147
Manatt, Phillips	Vitro	—	0.036	0.085	0.121
Pantin and Partners	SECOFI	—	0.06	0.06	0.12
Total		8.78	413.04	15.959	37.811

Source: Author's calculations.

The Origins of the Mexico Lobby in Washington

In the realm of foreign relations, Mexico has long sought to overcome the asymmetrical interdependence that dominates other spheres of the binational relationship. If the United States' relationship with Mexico has been characterized by paternalistic interventionism, Mexico's relationship with the United States has been one of cautious rebellion through the assertion of nationalist impulses and sovereignty, but within measured limits. Depending in part on its economic well-being (and thus independence from the U.S. economy), Mexico has pursued fiercely independent foreign policies when it felt able to—most recently in the late 1970s and early 1980s when Luis Echeverría carried the banner of the Third World-ist nonallied powers, and José López Portillo, riding the crest of the 1976 oil boom, advocated for social revolutionaries in Central America, much to the disdain of the zealously anti-Sandinista Reagan administration. However, the 1982 debt crisis decisively constricted Mexico's foreign policy space, and by the mid-1980s a confluence of several structural factors made Mexico increasingly dependent on the United States. The rise of the U.S. Congress in foreign policy (particularly in the debates over Central America policy) left Mexico ill-equipped to express its position in the United States. Mexico's failures to achieve diplomatic success via its narrow interaction with the U.S. executive branch resulted in greater misunderstandings in other areas as well, including drug policy and immigration. The "intermestic agenda" (issues treated at both the international and domestic levels) grew ever more complex, rendering Mexico's traditional diplomatic approach out of date. And Mexico's ever-increasing dependence on the U.S. economy made effective diplomacy in Washington absolutely critical (Eisenstadt 1992a: 671–679).

There exists a consensus among political analysts that by the mid-1980s, U.S.–Mexico relations were at their nadir, at least since Lázaro Cárdenas' 1938 nationalization of British and U.S. oil companies.[6] The Reagan administration was woefully out of touch with Mexican reality, and the Mexicans, fearing for their sovereignty, steadfastly refused to hire U.S. "fixers" to intervene on their behalf. The low point of bilateral relations was probably exemplified by Senator Jesse Helms' notorious "Mexico-bashing" hearings in June 1986. Against an already discordant backdrop, Helms managed to touch on almost every sensitive issue—calling on Mexican citizens to impeach President de la Madrid, who his "secret" sources told him was illegitimately elected, and accusing the Mexican government of promoting communism in Central America through its support of the Sandinistas. At the same hearings, high-level Reagan administration officials accused the Mexican government of widespread corruption, just weeks after outspoken U.S. Customs Commissioner William von Raab had publicly characterized the Mexican government as "a bunch of crooks" and asked for a list of the Mexican officials who were not corrupt so that he would know whom to trust with drug-trafficking intelligence (Brinkley 1986). Helms' response to the outraged Mexican government was to declare that "All Latins are volatile people. Hence I was not surprised at the volatile reaction [to the hearings]" (*Washington Post* 1986). The sum total of this chorus of Reagan administration voices against Mexico did not add up to any coherent policy. As summarized in one account, "the overall [Mexico] policy may be so broadly stated that it is not a policy at all" (Omang 1986).

The Mexican counter to this tremendous insensitivity by the United States was an irrational clinging to its sacred principle of noninterventionism. Steeped in a history of U.S. interventionism in some of the most critical moments of Mexico's national development, Mexicans viewed lobbying as at best distasteful and at worst disingenuous. The logic of their argument was always that if they did not seek to intervene in U.S. affairs, then the U.S. could not justify intervening in Mexico. It was a naive view, as stated by longtime U.S. trade negotiator Timothy Bennett, who was met with this attitude when he led a trade mission to Mexico City in 1987 to protest discrimination against U.S. goods in the electronics sector: "I remember telling the Mexicans at the table how misled they were to think that the U.S. would not represent its interests in Mexico City if Mexico was trying to implement certain restrictive trade measures . . . Even if they didn't want to do anything in Washington, they could bet the house that we were going to be down there venting our concerns in Mexico City" (Bennett 1991).[7]

Furthermore, the Mexicans had little understanding of interest group politics, and thus would have been unable to properly undertake a lobbying effort even if they had wanted to. For example, Mexican officials recalled that in the late 1970s, when a minor bilateral trade agreement regulating tropical fruit imports was derailed by the U.S. Congress, the Mexican government was stunned. Similarly, the suspension of the construction of a natural gas pipeline from Mexico to the United States blindsided the Mexicans, who did not know where to apply pressure within the U.S. government, or even how to minimize damage (Bernal 1991). Indeed, the Mexicans were limited by their intimate familiarity with their own traditional executive-only strategy, which was precisely the only form of interest articulation that worked at home in Mexico City, where the Congress, media, and public opinion were not yet players.

With U.S.–Mexico relations spinning out of control in the summer of 1986, the Mexican government decided to seek professional help. Between the June Helms hearings and President de la Madrid's August visit to the United States, the Mexican Office of the Presidency signed an unprecedented lobbying contract with Peter D. Hannaford for a considerable $419,643 to contact "administration officials, members and staff of Congress, and journalists to discuss the visit of the president of Mexico to the United States, Mexican efforts against illegal drugs, Mexican elections, and other issues. . . ."[8] While that contract marked a stride by Mexico to improve its Washington image, it was not an unqualified first, as other Mexican federal agencies, state governments such as Yucatan and Baja California Norte, and several private firms had retained lobbyists on minor contracts (not to mention the millions in Mexican public and private financing that supported the country's ongoing tourism promotion campaign in Washington, New York, and some half dozen U.S. regional outlets of the Mexican Office of Tourism).

Ironically, it was perhaps one of those lesser Mexican government contracts that had the greatest impact on Mexico's internal debate about whether to sustain its increasing lobbyist presence. The contract was rather insignificant: a $62,500 premium exchanged for the monitoring of economic issues such as Mexico's accession to the General Agreement on Tariffs and Trade (GATT), U.S. oil import fees, the Baker Plan for debt forgiveness, U.S. intellectual property protection laws, and World Bank lending for the Secretariat of Commerce and Industrial Development (SECOFI). However, the contract just happened to be with former Hannaford associate and ex–White House Deputy Chief of Staff Michael K. Deaver, whose 1986 federal indictment on charges of lying to Congress on behalf of his foreign clients (including Canada, South Korea, and Mexico) brought out the excesses of the influence-peddling cronyism deployed by the "super-lobbyists," and prompted at least a partial reconsideration by Mexico of whether that was how it wanted to do business.

Deaver did exert some effort for Mexico. According to his Department of Justice filings, Deaver and his assistants made twenty-three contacts with the U.S. Trade Representative's Office, fourteen with the Commerce Department, two with the Department of the Treasury, and two with the U.S. Customs Service (U.S. Department of Justice, File 3734). Taking advantage of his longtime friendship with President Reagan and many other top officials, Deaver parlayed these contacts into access for his clients. Less than a year after resigning from his high-profile government post, the quintessential super-lobbyist had cashed in his mere six-figure government income for a multimillion-dollar lobbying empire. However, Deaver's business collapsed with his highly publicized indictment and legal proceedings (and the finding of his guilt on perjury charges), which led to a short-lived movement to reform conflict-of-interest legislation and slow the revolving door of officials-turned-lobbyists.[9] Deaver's peccadilloes caused a resurgence of the Mexican anti-intervention, antilobbying advocates. But some of Deaver's more pragmatic critics in Mexico, already versed in their new diplomacy in Washington, raised doubts—but not predictable ones—from the traditional moral high ground of Mexican foreign policy. Rather, they asked why it was necessary to pay so much for access to the Republican White House when in fact where the Mexican government lacked contacts was in the Democratic Congress (Castañeda 1986).

While this Mexican opposition on pragmatic grounds represented a tacit recognition of a need to hire lobbyists, the dramatic finish to Deaver's short-lived lobbying career is seen more generally as a watershed in U.S. lobbying strategy. One analyst even pinpointed the sea change in Washington lobbying as the *Time* magazine 3 March 1986 cover photo. It showed Deaver talking on the telephone from the back seat of his limousine, with the caption, "Who is this man calling?"[10] To many, that image represented what was wrong with the old-fashioned influence-peddling that Deaver epitomized. The demise of Deaver, the increasing obsolescence of other super-lobbyists, public fatigue with Washington cronyism (tapped so effectively by "outsiders" like Ross Perot), the rise of grass-roots lobby groups like Ralph Nader's Public Citizen, and the technological advancements that have made direct appeals to citizen networks both cheap and far-reaching, have all contributed to the change in lobbying tactics over the last decade (Brinkley 1993; Tackett and Drew 1992a: A-1). Direct mail campaigns, computer address sort programs, and phone banks—all striving to generate grass-roots campaigns that galvanize ordinary voters into writing, E-mailing, or faxing their congressional members—have replaced the Rolodexes of influence merchants like Deaver as the primary tools of the trade. In direct obeisance of "the electoral connection" (Mayhew 1987) that governs relations between members of Congress and their constituents, lobbyists have sought a more indirect role of persuading voters to convince their elected representatives, rather than undertaking the persuasion directly. Mexico adapted gracefully to these new rules under the tutelage of its high-powered NAFTA lobbyists.

The Design and Execution of Mexico's NAFTA Strategy

The ascendancy of Mexican President Carlos Salinas' prointernationalist foreign policy starting in 1988, his close relationship with President George Bush, and his reckoning with Mexico's increasing economic dependence on the United States in the late 1980s are all credited with the Mexican decision to seek a free trade agreement with the United States starting in 1990. Traditional nationalist opposition persisted and was fanned by public venting among scorned Mexican diplomats who were passed over in favor of Salinas' trade ministry technocrats. The public dissent of these bureaucrats offers evidence of the scope of the changes, as their Foreign Relations Secretariat was replaced by SECOFI as the lead agency presiding over U.S.–Mexican relations in Washington, starting with the NAFTA negotiations in 1991 (Ibarra 1991). Furthermore, the untimely leak of an internal State Department cable articulated Mexicans' worst fears: that U.S. diplomats viewed a trade agreement as a means to "institutionalize acceptance of a North American orientation to Mexico's foreign relations," conditioning Mexico's freedom of maneuver in pursuing its traditional "third world demagoguery" in international forums. This leak rankled Mexico's considerable population of nationalists.[11] Such dissent was nevertheless the exception, as the public debate in Mexico was quite controlled. The government was sensitive about its Washington lobby and sought to underplay this new policy (Franco Hijuelos 1995: 26).

In the United States, contrarily, an extensive debate arose, which Mexico sought to condition through the services of a new ally, the lobbying behemoth Burson-Marsteller. Before placing the public relations and lobbying agency on a multimillion-dollar retainer for the duration of the NAFTA debates, the Mexican government tried out Burson-Marsteller in 1990 with smaller targeted public relations campaigns to improve Mexico's image in fighting drug traffic and to prompt a repeal of the U.S. ban on Mexican tuna for its danger to Pacific dolphins (U.S. Department of Justice, File 2469). According to Department of Justice documents, Burson-Marsteller collected $1.13 million from SECOFI in 1990 for "general public relations services" including "the development and implementation of an ad campaign concerning the war on drugs, including the production of a commercial and press kit," and $3.84 million in 1991 for continuing the "war on drugs" campaign for the Office of the Presidency, its work for the Ministry of Fisheries, and "general media relations counseling" for the Mexican Embassy in Washington (U.S. Department of Justice 1992: 834). Abandoning previous Deaveresque "influence merchant" tactics, Burson-Marsteller General Manager Timothy Brosnahan explained that Mexico's drug war campaign "justified by the facts and disseminated to a variety of audiences through the media, could presumably impact the attitude of the U.S. general public" (U.S. Department of Justice, File 2469).

Such "direct to the people" grass-roots lobbying tactics also came to characterize Burson-Marsteller's work for SECOFI on NAFTA. Concurrent with the opening of formal negotiations in the spring of 1991, Burson-Marsteller constructed its multimillion dollar "Public Affairs Program for Building Support for a Mexico–U.S. Free Trade Agreement" (U.S. Department of Justice, File 4310). The project bid, constructed with subcontractors Gold and Liebengood and The Brock Group, included jargon-riddled mention of strategies to "maximize the value of current relationships with influencers, create new relationships with influencers, coordinate FTA support activities with and among U.S. business coalitions, [and] counter/negate efforts of critics."[12] The Brock Group, headed by former U.S. Trade Representative and Labor Secretary William E. Brock, also emphasized coalition building in its agreement, promising to: "forecast and interpret executive branch actions and responses, provide policy and political counsel on trade and labor issues, personal outreach to leaders of organized labor, counsel on handling non-trade issues during negotiations, advice on managing relationship with private sector advisory process in trade negotiations, and advice on managing business coalition in support of Mexican objectives" (U.S. Department of Justice, File 4310).

Besides Burson-Marsteller (which received $11 million between 1991 and 1993), SECOFI's other flagship foreign agent was Shearman & Sterling, which was paid almost $7 million over the three-year period for both lobbying and legal counsel. According to descriptions of Mexico's NAFTA lobby by the Center for Public Integrity and George Grayson, Shearman & Sterling's lead consultant on the Mexico account was former Under Secretary of Commerce Robert Herzstein. The Mexico team also included Daniel Tarullo, who was nominated by incoming President Clinton to serve as Assistant Secretary of State for Economic and Business Affairs soon after starting work on the SECOFI account (Lewis et al. 1993: 20–25; Grayson 1995: 160). Other major lobbying contracts awarded in Washington by early 1992 were granted to target particular audiences and were based more on an old-fashioned logic of influence peddling than on the newfangled grass-roots lobbying concept. The influence-peddling approach was also reinforced by the sponsorship of more than a half dozen junkets to Mexico for at least forty-eight congressional aides, three congressional members, and a governor, paid for by the Mexican private sector and organized by COECE (Mexico's Association of Exporting Companies) (Lewis et al. 1993: 26–28; U.S. Department of Justice, File 4498).

The recipients of these old-fashioned influence-peddling calls over the first eighteen months of the NAFTA campaign were logged by Lewis et al. (1993), based on U.S. Department of Justice Foreign Agent Registration Act (FARA) disclosures. The results show the most frequent legislative and executive "targets," as well as indicate how redundant the whole effort was (the most popular recipients had received dozens of contacts a full year before the vote) (see Table 5.4). It bears considering that the Center for Public Integrity study was never extended through 1993; one can well imagine that the number of contacts must have tripled or quadrupled in the final months of the campaign.

Public Strategies, Inc. was paid $840,000 over three years to focus on California and Texas congressional members, utilizing the influence of its president, Joseph O'Neill, a former key assistant to Clinton Treasury Secretary Lloyd Bentsen, the longtime Texas senator and head of the powerful Senate Finance Committee before being tapped by Clinton. Walker/Free Associates, headed by former U.S. Treasury official Charles Walker, was designated as the key lobbyist of the midwestern congressional delegations, and was paid $1.25 million for his services between 1991 and 1993. Gold and Liebengood was the designated lobbyist of congressional Republicans (on a stipend of $650,000 through 1993), fully utilizing both Martin Gold and Howard Liebengood's extensive experience working for former Senate Minority Leader Howard H. Baker Jr. (R–TN), and Liebengood's tour in the all-important post of sergeant-at-arms in the Senate during the early 1980s. TKC International, headed by Gabriel Guerra-Mondragón, a former special assistant to the U.S. ambassador in Mexico and Clinton transition team foreign policy advisor, was assigned to cover the emergent congressional Hispanic Caucus (Lewis et al. 1993: 22, 97–104).

SECOFI's NAFTA office director Hermann von Bertrab disparaged interviewer questions about whether Mexico had sought out such well-connected lobbyists. He answered that his government had not expressly recruited former U.S. officials, "just good, competent, well-connected Washington 'professionals'" (Lewis et al. 1993: 23). It is clear from Center for Public Integrity descriptions of the workaday functioning of the SECOFI office that while the Mexicans may have continued to rely on the Deaveresque influence peddlers to make their congressional contacts, their strategy was much more complex. The division of labor within the SECOFI trade office indicates the breadth of their responsibilities. One of von Bertrab's top assistants tracked congressional member positions with a database program. Another handled travel arrangements for visiting

Mexican dignitaries who crisscrossed the United States to publicize NAFTA. A third assistant conducted liaison work with U.S. environmental groups, a fourth handled Hispanic outreach throughout the United States, while a fifth top assistant coordinated with U.S. business interests that had gathered together under an umbrella group called USA*NAFTA (Lewis et al. 1993: 18–19).

As quantified in Table 5.4, Mexico clearly covered its bases by smoothly

**Table 5.4 U.S. Officials Most Frequently Contacted by
Mexican Officials or Their Foreign Agents during 1991 and 1992**

Dates	U.S. Official	Contactor	Number of Contacts
7/91–7/92	John Scheibel, House Foreign Affairs Committee	Gold & Liebengood	45
5/91–9/92	Barry Moehring, Office of Rep. Kolbe (D–AZ)	COECE Gold & Liebengood	30
3/91–12/92	Rep. Bill Richardson (D–NM)	COECE Gold & Liebengood Public Strategies, Inc. Solar & Ellis TKC International, Inc. Toney Anaya Abelardo Valdéz	26
2/91–9/92	Robert Kyle, Senate Finance Committee	Burson-Marsteller COECE Public Strategies, Inc. Walker/Free Associates	23
5/91–12/92	Patricia Kery, Office of Rep. Kennelly (D–CT)	COECE Gold & Liebengood	20
6/91–4/92	Mary Irace, Office of Sen. Roth (R–DE)	COECE Gold & Liebengood	17
3/91–9/92	Richard Kiy, Environmental Protection Agency	Abelardo Valdéz COECE Burson-Marsteller Gold & Liebengood Toney Anaya Walker/Free Associates	16
3/91–9/92	George Weise, House Ways & Means Committee	COECE Public Strategies, Inc. Walker/Free Associates	16
8/91–6/92	Mary Latimer, Office of Rep. Pease (D–OH)	Gold & Liebengood	15
1/92–12/92	Todd Malan, Office of U.S. Trade Representative	Brownstein, Zeidman Walker/Free Associates	14

Source: Author's calculations.

deploying lobbyists with connections in both the Republican and Democratic administrations. This tactic was combined with the increasingly common lobbying practice of grass-roots interest group mobilization. These proven strategies, which in the Mexican case included grass-roots efforts to mobilize Latinos, border region communities, and the pro-NAFTA U.S. business coalition, were also well-funded. The Mexican government and private sector spent immense sums of money to hedge their bets by complementing their elite-induced pressure from above with interest group pressures from below. The success of this strategy depended on the domestic influence of the Mexican foreign agents' targeted U.S. interest partners, which varied. While the USA*NAFTA business coalition seems to have mustered clout gradually based on its own funding and organizing (albeit not until the summer of 1993), the Mexican agents' efforts in the regions and in the Latino community did seem to have a broad, catalyzing impact.

Harvesting the Grass Roots

Upon filling all the gaps in its congressional coverage with well-heeled Washington insiders, SECOFI launched a second, less direct strategy to appeal directly to U.S. voters in states that would prove important to NAFTA, either because of their size, position on the Mexican border, or Latino populations. In 1992, SECOFI retained four freelance Latino lobbyists to canvass the United States identifying and motivating Latino interest groups to pressure the U.S. Congress. The Mexican trade ministry also hired public relations firms in important regions—mainly Los Angeles, Houston, and Miami—to manage local and regional pro-NAFTA activities. Most importantly, the SECOFI team worked closely with USA*NAFTA, both through its own private sector pro-NAFTA lobby, COECE, and through direct contact with USA*NAFTA. Each of these three grass-roots strategies will be considered in turn.

The Latino Lobby

The Latino lobbyists each had extensive public service records. But while they seemed to share public profiles, they were not necessarily congressional operatives, and they did not need to be. Their task was more one of spreading Mexican goodwill to the heartland. These roving Latino lobbyists were: Toney Anaya (a former governor of New Mexico who received $490,000 in 1992 and 1993); Jerry Apodaca (also a former governor of New Mexico who along with his associate Juan Sosa received $150,000 in 1992 and 1993); Eduardo Hidalgo (Carter's Navy Secretary who was paid $350,000 over these two years); and Abelardo Valdéz (a former State Department and U.S. AID official who received $450,000 over the two years). A fourth firm, the Houston-based Solar & Ellis, was commissioned to provide SECOFI with outreach to the African American and Latino communities.

Anaya, Apodaca and Sosa, and Solar & Ellis clarified their grass-roots coalition-building objectives in their FARA filings. Anaya described his function as the following: "In consultation with appropriate officials of Mexico and other consultants they retain, [I will] help develop and implement a plan of action to obtain the input of ethnic and racial minority groups, workers, environmentalists, and other interest groups on provisions of a proposed Free Trade Agreement" (U.S. Department of Justice, File 4568).

Apodaca and Sosa sought to establish links with a narrower constituency— Latino business leaders—by seeking "the names of members of the Hispanic business community in various cities in the United States and invite[ing] them to a panel discussion at a local site," with the hope that "the result of a positive response to this series of seminars could be support for passage of the North American Free Trade Agreement." FARA filings indicate that these seminars, usually sponsored by local Hispanic Chambers of Commerce, were held from June 1992 through June 1993 in San Francisco, Sacramento, Kansas City, Atlanta, Indianapolis, Oklahoma City, Tampa, and Philadelphia (U.S. Department of Justice, File 4640). Solar & Ellis emphasized providing SECOFI with "a better understanding of the rich cultural diversity that is present throughout the United States." Specifically, they organized delegations to Mexico for African American business leaders and the U.S. Conference of Mayors, and met with groups such as the National Association for the Advancement of Colored People (NAACP) and the Congressional Black Caucus (U.S. Department of Justice, File 4630).

Hidalgo and Valdéz each filed less revealing overall statements of their activities, but in itemizing their activities, it was clear that their role was also to cull Latino support. Hidalgo, for example, spoke to Latino audiences in Palm Beach and Dallas about NAFTA negotiations, escorted thirteen prominent Latinos to Mexico to meet with officials, and formally lobbied congressional members (U.S. Department of Justice, File 4509). Valdéz' contacts were almost entirely with U.S. Latino leaders, congressional members, and interest groups, such as the National Council of La Raza, the Hispanic National Bar Association, the Mexican American Legal Defense and Education Fund (MALDEF), and the League of United Latin American Citizens (U.S. Department of Justice, File 4567).

Regional Ambassadors

The second prong of SECOFI's regional grass-roots strategy, in addition to sending Latino messengers out to Mexico's regions, was to hire representatives in the regions themselves. In this capacity, several local public relations firms, mostly Latino-run firms that had extensive contact with local and regional

Latino businesses, were contracted. These included the Los Angeles–based Moya, Villanueva & Associates ($690,000 in 1992–1993), Houston's Campos Communications ($450,000 in 1992–1993), the Pantin Partnership of Miami ($120,000 in 1992–1993), and Kathleen Ann Griffith of the San Diego area ($70,000 in 1991–1993). Griffith was the SECOFI consultant with the grandest vision of the role of these regional representatives in her FARA filing:

> . . . I have assumed the special mission of aiding in the dissemination of information and promoting goodwill as an "ambassador for NAFTA" in the State of California. This includes participating in conferences, seminars, trade shows, conventions, and meetings with committees and private individuals. Hence, I have engaged in educating local non-government organizations, academicians, business people, government officials, and elected politicians on the facts concerning NAFTA and the negotiation of parallel agreements (U.S. Department of Justice, File 4655).

Among her duties for SECOFI, Griffith lists pro-NAFTA presentations at Southern California trade shows, the San Diego Convention and Visitors' Bureau, and the Columbia University Club of San Diego, as well as authorship of articles including an interview with SECOFI Secretary Jaime Serra Puche and an academic article on the environmental provisions of NAFTA (U.S. Department of Justice, File 4655). Her filings do not reveal extensive coordination with the Washington office, as do the reports of other regional ambassadors of NAFTA, especially those of Moya, Villanueva & Associates, and Campos Communications. Before analyzing the work of SECOFI's active California and Texas outposts, it is worth mentioning that the Pantin Partnership also did not exhibit evidence that it played a coordinated role in the SECOFI campaign. Although its FARA filings are incomplete, the only evidence it offered as work on behalf of the Mexican government was a memo titled "Local Spokespersons Available for Interviews on NAFTA," encouraging local media interviews and listing the addresses and phone numbers of three South Florida "experts": Nino Lucio, a Miami attorney who headed the "MiaMex" committee of the Greater Miami Chamber of Commerce; Mark Rosenberg, a Florida International University professor who headed the university's Latin American and Caribbean Center; and Alberto Cárdenas, a Miami attorney, Republican committeeman, and member of the local Hispanic Alliance for Free Trade (U.S. Department of Justice, File 4617).

The filings of Moya-Villanueva and Campos demonstrate extensive interaction with SECOFI's other foreign agents and with the Mexican government. In the final months of 1992, for example, Moya-Villanueva handled local arrangements for Southern California visits by Serra Puche, lead Mexican NAFTA negotiator Herminio Blanco, and von Bertrab; reported to Mexico's Los Angeles consulate on a Blanco "Hispanic influential meeting;" reviewed and analyzed California media news clippings; "reviewed all national press clipping updates received from Burson-Marsteller;" distributed hundreds of "NAFTA information kits;" and researched Hispanic political figures in California for SECOFI. In the first half of 1993, the public relations firm attended several local Hispanic trade conferences; worked to "enhance the community-based organization list and began inputting to create a data base;" drafted a "California Doing Business with Mexico" pamphlet; edited and distributed a von Bertrab opinion piece to statewide English- and Spanish-language print media; "began to draft materials for a network volunteer kit, including industry fact sheets, glossary of NAFTA terms and regionalized media lists;" produced and distributed two Spanish-language radio news releases based on a Serra Puche speech to San Diego business leaders; solicited a NAFTA opinion piece from Robert Guzmán, president of the Society for Professional Hispanic Engineers; and "developed an in-house rough draft of the article" (U.S. Department of Justice, File 4629).

Additionally, in the winter of 1993, Moya-Villanueva planned a Latino journalist Mexico trip; "continued to recruit members and develop regional NAFTA committees for the statewide NAFTA network;" promoted a Southwest NAFTA conference among "Hispanic influentials;" and developed talking points in response to a 3 March *Wall Street Journal* article "U.S. Hispanics Flex Political Muscles as Mexico Lobbies for NAFTA." According to spring 1993 FARA filings, Moya-Villanueva continued developing a "statewide business leadership network;" finalized the Robert Guzmán guest column; translated a Burson-Marsteller press release, "Cinco de Mayo: Much to Celebrate in Mexico-California Relationship," and distributed it "to print publications in Northern California with Jim's [Lopez, network co-chair] and in Southern California with Ana's [Barbosa, president of the Latin Business Association] name;" distributed hundreds of "NAFTA information kits;" "pitched media interviews and community presentations in Fresno and Bakersfield for a two-day media tour with Toney Anaya" in July as well as another Anaya (statewide) in September; held talks with the Los Angeles Chamber of Commerce and the Fresno Hispanic Chamber of Commerce about "getting both NAFTA seminars off the ground;" and participated in two Washington team meetings where they "provided the client with a detailed report on proposed public relations activities for each of the 13 target congressional districts in California" (U.S. Department of Justice, File 4629).

Campos Communications' FARA filings demonstrate a similarly hectic schedule of intelligence gathering on Latino influentials and Texas politicos' positions on NAFTA more generally, coalition building with local Latino business and political groups, event planning and publicity, and drafting press releases. The Campos filings were less explicit than those of Moya-Villanueva about soliciting and ghostwriting "influencer" opinion pieces, and also about the closeness of their contact with Burson-Marsteller and SECOFI's other Washington agents. However, the Campos filings do demonstrate extensive efforts in promoting a Texas-wide pro-NAFTA coalition. In 1992, agency representatives reported having arranged Houston appearances of von Bertrab and a Dallas appearance by Serra Puche; distributed hundreds of copies of a poster commemorating free trade sponsored by AT&T; "selected business and political leaders to participate in a delegation to Mexico City sponsored by the Mexican government;" appeared at both the state Democratic and Republican conventions; and arranged a speech for Idelfonso Guajardo of the Washington SECOFI office at a Houston meeting of the Coalition for Free Trade with Mexico. Also in 1992, Campos representatives met several times with Houston Council Member Gracie Saenz "to discuss the formation of a free trade coalition" (she subsequently hosted meetings for this coalition), and met with the leadership of Hispanic Chambers of Commerce in Fort Worth, Dallas, Lubbock, Midland, and San Antonio. In 1993, Campos' filings report having met with Hispanic journalists, accountants, and business groups in Houston; attended a Latino NAFTA Strategy Session and meetings with SECOFI in Washington, as well as the National Association of Latino Elected and Appointed Officials (NALEO) conference in Las Vegas, the national League of United Latin American Citizens (LULAC) convention in Miami, and the National Council of La Raza convention in Detroit (U.S. Department of Justice, File 4609).

Private Sector Ambassadors

The third prong of the grass-roots portion of SECOFI's campaign involved working directly with the U.S. private sector. This involved close contact with USA*NAFTA, the ad hoc trade association of U.S. pro-NAFTA corporations, which seemed to sputter until August 1993, when negotiations of the controversial side agreements were concluded, as many of the Fortune 500 members of the USA*NAFTA coalition hesitated to commit resources until knowing the content of the side agreements. Also, USA*NAFTA seemed to lack the singularly determined leadership demonstrated by SECOFI in its efforts. The coalition's first head, Kay R. Whitmore, was removed from her position as chief executive officer of Eastman Kodak Co. in mid-1993, and not replaced until September 1993 by Allied-Signal CEO Lawrence A. Bossidy. In the fall of 1993, however, USA*NAFTA did become quite effective as it purchased prime-time television commercials, and a full-blown print media campaign, contracted Washington firms like Grunwald, Eskew, and Donilan (public relations), and Nick Calio (formerly President Bush's legislative liaison) who targeted Republican congressional votes for NAFTA (Grayson 1995: 161–162).

Prior to the eleventh hour—autumn of 1993—USA*NAFTA's activities were conducted with a much lower profile, but the coalition did conduct extensive local, regional, and national grass-roots campaigning. In the spring of 1993, Lewis et al. (1993) identified the "most committed" members of a twelve-hundred-organization umbrella as the following: Whitmore; Harold A. Wagner,

CEO of Airproducts and Chemicals; James R. Jones, formerly chairman of the American Stock Exchange and currently Clinton's ambassador in Mexico; José F. Niño, president of the United States Hispanic Chamber of Commerce; and James Robinson, formerly CEO of American Express, who founded USA*NAFTA along with Whitmore in October 1992 (Lewis et al. 1993). The coalition named state captains to preside over pro-NAFTA organizing in their states. Performing regional ambassador roles similar to those of SECOFI hires Moya-Villanueva and Campos Communications (but acting directly out of their own business self-interest, rather than as hired agents of any contractor). Lewis et al. described the function of the state captains as mobilizing businesses, particularly small and medium-sized companies, interacting with state and local political leaders, monitoring positions of these influencers, and advocating for their public support of NAFTA. At the national level, USA*NAFTA retained several lobbyists starting in 1992, including Gail Harrison, senior vice president of the Wexler Group, a consulting firm affiliated with the lobbying giant Hill and Knowlton, to coordinate grass-roots organizing (Lewis et al. 1993: 31–34).

While USA*NAFTA officials reported maintaining a separation between their activities and those of the Mexicans, von Bertrab acknowledged that the primary task of one of his top assistants in the SECOFI office, Idelfonso Guajardo, was to coordinate with Harrison and USA*NAFTA (Lewis et al. 1993: 18–19, 33). Furthermore, while documentation of the U.S. NAFTA coalition's activities is scarce (domestic lobbyists face none of the reporting requirements of foreign agents), it is obvious that the work of Mexican agents such as Moya-Villanueva and Campos in courting support from local and national Hispanic chambers of commerce overlapped greatly with USA*NAFTA, whose active members included the president of the U.S. Hispanic Chamber of Commerce. Moreover, the Mexican government and USA*NAFTA seemed to share data, such as positive impact studies of NAFTA on states or congressional districts, and firms in each state or district actively campaigning for (or against) the agreement. As stated by an aide to pro-NAFTA Senator John McCain (R–AZ), "Many times we would ask lobbyists hired by USA*NAFTA or Mexico if there were any companies in the congressman's home district or state and get them to get in contact with us" (Hernández 1995: 17).

The Last, Best Lobby: Clinton, Pork Barrel Politics, and NAFTA's Passage

The irony of all the effort exerted by SECOFI is that NAFTA's passage ultimately depended on one person: President Bill Clinton. The enlightened new premises of Mexico's pluralistic diplomacy were all undermined; their antiquated and doctrinaire executive-only policy would have been more effective in the final days before the roll-call vote. By the end of October, all the grass-roots business and Latino activists had conveyed their messages, and NAFTA was still short by dozens of votes in the House of Representatives. President Clinton, having adopted NAFTA as one of his foreign policy cornerstones (and indeed the only one with prospects for success at a moment when U.S. involvements in Bosnia and Haiti were not generating high approval ratings), undertook one of the most expensive congressional vote-buying sprees in modern U.S. history. At a cost of billions of dollars in incentives and inducements for undecided House members who would "sell" their votes for pork barrel projects for their districts or important constituency groups, Clinton won approval of NAFTA. The most notable of these deals and their recipients are summarized in Table 5.5. According to Diana Evans' analysis of data from Ralph Nader's non-profit group, Public Citizen, 76 House members were offered deals that helped convince 84.2 percent (or 64) of them to vote for the agreement. Only 47.5 percent (or 170) of the House members not tendering offers from Clinton supported the trade bill, which ultimately passed on November 17 by a vote of 234 to 200 (Evans 1995: 10–11). At that rate, without Clinton's offers, NAFTA would not have received the simple majority needed to pass the House.

When some of the more notorious of these deals are compared to the roll-call pronouncements of the House members who took them, it becomes clear that a huge disparity exists between what congressional members say motivates their votes, and the financial and "electoral connection" incentives that theories of U.S. congressional behavior tell us truly stimulate them (Jacobson 1987; Mayhew 1987). True, it could hardly be expected that a fence-sitting House member would declare himself or herself a pro-NAFTA supporter, because "President Clinton offered me $32 million for a new highway in my district, as well as special protection for sugar producers, who have given $650,000 to my campaigns over the years, and promised to support my reelection 'handsomely' if I bring them some protection." That would be a cynical statement, but perhaps more honest than the declarations in favor of "Mexican democracy" and "the benefits of free trade throughout our hemisphere" made by the pork barrel recipients. Indeed, a review of the 17 November 1993 *Congressional Record* indicates that while some House members explained the ambivalence of their decisions, none of the fence-sitters mentioned the deals they cut in exchange for votes (*Congressional Record* 1993: 9875–10049).

President Clinton's NAFTA-clinching deals after Mexico and U.S. lobbying efforts fell shy offer at least circumstantial evidence that generalized public relations campaigns, and phone calls and meetings by congressional members and staff with hired foreign agents can have only a nominal impact on policy making. At its best moments, the Mexican government seemed to abide by this broadly understood truism. The government's economic studies of congressional district impacts, and mobilization of pro-NAFTA businesses by district demonstrated a combination of savvy and cynicism appropriate to Washington

Table 5.5 Clinton Administration Deals for Pro-NAFTA Votes

Representative	Clinton's Offer of Particularistic Benefits	Value in Billions
Allard, Wayne (R-CO)	Reduction of airline and ship passenger tax	inexact
Allard, Wayne (R-CO)	Reversal of federal grazing fee increase	inexact
Bacchus, Jim (D-FL)	Protection for Fla. and La. sugar and produce	$1.4 divided by 12
Becerra, Xavier (D-CA)	NADB funds for infrastructure projects	$.25 divided by 6
Brewster, Bill (D-OK)	Limits on Canadian durum wheat import	inexact
Bryant, John (D-TX)	NADB funds for infrastructure projects	$.25 divided by 6
Cardin, Benjamin L. (D-MD)	Heat on Canada to lower chemical subsidies	inexact
Clement, Bob (D-TN)	More American Airlines London routes	inexact
Combest, Larry (R-TX)	Limits on Canadian durum wheat import	inexact
Deal, Nathan (D-GA)	Stepped-up enforcement of textile import laws	$.015 divided by 3
Dunn, Jennifer (R-WA)	Reduction of airline and ship passenger tax	inexact
English, Glenn (D-OK)	Limits on Canadian durum wheat import	inexact
Ewing, Thomas (R-IL)	Reduction of airline and ship passenger tax	inexact
Fowler, Tillie (R-FL)	Protection for Fla. and La. sugar and produce	$1.4 divided by 12
Frost, Martin (D-TX)	Federal pledge to protect glass producers	inexact
Goss, Porter (R-FL)	Protection for Fla. and La. sugar and produce	$1.4 divided by 12
Grandy, Fred (R-IA)	Heat on Mexico to reduce appliance tariffs	inexact
Hastert, Dennis (R-IL)	Reduction of airline and ship passenger tax	inexact
Hastings, Alcee (D-FL)	Protection for Fla. and La. sugar and produce	$1.4 divided by 12
Hayes, James (D-LA)	Protection for Fla. and La. sugar and produce	$1.4 divided by 12
Hefley, Joel (R-CO)	Reversal of federal grazing fee increase	inexact
Hefner, W. G. (D-NC)	Stepped-up enforcement of textile import laws	$.015 divided by 3
Hobson, David (R-OH)	Protection for flat glass and broomcorn	inexact
Hoekstra, Peter (R-MI)	Federal promise to protect asparagus growers	inexact
Hutto, Earl (D-FL)	Protection for Fla. and La. sugar and produce	$1.4 divided by 12
Jefferson, William (D-LA)	Protection for Fla. and La. sugar and produce	$1.4 divided by 12
Johnson, Eddie Bernice (D-TX)	Construction of two C-17 military planes	$1.40
Johnson, Sam (R-TX)	Reduction of airline and ship passenger tax	inexact
Johnston, Harry (D-FL)	Protection for Fla. and La. sugar and produce	$1.4 divided by 12
Lewis, Tom (R-FL)	Protection for Fla. and La. sugar and produce	$1.4 divided by 12
McCrery, Jim (R-LA)	Protection for Fla. and La. sugar and produce	$1.4 divided by 12
Meek, Carrie (D-FL)	Protection for Fla. and La. sugar and produce	$1.4 divided by 12
Miller, Dan (R-FL)	Protection for Fla. and La. sugar and produce	$1.4 divided by 12
Mineta, Norman (D-CA)	Promise of protection for cut-flower industry	inexact
Packard, Ron (R-CA)	Reduction of airline and ship passenger tax	inexact
Pastor, Ed (D-AZ)	NADB funds for infrastructure projects	$.25 divided by 6
Payne, Lewis (D-VA)	National Institute of Standards consideration	$.5 to $3 federal
Pelosi, Nancy (D-CA)	NADB funds for infrastructure projects	$.25 divided by 6
Pickle, J. J. (D-TX)	Creation of Center for Study of Trade in Western Hemisphere	$0.01
Price, David (D-NC)	More American Airlines London routes	inexact
Rowland, J. Roy (D-GA)	Limits on Canadian peanut butter imports	inexact
Roybal-Allard, Lucille (D-CA)	NADB funds for infrastructure projects	$.25 divided by 6
Sarpalius, Bill (D-TX)	Limits on Canadian durum wheat imports	inexact
Sarpalius, Bill (D-TX)	Reversal of Clinton effort to cut helium subsidy	$0.047
Shaw, Clay (R-FL)	Heat on Mexico to extradite rape suspect	inexact
Smith, Bob (R-OR)	Reversal of federal grazing fee increase	inexact
Smith, Neal (D-IA)	Heat on Mexico to reduce appliance tariffs	inexact
Spratt, John (D-SC)	Stepped-up enforcement of textile import laws	$.015 divided by 3
Stump, Bob (R-AZ)	Reversal of federal grazing fee increase	inexact
Torres, Esteban (D-CA)	NADB funds for infrastructure projects	$.25 divided by 6
Valentine, Tim (D-NC)	American Airlines London routes	inexact
Total of 51		**19 deals struck**

Note: NADB = North American Development Bank.
This table mentions only the recipients of the most overt deals.
Source: Anderson and Silverstein 1993. Reprinted with permission from the 20 December 1993 issue of *The Nation*.

politics. Their indirect grass-roots approach of pressuring Congress through Latino and other private sector influencers out in the district was also well-conceived. However, there is a quick saturation point reached by any third-party efforts to influence the special relationship between congressional members and constituents. When they "went it alone" (i.e., all their expenditures on direct lobbying: Burson-Marsteller, the Brock Group, Gold and Liebengood, Walker & Associates, Public Strategies, Inc.), there was only so much impact the Mexican agents could have once they had accomplished the minimum achievement of merely informing the congressional members of exactly what the Mexican position was (and more practically, which members could find an ally in them) (McCormick 1995; Hernández 1995.)

While it may never be precisely understood exactly how strong the relationship was between SECOFI and USA*NAFTA, it would appear that the Mexicans might have gotten more for their money by either donating some of it to USA*NAFTA's campaign (and indeed they may have without the knowledge of FARA archive researchers, as domestic lobbying expenditures need not be reported), or by coordinating its efforts more directly under the U.S. private sector's umbrella. There is no doubt that all the Mexican government's public relations and lobbying firms created some intangible quantity of goodwill toward Mexico both in Washington and in the U.S. heartland. But even constituent interest groups could not convert that goodwill directly into congressional votes. It took a hell-bent executive bearing gifts to achieve what the expensive consultants could not. And any consideration of the efficacy of the Mexicans' conveying information to a third party (i.e., hired lobbyists) involves transaction costs, that is, the resources required (time and money) to fully transfer the information to the third party, which in turn must assimilate it only to retransfer it to political elites, the media, and other purveyors of public opinion. Furthermore, lobbyists necessarily represent their own interests first. Thus, the pure objective of winning causes for their client is second to winning them after staging a high-profile fight in which they log public and even ostentatious victories.[13] Such public "scores" enhance lobbyists' reputations and make them more desirable to prospective future clients.

Certainly, the lobbyists perform a service by monitoring the foreign agent's interests, identifying coalitions with which their contractor can merge, and informing congressional members and their staffs, for the record, of their client's exact position. But perhaps that level of service could have been provided for less than what the Mexican government paid (and again it should be noted that the Mexican government probably spent two or three times its documented expenditures). There is no way to definitely measure the precise marginal value of the services received by the Mexican government, above and beyond the benefits derived from U.S. executive branch and nongovernment interest group mobilization and lobbying, and Mexican' officials direct advocacy in their meetings with U.S. counterparts. But there is at least suggestive evidence of counterfactual examples in which the U.S. executive alone carried pro-NAFTA policies, and further evidence of testimony by congressional aides and even candid lobbyists that lobbying has finite limits. These limits may also be evidenced through brief considerations of Mexico's other recent policy crisis in Washington, the winter 1995 bailout package, in which lobbyists played no role, as the entire legislative branch grew increasingly irrelevant as Mexico's crisis escalated (along with the U.S. search for a policy response).

The Mexican Bailout, or Life After Lobbyists

In many ways an extension of his heavy political investment in the last-minute NAFTA campaign, President Clinton on 30 January 1995 cobbled together an emergency $40 billion loan guarantee package using his discretion over the Treasury's exchange stabilization fund and some expeditious negotiating with the International Monetary Fund (IMF), the Bank for International Settlements (BIS), and the Canadian government. The president had hoped to have a $20 billion U.S. loan guarantee program approved by Congress and he campaigned during January for legislative sponsorship of such a bill. Several reasons have been cited for the failure of the bill, particularly on the House side, where the brunt of the negotiations took place. None involved the ineffectiveness of the Mexico lobby, as there was none.

Postmortems of the congressional package blame its failure on several factors: the executive's hasty conception of the proposal and President Clinton's insufficient campaign to sell the bill to the public, squabbling in Congress both between parties and between the prorescue package leadership and the anti-assistance "back benchers," and a general lack of will by Congress to pass unpopular legislation at a difficult political moment. House Republicans, spearheaded by Banking Committee Chair James Leach (R–IA), supported the president's proposal more than did the Democrats, who sought to condition support on inclusion of clauses to influence Mexico's oversight of its central bank, foreign policy towards Cuba, and wage and labor policies, to name just a few of the conditionality clauses suggested by posturing House members eager to please diverse constituencies (even if they knew their "clause" had no chance of even reaching the House floor for debate).

According to James McCormick, assistant staff director of the House Banking Committee's Domestic and International Policy Subcommittee, Leach and the House leadership recognized the broad potential scope of the financial crisis if it were not contained, and did draft a bill, but "The White House could not deliver language which would bring along the congressional Democrats in a timely manner. The more time the bill was just laying out there, the more time there was to criticize it and soon it was clear that the votes [for approval] no longer existed" (McCormick 1995).

Different congressional members needed different conditions attached to the bill for "political cover" with their constituents, and no common ground could be found. McCormick said this lack of consensus had nothing to do with lobbying and everything to do with the composition of members' constituencies and bases of support.

"There was no lobbying visible to us," said McCormick. "There were efforts to get the pro-NAFTA business roundtable back together, but ironically that effort reached its apex precisely at the time we decided we could not bring a bill to the floor for a vote" (McCormick 1995). A 23 January meeting by the Business Roundtable, lead by John W. Snow of CSX Corporation and Lawrence A. Bossidy of Allied-Signal Inc. (who led the USA*NAFTA campaign) was attended by some one hundred lobbyists, but they never had the chance to discuss more than "strategies and assignments for the Mexico package" (Graham et al. 1995). According to McCormick, it was just as well that no lobby campaign was organized, as "this was an issue where our national interests were at stake. Lobbying by Mexico would have been superfluous or even counterproductive. Their lobbying was directed at Wall Street, not Congress" (McCormick 1995).

Indeed, neither of the pivotal players were strangers to Wall Street. Treasury Secretary Robert Rubin, a former partner at the Wall Street trading giant Goldman-Sachs was accused by political enemies of parlaying the Mexican crisis into profit through his extensive network of financial sector contacts. Mexican Finance Minister Guillermo Ortiz' Wall Street network had just been bolstered by a month of shuttling between New York and Mexico City in December 1994, when he sought to assure U.S. investors not to pull out of Mexico in the wake of President Ernesto Zedillo's alarming peso devaluation. But even if the focal point of the bargaining was outside the beltway, the deals had to be consummated in Washington, where the Mexican government did make its presence felt, but not via the usual contracted labor. Instead, the Mexicans adopted a refreshingly direct lobbying approach. They resorted to an old-fashioned but proven strategy of direct face-to-face meetings with their U.S. counterparts.

Press accounts depict a full-fledged and desperate effort by Mexican officials to convince their U.S. counterparts in Congress, the Treasury Department, and the State Department of the desperate plight of Mexico's economy and the U.S. economic stakes in preventing a Mexican default. By the end of January, Mexican Foreign Minister José Angel Gurría had "virtually set up shop" at the State Department, and former Finance Minister Pedro Aspe and presidential Chief of Staff Luis Tellez had made low-profile trips to Washington as congressional support dissipated (Graham et al. 1995: 1). As the House leadership held heated discussions in the waning days of the effort, even President Zedillo became personally engaged in calling in chips. Zedillo telephoned Arizona Governor Fife Symington, who was in Washington for a National Governors' Association meeting and to lobby Congress on some Arizona-related matters. "He told me he was in desperate trouble and that he hoped I would do everything I can to help," Symington reported. On 30 January, Symington conveyed Zedillo's concerns to House Speaker Newt Gingrich (R–GA) who invited the governor to a Republican congressional leaders' meeting. Symington's candid observations of the meeting depict the plight of congressional approval of the loan guarantees: "It was an absolute free-for-all. Alfonse D'Amato [Republican senator from New York] was yelling at Phil Gramm [Republican senator and presidential candidate from Texas]. Gramm was yelling at D'Amato. At one point, I thought D'Amato came lurching up out of his chair" (Sidener 1995).

By that time, congressional approval was impossible, despite extensive foreign and domestic pressures. Direct pressure by foreign officials, such as the campaign by Mexico's highest officials, when exerted on the proper U.S. officials, appears more effective than hired lobbyists, said McCormick, as the officials' interests are much more transparent and the whole transaction less "unseemly" (McCormick 1995). But even boosted by their direct intervention, there was little the Mexicans could do. Again, the entire burden fell upon the president, who was sympathetic to the NAFTA partner upon which he had already staked considerable political capital. And beyond these personal concerns, President Clinton expressed trepidation about broader dangers to world financial flows that could result from a Mexican default. President Clinton had been negotiating his executive-only solution with the international financial community and the Treasury Department since 28 January, when it became clear to him there was to be no congressional package.

The Foibles of Lobbying—Foreign and Otherwise

Given the innumerable factors beyond lobbyists' control involved in U.S. foreign policy making, the question begs to be revisited: "Was Mexico's NAFTA effort worth the price?" Considering that the $37 million in recorded earnings by Mexico's biggest foreign agents over the three years of the NAFTA lobby probably represents only a minority of the Mexicans' total expenditures on the pact, and none of the lobbying price tag on the U.S. side, it is hard to imagine that some of that money could not have been better spent, especially given that Mexico is still a developing economy that can ill afford to pay exorbitant lobbyist fees at an hourly rate that can top one hundred times the country's daily minimum wage in exchange for dubious services. Questions also remain from the U.S. perspective about who these foreign lobbyists are, how they are regulated, and the quality of the information they "sell," and more broadly, about the role of lobbyists in the promulgation of public policy. Are lobbyists useful to the democratic policy making process, or do they merely obfuscate facts and manipulate public opinion while the real decisions continue to be made behind closed doors? I will reconsider the effectiveness of Mexico's lobby, and then utilize the context of the NAFTA debates to address the microlevel issues related to lobbying regulations and ethics and the bigger, normative issue of where such lobbying fits into interest group pluralism.

My argument, based on suggestive evidence only, is that Mexico's lobbying presence went from underrepresentation to overkill in less than five years. Indeed, there is a need for foreign governments to closely monitor their interests, and some need for Washington insider-ness and economic and legal consultants is inevitable. However, as McCormick and other congressional aides have made quite clear, these hired guns are no substitute for the real thing—well-trained diplomatic staff who steward their own issues. Congressional aides tend to receive foreign agent lobbyists skeptically, especially if they represent generalist public relations firms rather than specialized expertise (usually legal or economic). Even one of Burson-Marsteller's chief "Mexico hands" acknowledged that the benefits to Mexico of his firm's public relations campaigns was at best ambiguous (Eisenstadt 1992a: 700). The real reason why so many countries pay so much for Washington representation may be that they cannot be absolutely certain that a high-quality lobbyist corps may not be a decisive factor or even the factor that puts them over the top in an issue critical to bilateral relations. In cases like NAFTA, where actual expenditures are still paled by what is actually at stake, foreign governments hire lobbyists as insurance. This becomes a self-fulfilling prophesy, as the more foreign countries and domestic interests hire lobbyists, the more their opponents over a particular legislative issue feel that they too must hire lobbyists as a necessary transaction cost, in order to present a formidable image, if not in expectation of actual benefits accrued from such an investment.

The trend towards grass-roots strategies (as opposed to influence peddlers) by both the public and private sectors stands as testimony to this tactic's better yield of results. This is especially true of narrowly focused domestic interest groups with large constituencies such as ethnic lobbies, the National Rifle Association, the Teamster's Union, and the Sierra Club. Of course, lobbyist-channeled grass-roots campaigns beg the question of how necessary the facilitating lobby group is if a true domestic grass-roots force is already mobilized over a particular issue. This is especially true in the case of foreign government lobbyists, since U.S. citizens only rarely care enough about foreign policy issues to respond to postcards, phone calls, faxes, or E-mails calling them to action.

If the domestic mobilization is not an extant social force but rather an ad hoc group manipulated by the foreign agent, then this raises normative questions about the validity of claims by the aroused populace that they are in fact a spontaneous social uprising (which they always claim). Close observers do credit the Mexican government and its agents with keeping NAFTA on the congressional agenda and framing it as a national security issue when, during the first half of 1993, President Clinton wavered under the attacks of Ross Perot, the AFL-CIO, the Sierra Club, and Ralph Nader's Public Citizen group, among others. Furthermore, SECOFI's extensive efforts, through its Houston and Los Angeles public relations firms, did cultivate Latino support where little had previously been organized. Whether this support constituted a grass-roots movement or was merely a construct of the PR firms is a valid question. And obviously, even the harshest detractors of Mexico's Washington lobby cannot argue with NAFTA's final vote. But again, circumstantial evidence and actor testimonials indicate that the Mexican and U.S. lobbies' impact on regional business elites, Latino activists, and other constituencies may have been necessary, but it was not sufficient.

Members of Congress responded to executive pork barrel overtures after both the influence-peddler and grass-roots-mobilizer lobbyists had peaked. Both strategies came up well shy of the needed votes, suggesting that legislators respond most favorably to those who can deliver resources or constituency services directly to their districts that they can harness for their reelection. The provision of indirect or less particularistic benefits to these lawmakers, through influence peddling or grass-roots mobilizing, is only a second-best strategy. Whether this information is presented as the number of companies in a given district with trade ties to Mexico, the estimated job loss in the district due to NAFTA implementation, or a roster of newly registered Latino voters favoring the agreement, this is the type of information that wins support in Washington.[14] The rest of the maximizing the value of relationships with influencers, forecasting and interpreting actions and responses, personal outreach, and personal outreach to leaders is at best of limited utility, and at worst frivolous and misleading. Economists and political analysts alike are increasingly suggesting that lobbying is a nonproductive means through which politicians and those who live off the policy-making economy raise the transaction costs of conducting politics, and thus enable themselves to extract greater rents.[15]

In addition to the costs that foreign lobbying exacts on governments (and ultimately, their taxpayers), there is at least suggestive evidence that foreign lobbying by hired agents can obfuscate the interests of both their client governments and the officials they lobby. Perhaps the most notorious recent example was the admission by one of Kuwait's Washington representatives, the public relations behemoth Hill & Knowlton, that account executives there arranged "impartial" congressional testimony by a fifteen-year-old Kuwaiti girl about atrocities against babies during the Gulf War. The Hill & Knowlton staffers knew but did not disclose that the girl was in fact the daughter of the Kuwaiti ambassador to the United States (McCrory 1992). In the NAFTA debate, a less extreme case of lobbyist misrepresentation was described by Lewis et al. (1993). Brock Group president Bill Brock, the former U.S. trade representative, was asked by the Senate Finance Committee to testify in favor of fast-track approval for NAFTA. At no time did Brock disclose his financial relationships with Burson-Marsteller or SECOFI. When called on this alleged impropriety, Brock responded that he had revealed the potential conflict of interest in his FARA disclosures, which were available for congressional staff review at the time of his testimony.

In fact it is quite unlikely any of the Finance Committee staff had reviewed Brock's FARA filings. As Lewis explained, the FARA files are "basically a joke." He likened them to the Salvation Army, as archivists "are happy to get whatever comes their way" (Hernández 1995). The FARA filing requirement has two major loopholes: it does not apply to lawyers appearing informally before courts or U.S. agencies or to activities by foreign-owned companies that also benefit U.S. subsidiaries. Furthermore, its reporting requirements are vague and unenforced. Recent efforts to legislate a tightening of the law and its enforcement have largely failed (Sachs 1995: 8).

The "free exchange of ideas, but for a price" mentality fostered by Washington's lobbyist culture was abundantly visible in the work of the SECOFI foreign agents. California public relations firms deceivingly drafted op-ed pieces and then sought appropriate influencers to sign their names to them. Former New Mexico governors crisscrossed the country on SECOFI-sponsored junkets with the zeal of newly converted missionaries of goodwill—all for a mere trade agreement. Meanwhile in Washington, congressional hearings misrepresented the interests of witnesses while public relations campaigns oversimplified and confused substance with image.

Still, the Mexicans cannot be faulted for recurring to full-scale lobbying campaigns—"doing as the Romans." Indeed, they won their vote and by the standards of the business, conducted a highly professional and successful campaign. Nor should foreign governments in general be singled out for blame for the excesses of lobbying. The Japan-bashers of the 1980s and the Perotian xenophobes of the 1990s should have nothing to fear from rational political debates undertaken with full information, even if one or more participants cannot have U.S. national interests in mind (not that these may easily be defined in any case). Free societies must provide forums for the views of all wishing to express them—either individually or collectively—even if through a foreign government. The danger lies in not properly disclosing the interests in play. Foreign agent (and domestic lobbyist) disclosures must be strengthened and enforced.[16] Regulations limiting campaign contributions by the Washington offices of corporations are also essential. These are only the first steps of what should be dramatic reforms to end the special interest groups' stranglehold on Washington.[17]

Very little has been written in the international relations literature directly about the role of foreign lobbies in the approval of trade pacts in Washington.[18] From a positivist perspective, there is little evidence to date that foreign lobbying has had a decisive impact in the signing of trade agreements, especially when considered with other variables such as level of trade openness with the foreign country prior to the pact, the cost-benefit ratio in terms of overall trade and job migration (and how these gains and losses are distributed across congressional districts), and most importantly, the domestic coalitions lining up in favor versus those against. From a normative perspective, the condition of U.S. pluralist democracy would be even worse off if levels of foreign lobbying had enough of an impact on U.S. policy making so as to be modeled as one of the variables affecting trade pact approval.

While it is impossible to measure the effect of foreign lobbying on U.S. policy making, political science theories and the testimony of politicians and their staffs attest to the relative success of targeting congressional members through their constituencies, rather than hiring influence peddlers to directly persuade, especially in an era when technology has lowered the barriers to accessing congressional members directly and to organizing mobilizations around particular issues. Observations of the success of interest coalitions across countries, as compared to direct government-to-government interaction only, do give cause for optimism that lobbyists can effectively serve as clearinghouses to match foreign governments with likely U.S. domestic coalition partners. And again, in its best moments, this was a true achievement of the Mexico lobby during the NAFTA debate, even though this low-overhead service could have been provided, by all indications, at a much lower cost.

Whatever its normative, ethical, and economic shortcomings, Mexico's lobby has become an important and permanent tool of the stewards of Mexico's increasingly complex political interests in Washington. As Mexico's foreign agents build a track record on promoting these interests, future studies may be able to address the cost-effectiveness of this expensive diplomatic tool. The formidable Mexican effort to harmonize its approaches to square with those of the Washington "K Street" lobbying community's other employers (domestic and foreign) cannot harm U.S.–Mexico relations, and in fact could continue to create some expectations of better bilateral understanding and closer relations, at least at the margins. Lest the Mexicans not forget a distinction lost on many K Street customers, however: lobbying success is defined by images, and images only. Government success is still measured primarily in deeds, both at home and abroad.

Notes

I would like to thank David Weiner, staff consultant to the U.S. House of Representatives Foreign Affairs Committee, for all of his assistance, both in training the author in the ways of Congress generally, and in directly helping in the research of this chapter. I would also like to acknowledge the comments of Jesús Velasco and Michael Coppedge on earlier versions of this work, and institutional and financial support from the Harold Rosenthal Fellowship in International Relations, which awarded me placement as a research fellow with the House Foreign Affairs Committee, where U.S. Representative Lee Hamilton (D–IN) and his staff granted me valuable firsthand exposure to the policy-making process over eighteen months during 1991 and 1992.

1. With apologies to the real author of the lament, "Pobre Mexico: tan lejos del

cielo y tan cerca a los Estados Unidos," (Poor Mexico: so far from God and so close to the United States), which is attributed to several historical figures.

2. In the early 1990s, the Mexico lobby became a "media darling" success story. The aforementioned characterizations are from Abramson 1991 and Golden 1991.

3. These are comments by Raul Hinojosa, UCLA public policy professor, as quoted in Hernández (1995: 16).

4. Indeed, in 1992, Chile signed a multimillion-dollar contract with the law and lobbying firm of Akin, Gump, Hauer & Feld to "assist the Republic of Chile in the various trade and legislative aspects related to negotiation and implementation of a free trade agreement between the United States and Chile . . ." (U.S. Department of Justice, File 3492). Similarly, Robinson, Lake, Lerer & Montgomery was hired in 1993 as the flagship public relations firm to "help promote through strategic communication support Chile's interest in free-trade relations with the United States. . . ." (U.S. Department of Justice, File 3911). Over the next two years, Chile spent well over a million dollars on Washington lobbying. Chilean officials disparaged comparisons to the Mexicans, but filings such as that by Robinson-Lake noting their plan of "coalition-building across different relevant groups and territorial locations," were remarkably similar to Burson-Marsteller's Public Affairs Program, designed for SECOFI. Needless to say, the Chileans have thus far not succeeded, having apparently discovered that without a domestic constituency upon which to piggyback, foreign lobbying is largely irrelevant. In December 1994, the Chileans suspended their major contract with Akin-Gump.

5. Japan's lobbying is so extensive, it is difficult to quantify. A broad attempt was made by Tackett and Drew (1992a and 1992b). See also Choate (1990: 65–76).

6. Commentators sharing this opinion include Cornelius (1988: 212) and Aguayo (1988: 160).

7. Similar conclusions were reached by an astute Mexican observer of U.S. politics, Jorge Castañeda. According to Castañeda, Mexico's non-interventionist "conservative reasoning omits an undeniable fact: the United States already intervenes in Mexico, already plays politics inside our country, already acts here [in Mexico] as we would there. The hypothetical moral authority we would lose if we did the same is a moot point: we cannot do anything to prevent the United States from playing politics with us" (Castañeda 1987: 25–26).

8. Hannaford had previously represented the Mexican President's Office in 1985, but on a much smaller scale, collecting only $58,861 for general "media and public affairs services" (U.S. Department of Justice 1986: 411, 456).

9. The Deaver-prompted debate over whether to tighten restrictions on lobbying activities by recently departed federal appointees died without major changes. However, early in the Clinton administration changes were made. An executive decree in 1993 prompted a one-year ban on lobbying by former senior government officials. In 1995, the Senate managed to pass a relatively minor bill limiting the size of gifts acceptable by senators and their staffs. In November 1995, both houses of Congress passed an historical tightening of disclosure requirements by foreign and domestic lobbyists. However, it remains to be seen how well the new law will be enforced. For an exhaustive description of recent legislative activities, see Sachs (1995: 8–12).

10. These are the comments of lobbyist Mark Cowan in Brinkley (1993: A-1).

11. The cable, from U.S. Ambassador to Mexico John D. Negroponte to Assistant Secretary of State for Inter-American Affairs Bernard Aronson, was reprinted in Puig (1991: 7).

12. The "Public Affairs Program for Building Support for a Mexico–U.S. Free Trade Agreement," is a 23 January 1991 submission by the three lobby firms contained in U.S. Department of Justice File 4310.

13. This cynical statement is the empirical result of dozens of interactions by the author with lobbyists and congressional staffers, and theoretically, it may be considered "agency loss," resulting from "delegation" by the principal (the foreign agent contractor) to the agent (the lobbyist). For more on delegation theory, see Kiewiet and McCubbins (1991). An alternative theoretical construct, yielding similar empirical results, is Olson's political economy of interest group articulation. In Olson's scenario of "pluralism run amuck," interest groups effectively hold policy makers captive to the economic "rents" and side payments they charge in exchange for allowing policy making to proceed. The complications arise, for Olson, when multitudes of competing interest groups deploy similar tactics, causing government gridlock, and even "the decline of nations" (Olson 1982).

14. Again, extensive practical experience as a legislative researcher during the run-up to the NAFTA bears out this statement, as do theoretical treatments by Jacobson and Mayhew (1987). Every time an anti-NAFTA letter from a glass factory or broom producer in Representative Hamilton's Indiana district lamented possible job losses from NAFTA, he wavered in his position and requested more evidence as to why he should support the bill. An ideological moderate from a safe district who lived up to his reputation as a true statesman on foreign policy (someone above politics and able to conceive of a broad national interest and advocate for it), Hamilton was nevertheless acutely sensitive to public opinion in his district. Members with less stature, greater electoral uncertainty, and narrower political interests were even more sensitive to special interest influences, both inside and outside their districts.

15. In 1982, political economist Mancur Olson predicted the increasing economic stagnation of interest-group–dominated societies that increasingly occupy themselves with skimming "rents" from existing wealth rather than generating new wealth (Olson 1982). Olson's work echoed economists such as Gordon Tullock and has been resurrected and popularized by premier political analysts such as Kevin Phillips (1994) and Jonathan Rauch (1994).

16. A bill mandating fuller disclosure of lobbyists' activities was passed on November 29, 1995. However, it remains to be seen how well the new law will be enforced.

17. Discussing such an agenda is beyond the scope of this work, but interested readers are referred to Greider (1992), Rauch (1994), and particularly Phillips (1994: 230–270), who advocates using electronic technology for more "direct democracy" referenda, adopting proportional representation as a way to break down entrenched interests and reinvigorate partisan politics from outside the extant two-party system, strongly regulating speculative finance and its effect on political decision making, improving tax collection and income distribution, and controlling national and international debt.

18. A prominent exception is Moon (1988: 67–89). However, Moon really only

establishes a typology for how nations lobby, rather than assessing the effectiveness of such efforts.

Explanatory Notes about the Tables

FARA filings were incomplete in several cases, making it impossible to discern whether a given foreign agent had ceased activities on behalf of Mexico or the other foreign governments considered, or simply had neglected to file, the proper documentation. Data were sorted into years based on when reporting periods ended, rather than on the dates when the reports were filed (there exists a lag of many months between the end of a reporting period and when the report is actually filed, and another between when it is reported and when it is logged in the Department of Justice computer files).

In Table 5.1, a distinction is drawn between "public sector" and "private sector" expenditures. "Public" refers to direct government expenditures on lobbying (naming particular ministries or agencies as the contractor), and expenditures by parastatal companies, where it can be discerned from their FARA filings that they are entirely public companies. Government–private sector coalitions, or companies that are not evidently "public only," were considered "private" for classification purposes.

Table 5.2 further disaggregated expenditures within the "public/private" distinction. For the Mexican case, it distinguishes between "legal and technical services" and "public relations and lobbying" within the broader, aforementioned dichotomy. "Legal and technical services" are considered here to be foreign agent activities emphasizing specialized information—such as the provision of economic forecasting or legal counsel. "Public relations and lobbying" covers more general activities, the objective of which is to convince particular subjects (lawmakers, the media, executive branch officials, public opinion) rather than solve specific problems or render technical advice.

For Tables 5.1 and 5.2, the principal source was the *Report of the Attorney General to the Congress of the United States on the Administration of the Foreign Agents Registration Act* for given years. However, due to reporting and compiling lags, that report existed only through 1991 as of late 1995, when I was last able to travel to Washington, D.C. to update this data. That source is a comprehensive compilation of all reported foreign agent activities. For Table 5.3, I compiled the data myself directly from each foreign agent's FARA reports. The results from each file may be less complete (some of the 1993 files may still not yet have been on line by late 1995), but this is the only way to obtain more updated information. It should be noted that Table 5.3 contains only the foreign agents who received at least $100,000 from Mexican contractors (the Mexican government and Mexican companies). The twenty-five foreign agents listed (Burson-Marsteller is listed for three separate, large accounts) represent well over three quarters of those hired by Mexican interests, but not all of them.

It should be noted that given the time lag of approximately two or three years between when a foreign agent files its FARA reports and when they are published in the *Report of the Attorney General*, it was impossible to obtain definitive data for any period later than 1993 as of September 1995. Thus this chapter is necessarily limited in scope to quantifying the Mexico lobby during the NAFTA debates. While I am aware that Mexico's foreign agent presence in Washington continues to be much greater in the mid-1990s than it was in the mid-1980s, proving this will unfortunately be the task of future researchers with access to later FARA filings.

References

Abramson, Jill. 1991. "U.S. Mexico Trade Pact is Pitting Vast Armies of Capitol Hill Lobbyists Against Each Other." *Wall Street Journal*. 25 April.

Aguayo, Sergio. 1988. "Mexico in Transition and the United States: Old Perceptions, New Problems." In Riordan Roett, ed., *Mexico and the United States: Managing the Relationship*. Boulder, Colo.: Westview Press.

Anderson, Sarah, and Ken Silverstein. 1993. "Oink, Oink." *The Nation*. 20 December, 752–753.

Arnson, Cynthia J. 1988. *Crossroads: Congress, the Reagan Administration, and Central America*. New York: Pantheon Books.

Bennett, Timothy B. 1991. SJS Advanced Strategies lobbyist, Interview by author, 18 December, Washington, D.C.

Bernal, José Luis. 1991. Director of Legislative Affairs, Mexican Embassy, Interview by author, 18 December, Washington, D.C.

Brinkley, Joel. 1986. "Angry Words and, Now, Silence on Mexico." *New York Times*. 9 July.

———. 1993. "Cultivating the Grass Roots to Reap Legislative Benefits." *New York Times*. 1 November.

Castañeda, Jorge. 1986. "Enjuiciado Deaver, el Gobierno Se Consigue Otro Gestor en Washington." *Proceso*. 5 May, 22–24.

———. 1987. "México en el Mundo: Más Allá de los Principios." *Nexos* 110.

Choate, Pat. 1990. *Agents of Influence—How Japan Manipulates America's Political and Economic System*. New York: Alfred A. Knopf.

Congressional Record. 1993. 103rd Cong., 1st sess., Vol. 139, Part II, 9875–10049.

Cornelius, Wayne A. 1988. "Las Relaciones de Estados Unidos con México: Fuentes de su Deterioro, 1986–1987." *Foro Internacional* 24.

Eisenstadt, Todd A. 1992a. "Nuevo Estilo Diplomático: Cabildeo y Relaciones Públicas (1986–1991)." *Foro Internacional* 37.

———. 1992b. "Prospects for Limiting Excesses of 'Deep Pocket' Foreign Governments and Restoring Vitality to the U.S. Foreign Policy Debate." Johns Hopkins University's School for Advanced International Studies (SAIS). Typescript.

Evans, Diana. 1995. "The NAFTA Sale: Presidential Vote Buying and Its Effects." Presented at the annual meeting of the Western Political Science Association, Portland, Ore.

Franco Hijuelos, Claudia. 1995. "El Cabildeo como Instrumento de Política Exterior: el Caso del Tratado de Libre Comercio (TLC)." *Revista Mexicana de Política Exterior* 46, 11–27.

Golden, Tim. 1991. "Mexico is Trying Hard to Lift Its Political Profile in the U.S." *New York Times*. 30 December.

Gourevitch, Peter. 1978. "The Second Image Reversed: The International Sources of Domestic Politics." *International Organization* 32, 881–911.

Graham, George, Peter Norman, and Ted Bardacke. 1995. "Bitter Legacy of Battle to Bail Out Mexico." *Financial Times*. 16 February.

Grayson, George. 1995. *The North American Free Trade Agreement: Regional Community and the New World Order*. Lanham, Md.: University Press of America.

Greider, William. 1992. *Who Will Tell the People?* New York: Simon and Schuster.

Hamilton, Lee H., and Michael H. Van Dusen. 1978. "Making the Separation of Powers Work." *Foreign Affairs* 57, 17–39.

Hernández, Saul. 1995. "The Impact of Mexican Lobbying Efforts during the NAFTA Debate." Princeton University. Typescript.

Ibarra, María Ester. 1991. "Ricardo Valero, Ex-subsecretario de Relaciones Exteriores, Enjuicia: el Servicio Exterior Subordinado a Washington." *Proceso*, 4 March, 6–13.

Jacobson, Gary C. 1987. "Running Scared: Elections and Congressional Politics in the 1980s." In Matthew D. McCubbins and Terry Sullivan, eds., *Congress: Structure and Policy*. New York: Cambridge University Press, 39–82.

Katz, Gregory. 1992. "Mexico Lobbies Hard for Free-Trade Accord: Millions Spent in Effort to Woo Congress." *Dallas Morning News*. 29 December.

Kiewiet, D. Roderick, and Matthew D. McCubbins. 1991. *The Logic of Delegation. Congressional Parties and the Appropriations Process*. Chicago: University of Chicago Press.

Lewis, Charles, et al. 1993. *The Trading Game—Inside Lobbying for the North American Free Trade Agreement*. Washington, D.C.: Center for Public Integrity.

Mayhew, David R. 1987. "The Electoral Connection and the Congress." In Matthew D. McCubbins and Terry Sullivan, eds., *Congress: Structure and Policy*. New York: Cambridge University Press, 18–29.

McCormick, James. 1995. Assistant staff director of the U.S. House Banking Committee's Domestic and International Policy Subcommittee, Interview by author, 20 November.

McGrory, Mary. 1992. "Capital Hill and Knowlton." *Washington Post*. 12 January.

McMathis, Charles, Jr. 1981. "Ethnic Groups and Foreign Policy." *Foreign Affairs* 59, 975–998.

Moon, Chung-in. 1988. "Complex Interdependence and Transnational Lobbying: South Korea in the United States." *International Studies Quarterly* 32, 67–89.

Moore, Richard, 1992. Burson-Marsteller Vice President, Interview by author, 26 May, Washington, D.C.

Olson, Mancur. 1982. *The Rise and Decline of Nations*. New Haven: Yale University Press.

Omang, Joanne. 1986. "Administration Reviewing Disjointed Policy on Mexico." *Washington Post*. 4 June.

Phillips, Kevin. 1994. *Arrogant Capital—the Acclaimed Indictment of Entrenched Washington*. New York: Little, Brown & Co.

Puig, Carlos. 1991. "Conclusión de Negroponte: con el Tratado de Libre Comercio, México Quedaría a Disposición de Washington." *Proceso*, 13 May.

Putnam, Robert. 1988. "Diplomacy and Domestic Politics: The Logic of Two-Level Games." *International Organization* 42, 427–60.

Rauch, Jonathan. 1994. *Democlerosis—The Silent Killer of American Government.* New York: Times Books.

Richardson, Bill. 1992. U.S. Congress Representative, Interview by author, 17 January, Washington, D.C.

Roett, Riordan, ed. 1988. *Mexico and the United States: Managing the Relationship.* Boulder, Colo.: Westview Press.

Sachs, Richard C. 1995. *CRS Issue Brief—Regulating Interest Groups and Lobbyists: Issues in the 104th Congress.* Washington, D.C.: Congressional Research Service.

Sidener, Jonathan. 1995. "Big 'Brawl' in Washington—with Symington at Center." *Arizona Republic.* 2 February.

Stone, Peter H. 1995. "From the K Street Corridor." *The National Journal,* 28 January, 235.

Tackett, Michael, and Christopher Drew. 1992a. "More and More, Lobbyists Call Shots in D.C." *Chicago Tribune.* 6 December.

———. 1992b. "Foreigners' Extra Asset: Lobbyists." *Chicago Tribune.* 9 December.

U.S. Department of Justice. Attorney General's Office. *Report of the Attorney General to the Congress of the United States on the Administration of the Foreign Agents Registration Act.* Washington, D.C.: U.S. Department of Justice. [various years]

———. Foreign Agents Registration Act. "Thomas Scanlon." File 03500.

———. Foreign Agents Registration Act. "Manatt, Phelps & Phillips." File 03736.

———. Foreign Agents Registration Act. "Steptoe & Johnson." File 03975.

———. Foreign Agents Registration Act. "Manchester Trade." File 04149.

———. Foreign Agents Registration Act. "Shearman and Sterling." File 04208.

———. Foreign Agents Registration Act. "SJS Advanced Strategies." File 04390.

———. Foreign Agents Registration Act. "Walker & Assoc." File 04446.

———. Foreign Agents Registration Act. "Public Strategies, Inc." File 04486.

———. Foreign Agents Registration Act. "Guerra & Assoc." File 04728.

———. Foreign Agents Registration Act. "Cleary, Gottlieb, Steen & Hamilton." File 508.

———. Foreign Agents Registration Act. "Burson Marsteller." File 2469.

———. Foreign Agents Registration Act. "Akin, Gump, Hauer & Feld." File 3492.

———. Foreign Agents Registration Act. "Gold & Liebengood, Inc." File 3700.

———. Foreign Agents Registration Act. "Michael K. Deaver." File 3734.

———. Foreign Agents Registration Act. "Robinson, Lake, Lerer & Montgomery/ Sawyer Miller Group." File 3911.

———. Foreign Agents Registration Act. "The Brock Group." File 4310.

———. Foreign Agents Registration Act. "COECE." File 4498.

———. Foreign Agents Registration Act. "Edward Hidalgo." File 4509.

———. Foreign Agents Registration Act. "Abelardo Valdéz." File 4567.

———. Foreign Agents Registration Act. "Toney Anaya." File 4568.

————. Foreign Agents Registration Act. "Campos Communications, Inc." File 4609.

————. Foreign Agents Registration Act. "The Pantin Partnership, Inc." File 4617.

————. Foreign Agents Registration Act. "Moya, Villanueva & Associates." File 4629.

————. Foreign Agents Registration Act. "Solar & Ellis." File 4630.

————. Foreign Agents Registration Act. "Apodaca-Sosa & Associates." File 4640.

————. Foreign Agents Registration Act. "Kathleen Ann Griffith." File 4655.

Washington Post. 1986. "Insulting the Latins." Editorial. 17 June.

Chapter 6

Selling Ideas, Buying Influence: Mexico and American Think Tanks in the Promotion of NAFTA

Jesús Velasco

In 1990, Mexico, the United States, and Canada negotiated the North American Free Trade Agreement (NAFTA). For Mexican President Carlos Salinas de Gortari's administration, NAFTA was not only a crucial piece of trade policy, it was a vital component of a broader economic strategy. According to the Mexican president, NAFTA was based on four principles: economic opening, deregulation, foreign investment, and privatization (Salinas de Gortari 1994: 395–396).

The authoritarian nature of the Mexican political system ensured NAFTA's approval in the Mexican Congress. In the United States, however, the situation was different. From the outset of the negotiations, American society was polarized over NAFTA. Aware of this polarization, Mexico adopted a strategy to persuade U.S. decision makers and various interest groups to support a free trade agreement with Mexico. This strategy consisted of four prongs: a Mexican lobby; the promotion of Mexican interests by Mexican consulates; the reinforcement of relationships with the Mexican American community in the United States; and the use of American think tanks as intermediaries in promoting a positive view of Mexico in general and of NAFTA in particular.[1] Never before had Mexico undertaken such a comprehensive effort to influence the decision-making process in the United States. This experience would be a learning process for both the United States and Mexico.

This chapter focuses on only one aspect of Mexico's campaign: the promotion of NAFTA through U.S. think tanks. In particular, it concentrates on four conservative think tanks: the Center for Strategic and International Studies (CSIS), the Heritage Foundation, the Hudson Institute, the Institute for International Economics (IIE),[2] and on one liberal think tank, the Brookings Institution. However, references will be made to other institutions and individual scholars that also supported NAFTA.[3]

The purpose of this chapter is to uncover the main traits of the alliances between the Mexican government and think tanks. During the debate over NAFTA, think tanks were an important channel of communication between Mexican interests and the U.S. government and American interest groups. They helped establish the boundaries of the NAFTA debate and were central allies of the Mexican government in shaping pro-NAFTA public opinion in the United States. This relationship illustrates an interesting phenomenon: the links between an underdeveloped country and nongovernmental organizations in a developed country. More significantly, the relationship also illustrates the ways in which a foreign government can and cannot influence the United States' decision-making process.

This chapter is divided into four main sections. First, it analyzes the role of think tanks in the United States, highlighting how ideas have become a relevant factor in the decision-making process since the late 1960s. It will also examine the main features of think tanks and their relations with some of the corporations that supported NAFTA. Second, it describes the Mexican strategy to use think tanks to increase awareness of NAFTA in the United States. This section studies the nexus between Mexico and American think tanks, the common strategy they created to influence both American public opinion and elite decision-making processes, and the measures taken by think tanks to defend Mexican interests. Third, it offers a preliminary evaluation of the impact of think tanks on NAFTA's passage.

The Rise of Think Tanks in the United States

Think tanks are not new institutions in the United States. During the first half of this century, organizations such as the Carnegie Endowment for International Peace (1910), the Hoover Institution on War, Revolution, and Peace (1919), the Brookings Institution (1927), and the American Enterprise Institute (1943) were established. However, beginning in the 1970s, think tanks began to take on a renewed importance, and many new ones were founded (Smith 1991a: xv). Approximately two-thirds of the hundred think tanks in Washington, D.C., were founded after 1970 (Matlack 1991: 1552).

The growth of think tanks can be explained by two factors. The first is the emergence of a political realignment in the late 1960s and early 1970s, characterized in part by the deterioration of political parties as organizers of collective action and the subsequent crowning of the mass media as the principal organizer of political life. Another feature of this new political order is the ascendance of what Martin Wattenberg calls candidate-centered politics (Wattenberg 1991; Aldrich and Niemi 1990). According to Walter Dean Burnham, the electoral system is ruled by what Sidney Blumenthal has called the "permanent campaign" and by a political order governed by the interregnum state—a state in which public policy is increasingly disassociated from a base of popular support.[4]A second factor explaining the recent proliferation of think tanks is the willingness of corporations and conservative foundations to finance conservative organizations (Vogel 1989).

It is important to stress that the new political order in the United States introduced a peculiar type of realignment. Historically, all realignments were partisan-channeled. Today, however, the eclipsing of parties has not only made the idea of partisan realignment problematic, but it has also paved the way for the rise of ideas as powerful political agents of change. For the first time in U.S. history, we are living in an era of "techno-ideological realignment," a term that is not common in political discourse (Velasco 1995). I use it to draw attention to the basic features of the current political order, i.e., the prominence of technology and ideology as articulators of electoral politics, political communication, education, and policy change. Technology, in the form of mass media, has replaced the political party as a means for organizing collective action. Today's candidates run individualistic campaigns using the media to directly communicate with voters, bypassing traditional party processes (Wattenberg 1990; Ranney 1983).

Further, the candidate-centered era equates the availability of economic resources with success at the ballot box. Candidates without parties depend heavily on funding to build their political campaigns and win in the electoral arena. As Benjamin Ginsberg and Martin Shefter have pointed out, the arrival of new communications technology has switched American electoral politics from being labor intensive to capital intensive (Ginsberg and Shefter 1990; Ginsberg 1984: 163–164). This phenomenon has considerably altered the balance of power among competing political groups. Today, wealthy groups or those with private fortunes—usually associated with conservative causes—have a greater likelihood of being politically effective. Likewise, a correlation exists between the decline of political parties and the rise of think tanks. Usually, political parties represent the link between the demands of the civil society and the state. When this nexus is broken or weakened, political and ideological organizations have a greater chance to fill the vacuum left by disintegrating parties.

According to Thomas S. Langston, the decline of political parties has facilitated the rise of ideas and ideologues as powerful political instruments of change (Langston 1992: 19–24). In a similar vein, David Ricci holds that changes in the United States since the late 1960s have facilitated the growth of think tanks dedicated primarily to the dissemination of ideas. In all, a distinctive feature of the current nonpartisan realignment era is the growth of ideas as sources of power and political change (Ricci 1993).

As this transformation was occurring, the balance sheet of corporations worsened with the economic problems of the 1970s. This situation, combined with increased governmental regulations in a wide variety of policy arenas, fostered an antagonism between the regulators and the regulated that has "no parallel outside the United States, traditionally considered the most conservative and pro-business capitalist democracy" (Vogel 1983: 24–25). This environment provoked corporate political mobilization on four fronts: lobbying the government through corporate interest groups such as the Business Roundtable; influencing electoral outcomes through political action committees (PACs); influencing political culture through advocacy advertising; and supporting think tanks and social organizations (Himmelstein 1990: 129–164). Private corporations used such measures to influence the conduct of American government directly and indirectly.

Marrying Ideas and Money

Conservative foundations supply a healthy portion of the annual budgets of the think tanks analyzed here (see Table 6.1). Indeed, the Bradley, Carthage, Coors, Olin, Nobel, Scaife, and Smith Richardson foundations were established in the 1970s to assist academics and think tanks, most of whom were conservative, in developing their work. Although these are not the nation's largest foundations, they have generously supported conservative institutions and individuals. In 1993, for example, the Bradley, Olin, Smith Richardson, and Scaife foundations made grants totaling $57 million (Howell 1995: 701). These foundations have also invested in disseminating the work that their funding has produced. From 1990 to 1993, four conservative journals—*The National Interest, Public Interest, The New Criterion,* and *The American Spectator* received a total of $2.7 million from conservative foundations. In this same period, four liberal and radical journals—*The Nation, The Progressive, In These Times,* and *Mother Jones* received one-tenth of this amount ($269,500) from liberal foundations (Schulman 1995: 11).

American corporations also worked with think tanks to promote NAFTA. The linkage between corporate interests and think tank activities is illustrated in the relationships between pro-NAFTA corporations and the think tanks they supported.

The Heritage Foundation

The Heritage Foundation was created in 1973 by two conservative entrepreneurs, Paul Weyrich and Edwin J. Feulner Jr., with an original donation of

Table 6.1 Foundation Grants to Selected Think Tanks, 1992–1993

Foundation	No. of Grants	Amount ($)	Foundation	No. of Grants	Amount ($)
Brookings Institution			*Institute for International*		
Brown Foundation	1	2,000,000	*Economics*		
Ford Foundation	6	1,072,000	Ford Foundation	2	1,500,000
Dillon	1	750,000	German Marshall Fund	4	970,000
W. Averell & Pamela Harriman	2	650,000	Andrew W. Mellon	1	400,000
Carnegie Corp. of New York	3	436,000	Pew Charitable Trust	1	300,000
United States–Japan Foundation	2	400,000	William and Flora Hewlett	1	300,000
Smith Richardson	2	204,000	GE Fund	2	120,000
W. Alton Jones Foundation	1	195,000	Ford Motor Company Fund	2	100,000
Lynde and Harry Bradley	2	175,000	Dayton Hudson Foundation	2	80,000
AT&T Foundation	2	150,000	American Express Foundation	1	33,400
Henry J. Kaiser Family	1	150,000	BT Foundation	1	30,000
Freedom Forum International	1	100,000	Tinker Foundation, Inc.	1	25,000
John & Catherine MacArthur	1	100,000	Rockefeller	1	25,000
Rockefeller Foundation	1	100,000	AT&T Foundation	1	25,000
Subtotal		*6,482,000*	W. Alton Jones	1	20,000
			Bank America Foundation	1	15,000
Center for Strategic and			General Motors Foundation	1	12,000
International Studies			Phillips Petroleum Foundation	1	10,000
Dr. Scholl	2	1,000,000	Texaco Foundation	1	10,000
Sarah Scaife	2	985,000	Alcoa Foundation	1	10,000
Andrew W. Mellon	2	975,000	*Subtotal*		*3,985,400*
United States–Japan Foundation	2	301,000			
Pew Charitable Trust	1	265,000	*Economic Policy Institute*		
Pritzker	2	250,000	Alfred P. Sloan	4	2,437,210
Amoco	2	200,000	Ford Foundation	8	1,580,000
Rockwell International Corp.	2	170,000	John and Catherine MacArthur	2	498,500
Metro. Atlanta Community	1	150,000	Carnegie Corp. of New York	2	125,000
William H. Donner	1	145,600	Joyce Foundation	3	125,000
Ford Foundation	1	100,000	Arca Foundation	2	120,000
Smith Richardson	1	100,000	Robert Wood Johnson	1	50,099
Sony USA Foundation	1	80,000	Henry J. Kaiser Family Found.	1	50,099
Subtotal		*4,271,600*	Rosenberg Foundation	2	50,000
			Metropolitan Life	1	45,000
Heritage Foundation			Joyce Mertz-Gilmore	1	25,000
Sarah Scaife	2	1,800,000	*Subtotal*		*5,105,809*
Lynde and Harry Bradley	7	1,520,177			
Samuel Roberts Nobel Found.	2	950,000	*Institute for Policy Studies*		
Jay and Betty Van Andel	2	500,000	John and Catherine MacArthur	2	676,910
Carthage	2	400,000	Samuel Rubin	2	413,000
Scaife Family	1	202,640	New-Land	3	80,000
Grover Hermann	1	200,000	W. Alton Jones	1	50,000
Henry Salvatori	1	200,000	Ford Foundation	1	50,000
M. J. Murdock Charitable Trust	1	200,000	Arca Foundation	2	45,000
John M. Olin	1	175,000	Jules and Doris Stein	1	40,000
Subtotal		*6,147,817*	S. H. Cowell Foundation	1	15,000
			Subtotal		*1,369,910*
Hudson Institute					
Lilly Endowment	3	1,550,000			
Lynde and Harry Bradley	7	641,250			
Pew Charitable Trust	1	500,000			
John M. Olin	3	407,000			
Jay and Betty Van Andel	1	250,000			
Sarah Scaife	2	208,000			
Carthage	1	150,000			
Retirement Research	1	111,100			
Eli Lilly and Company	1	99,100			
Subtotal		*3,916,450*			

$250,000 from beer producer Joseph Coors. When the organization was established, ideas and interests formed an unbreakable alliance. Since its early days, Heritage—its people, corporations, and foundations—has been committed to a free-market economy and free trade. In the view of one Heritage staffer, since the mid-1980s "Heritage was out there pushing for a North American free trade zone in the whole Western Hemisphere" (Franc 1993). When the NAFTA negotiations started, it was natural that Heritage would be one of the agreement's backers.

In 1980, Heritage received funds from the Scaife Family Trust, from the Nobel and John M. Olin foundations, and from 87 corporate grants from the Fortune 500 (Kondracke 1980: 12). In 1991 Heritage created a department to communicate with business leaders and began two programs: the Corporate Associates program, for companies that contributed more than $100,000 annually; and the Washington Policy Roundtable, to brief corporate executives on selected topics. That same year, Heritage organized a private luncheon for corporate leaders to inform them about the investment climate in Mexico (Heritage Foundation 1991: 24).

Although Heritage has tried to increase its corporate contributions, such donations are a small percentage of its total income. Heritage's income for 1992 was as follows: 44 percent from individual donations; 28 percent from foundation grants; 13 percent from investment income; 10 percent from corporations; and 5 percent from publication sales and other sources. Twenty-two funders gave $100,000 or more, among them: the Adolph Coors Foundation; the Carthage Foundation; the Lynde and Harry Bradley Foundation; the Korea Foundation; the John M. Olin Foundation; the Sarah Scaife Foundation; the Starr Foundation; Amway Corporation; and Taiwan Cement Corporation (Heritage Foundation 1992: 25).

Hudson Institute
The Hudson Institute was founded in 1961 by Herman Kahn. In its early days, the Institute obtained sizable contracts from government agencies. By the 1980s Hudson almost collapsed due to financial problems but was rescued by a "consortium of local business leaders" in Indianapolis and foundation executives backed by the Lilly Endowment (Smith 1991a: 158). By 1992, the rejuvenated Hudson had revenue of more than $5 million, and the trustee circle—members who contribute $25,000 or more each year—comprised several business groups and conservative foundations, among them: BancOne, Indiana Bell Telephone, Lilly Endowment Inc., the John M. Olin Foundation, the Sarah Scaife Foundation, and the Smith Richardson Foundation.

The Center for Strategic and International Studies
The Center for Strategic and International Studies was established in 1962 with a budget of $120,000 from the Scaife Foundation of Pittsburgh and Justin Dart.

In 1992, fifty-two of the Fortune 100 companies actively participated in CSIS' work.

The Institute for International Economics
The Institute for International Economics was founded in 1981 with a five-year grant of $4 million from the German Marshall Fund, an organization formed to oppose "progressive excesses," according to one analyst (Nobel 1981: 337).

The Brookings Institution
The Brookings Institution was established in 1927 when three groups previously organized by St. Louis businessman Robert S. Brookings coalesced. In its early years, Brookings received financial support from corporations such as Carnegie, which donated $1.65 million over a period of ten years. Brookings consolidated its position as a distinguished liberal research institution in the 1950s and 1960s. By the 1970s, the nation's general economic difficulties, together with the decline in foundation economic support and the ascent of conservative think tanks with better marketing strategies, coincided with Brookings' ideological journey to the center.

In the late 1970s Brookings both moderated its views and expanded its corporate financial aid—"a relatively untapped resource for Brookings" (Smith 1991b). Through the work of its office of external affairs, "corporate contributions rose from $200,000 in the late 1970s to about $1.5 million annually by the mid-1980s" (Smith 1991b: 115). Brookings also enhanced the role of trustees in the institution, giving them "increased power over the selection of research subjects" (Critchlow 1993: 294). The organization also expanded its government contracts from 5 percent at the beginning of the 1970s to almost 20 percent by the end of the same decade (Smith 1991b: 115). By the 1990s, Brookings' board of trustees included many pro-NAFTA CEOs from corporations such as American Express, IBM, and Chase Manhattan.

The Evolution of Think Tanks

Most of the think tanks that endorsed NAFTA were either created or supported by corporations or conservative foundations that also supported the agreement. It is therefore difficult to disentangle the extent to which the behavior of the think tanks reflects intellectual conviction, ideology, or material interests. Clearly, corporations do not dictate what the think tanks will produce, but their support can shape an institution's agenda and reward institutions that share their policy preferences. Brookings may be an example of the former, while the Heritage Foundation illustrates the latter.

Think tanks have five roles: 1) as sources of policy ideas; 2) as evaluators of policy proposals; 3) as evaluators of government programs; 4) as sources of personnel; and 5) as punditry (Weaver 1989: 568–569). They are credible institutions that spread or censor ideas and seek to link policy analysis with politics, while serving as a "bridge between policy and intellectuals" (Baer 1993b). Their roles have grown in importance during the last decade. In an era in which members of Congress read an average of eleven minutes in an eleven-hour day, think tanks have the opportunity to reach congressional staff and public officials with concise ideas and concrete policy recommendations (Adams 1979: 546). "Our business," asserts Heritage's founder Edwin J. Feulner Jr., "is influencing policy; causing changes" (Feulner 1985: 5).

Think tanks, furthermore, are not necessarily committed to objective research. Instead, many are now in the business of selling ideas from a specific ideological viewpoint. Indeed, an "obvious and significant development concerning the major Washington think tanks is the gradual transformation of the nonpartisan ideal that gave purpose to the early ones into an outlook that accepted ideological commitments and sometimes even partisan linkage" (Critchlow 1993: 319).

Think tanks work assiduously to disseminate their messages. They organize luncheons, conferences, and study groups involving businesspeople and legislators. They publish newsletters and books and endeavor to avoid academic jargon in favor of more accessible prose. They produce radio and television programs and have a significant presence in newspapers and the electronic media. Norman Ornstein of the American Enterprise Institute (AEI), for example, has been called "the king of quotes" because of his frequent appearances on television programs and his many press citations (Waldman 1986). More significantly, a six-month study of the guest list of the McNeil/Lehrer NewsHour conducted in 1989 revealed that AEI fellows appeared on this program six times and CSIS representatives appeared eight times. Neither the Institute for Policy Studies nor the World Policy Institute, both progressive think tanks, appeared even once, and liberal think tanks seldom appeared (Hoynes and Croteau 1990: 5). In a similar vein, between 1987 and 1989, CSIS fellows "made more than 1,200 local and network news appearances, did more than 1,000 radio interviews, were quoted in print almost 2,500 times, and placed more than 2,000 op-ed pieces in U.S. newspapers" (Abelson 1992: 862).

Thus, think tanks have the capacity to popularize unexplored issues and to increase awareness of topics already in the media and public discussions. They have the ability to persuade government officials of the pertinence of policy measures and to educate congressional staff and members about particular subjects. These were important assets that the Mexican authorities could not ignore. Accordingly, the Mexican government invested time, resources, and money to cultivate a strong relationship with them. The final outcome of this strategy was an intellectual lobby on behalf of NAFTA.

The Mexican Strategy

Mexico's effort to ensure the approval of the free trade agreement with the United States began in 1989, when the Mexican government finally decided to negotiate the treaty. According to José Luis Bernal, formerly in charge of congressional relations for the Mexican Embassy in Washington, "our only antecedent was the free trade negotiations between Canada and the United States" (Bernal 1995). Bernal said that after examining the U.S.–Canadian negotiations, the Mexican government asked different officials in several ministries—mainly Commerce, Foreign Affairs, and the presidency—to outline a general negotiation strategy. In the Mexican Embassy in Washington, Bernal and Minister for Economic Affairs Manuel Suárez Mier each presented his own ideas. Subsequently, Ambassador Gustavo Petricioli finalized the proposal incorporating his own ideas.

At the same time, the Ministry of Foreign Relations organized a group to study the importance and wisdom of hiring a permanent lobbyist in Washington. According to Bernal, the other ministries participating in the deliberations also proposed hiring a lobbyist. Based on the Canadian experience and at the suggestion of several officials, Mexico established a permanent office in Washington, D.C., appointed a chief negotiator, and created an office to coordinate relations with Congress. A function of this office was to establish permanent contacts with think tanks (Bernal 1995).

The "Group of Undersecretaries"

On 2 September 1992, the Mexican government established an important bureaucratic unit: the Group of Undersecretaries to Follow and Coordinate the Relationships with Canada and the United States. The group, created with the approval of President Salinas, had five goals: 1) to prepare agreements for the foreign policy cabinet; 2) to define foreign policy priorities toward Canada and the United States; 3) to design foreign policy strategies; 4) to exchange information; and 5) to increase congruency and coordination in Mexico's relations with North American countries (Secretary of Foreign Affairs n.d. - a). The group comprised the officials listed in Table 6.2.

The group designed a general strategy to increase awareness of NAFTA in Canada and the United States. Different agents of influence within the United States were enlisted, including those opposed to the agreement. The Salinas administration coordinated its efforts with those of the U.S. and Canadian governments.

The group identified two levels of action: the specific and the general. The former included three key actors, four main allies, and three leading adversaries. The three actors were: congressional committee chairs, leaders of political parties, and opinion makers, including think tanks. The group considered Mexico's allies to be business entrepreneurs, academics, journalists, and

Table 6.2 Members of the Group of Undersecretaries

Name	Agency
Andrés Rozental	Relaciones Exteriores (Coordinador)
Miguel Limón	Secretaría de Gobernación
Rafael García	Secretaría de la Defensa
José Angel Gurría	Secretaría de Hacienda
Herminio Blanco	Secretaría de Comercio
Luis Tellez	Secretaría de Agricultura
Gustavo Patiño	Secretaría de Comunicaciones
Juan A. Mateos	Secretaría de Desarrollo Social
Bruno Kiehnle	Secretaría de Turismo
Carlos Camacho	Secretaría de Pesca
Jorge Carrillo Olea	Procuraduría General
José N. González	Secretaría Técnica, Gabinete de Política Exterior

Source: Secretary of Foreign Affairs. n.d. - a.

government officials. The main adversaries were union leaders, environmental leaders, and certain legislators. At the general level, the group proposed a mass-media campaign and participation in events with national and regional business organizations, universities, think tanks, and specialized forums. Thus a central component of Mexico's strategy was the use of think tanks and academics as intermediaries for Mexican interests.

Enter the Think Tanks

Other Mexican officials apart from the group of undersecretaries recognized the role think tanks could play in promoting the free trade agreement. Minister Suárez Mier of the Mexican Embassy in Washington said think tanks played a "predominant and protagonistic role" (Suárez Mier 1993). Rosalva Ojeda, general director of the North American division of the Ministry of Foreign Relations, said think tanks were an "ideal vehicle to diffuse the Mexican view" (Ojeda 1995). Herman von Bertrab, director of the Mexican Office of Free Trade Negotiations in Washington, said think tanks played a "very important role, especially during the fast-track period" (von Bertrab 1993). Finally, a high-ranking politician with intimate knowledge of the subject said "without the help of think tanks the approval of NAFTA would have been very difficult."

The Salinas administration was certainly aware of the primary role that the U.S. Congress would play in the approval of NAFTA, especially after the authorization of the fast-track approach. Consequently, think tanks were used to develop congressional relations and to communicate the benefits of NAFTA to Congress. The congressional affairs office in Mexico's Washington Embassy monitored congressional hearings, contacted staffers and legislators, established pro-NAFTA campaigns in states and specific congressional districts, and examined the themes that could affect the negotiations. The Mexican government believed think tanks would play a central role because of their close contact with staffers and legislators, and because they were active in organizing study groups with members of Congress and business groups.

Think tanks were considered to be an ideal vehicle to diffuse Mexican views to American elites and opinion leaders for three reasons. First, think tanks influence opinion leaders in the media; second, think tanks are themselves opinion leaders; and third, they can influence American economic and political elites with their ideas and viewpoints. Think tanks were, in sum, a suitable vehicle to counterbalance negative information about Mexico that was being disseminated by anti-NAFTA organizations. According to a high-ranking politician who asked to remain unnamed, "Mexico's communications campaign was specifically directed to elites and opinion leaders." In his view, Mexico did not have sufficient time or resources "to go to the general public. In future negotiations we have to penetrate the general public through local radio and television stations."

A central component of the "strategy with think tanks and academics," asserted one politician who wished to remain unnamed, was to "provide them with first-hand information." Academics and think tank analysts were important because they "became sources for people who were writing newspaper articles on Mexico. If somebody was writing for the *New York Times* or the *Washington Post* the first thing that they did was to call CSIS to find an expert on Mexico and to ask him or her about any Mexican topic. That worked well for us. We were very interested that those experts knew exactly was going on in Mexico."

Rosalva Ojeda, a former Ministry of Foreign Relations official, pointed out that "academics were an excellent vehicle to promote both Mexico and the benefits of free trade." In her view, academics perform a role that "neither a Mexican politician nor a businessman can accomplish. It is not the same for an official from SECOFI [the Secretariat of Commerce and Industrial Development] to talk to a group of Americans as it is for U.S. researchers to address a particular audience. Academics are persons who have studied, who are independent, and who after some time of deliberation are convinced that something is good" (Ojeda 1995). In a similar vein, Herman von Bertrab argued: "we could not sell NAFTA to the Americans because we were not credible. The selling of NAFTA to the Americans had to come from the Americans." In the United States "think tanks had a lot of credibility" (von Bertrab 1993).

Mexico established its first communication with think tanks and academics during the first year of the Salinas administration. Some of President Salinas' closest associates attended American universities. During their stay in the United States they not only became exposed to basic traits of the American political system, but also established contacts with important members of the academic community. The friendship between Carlos Salinas and Wayne Cornelius, director of the prestigious Center for U.S.–Mexico Studies at the University of California at San Diego, is one manifestation of this phenomenon; another is the friendship between Jaime Serra Puche, Salinas' secretary of commerce, and Clark Reynolds, Stanford University's internationally respected specialist on the Mexican economy. Relationships with other academics were also cultivated as part of the NAFTA strategy.

Likewise, the Mexican government identified individuals with some knowledge about Mexico using contacts previously developed by the embassy and the consulates. Often, they were friends of Mexican diplomats. These "scholars and think tankers," asserted one prominent politician with close knowledge of the topic, "suggested that we should talk with individuals who were interested in NAFTA, and they also recommended other people to us." Through this snowballing process Mexico built a broad network with think tanks and academics.

Some think tankers and academics emerged as prominent architects in the diffusion of Mexican views in the United States. Delal Baer, Nora Lustig, Gary Haufbauer, Jeffrey Schott, Sidney Weintraub, and Michael Wilson, to mention but a few, became spokespeople for both the Mexican government and the American forces behind NAFTA. The relationship of the Mexican government with Delal Baer exemplifies this modus operandi. According to one high-ranking politician who asked to remain unnamed, in the

> particular case of Delal, I asked her directly: do you believe in a free trade agreement? Her answer was yes. When I knew that she was on our side, I decided to present myself as more ignorant than I really was. I determined to ask her openly, where would you start? what are the most convincing political, economic, and commercial arguments that we have to present? what does the message have to be? She and many others like Sidney Weintraub became our advisors.

Delal Baer and Sidney Weintraub also mobilized some American scholars in support of NAFTA. In 1991, at a time when opponents of the fast-track approach were increasing in number, Baer and Weintraub sent a letter to several academics who specialized in Mexico. According to José Luis Bernal, "circulating the letter was a project if not arranged, at least discussed among Mexican officials and American academics. I don't know when we agreed to circulate the letter, but I can assure you that it was something that we in the embassy discussed with American think tankers and academics as their contribution to the process of getting NAFTA approved" (Bernal 1996). In the letter Baer and Weintraub asserted that the future of NAFTA was "in jeopardy," and that the "voice of U.S. scholarly community could be helpful." They argued that the institutional affiliation of each signatory "will be listed for identification purposes only."

Baer and Weintraub sent two letters to academics who might sign a letter to Congress in support of NAFTA. The first, signed by Baer and Weintraub, advocated publicly supporting NAFTA. Attached to this letter was a letter that was ultimately sent to Congress. The signers of this second letter asserted that they did not "represent any special interests. Our only motive in sending this letter," they claimed, was "to promote the national U.S. interest." They rejected what they considered the three major arguments of the opposition: "1) Mexico would have an "unfair" advantage because of its wage rates; 2) the economic development of Mexico would pollute the environment; and 3) Mexico is not a democracy in the U.S. mold and therefore is not worthy of such an agreement."[5]

Baer and Weintraub argued that "better education" and not low wages was the "hallmark of trade success." They also claimed that "Mexico's environmental laws [are] similar" to those in the United States but "the country lacks the resources to enforce them." Nonetheless, Baer, Weintraub, and the other letters' signatories supported the incorporation of some environmental issues. Finally, they maintained that political choices in Mexico had recently expanded. Moreover, they asserted that the "free trade agreement would give an impulse to political democracy that cannot be achieved by outside exhortation or flagrant U.S. interference in Mexican domestic affairs. This latter approach is the surest way to stifle the growing democratic impulse in Mexico" (Secretary of Foreign Affairs n.d. - b).

The scholars who spearheaded these pro-NAFTA activities were well-rewarded by the Salinas administration. Mexico offered them enormous access to both political elites and information and paid for them to visit Mexico to get acquainted with the country and meet government officials, where they obtained firsthand information on Mexico's economic and political conditions and an inside view of the strategy to improve the economy and promote NAFTA. Likewise, these think tankers and scholars had ready access to information that they subsequently used in their speeches and writings. Thus, as one prominent politician asserted, Mexico offered these people the chance "to sparkle, to display their knowledge."

Different agencies of the Mexican government also contributed money to American think tanks. According to José Luis Bernal, the Mexican government contributed to the general support of these organizations, but not necessarily to the individual researchers (Bernal 1995). However, one scholar reported that "Mexican officials offered me money for my commitment to write pro-NAFTA articles." According to the monthly report of the Mexican Embassy in Washington, the Mexican ambassador contributed to the Interamerican Dialogue, a Washington, D.C., research and advocacy organization that favored NAFTA (Secretary of Foreign Affairs n.d. - c). In American society ideas often need to be funded to have a voice, and the Mexican government had the money to make them resonate.

As has been noted, Mexico established a close link with key researchers in different think tanks: Nora Lustig at Brookings; Delal Baer at CSIS; Alan Reynolds at the Hudson Institute; Fred Bergsten, Jeffrey Schott, and Gary Haufbauer at the IIE; and Michael Wilson at the Heritage Foundation. These individuals and their respective think tanks organized various events with the Mexican government and encouraged the work of study groups.[6] Usually, Mexico provided information to think tanks and arranged the participation of high-ranking politicians in their conferences, while the think tanks were responsible for organizing the events. Four examples of the innumerable events organized by think tanks in coordination with, or with the consent of, the Mexican government illustrate this arrangement. In April 1991, Heritage organized a panel discussion on "The U.S.–Mexico Free Trade Agreement: What Prospects for Passage of the FTA?" Speaking at this event were Brian Timothy Bennett, former deputy assistant of the U.S. trade representative for Mexico; José Luis Bernal of the Mexican Embassy; and John J. St. John, former director of the Office of Mexican Affairs, U.S. State Department.

In a similar vein, in November 1991, Heritage sponsored a conference entitled "U.S.–Mexico–Canada: A Free Trade Partnership for the 21st Century." On the Mexican side, participating were Herman von Bertrab and Manuel Suárez Mier, in addition to Roberto Salina of the Center for the Study of Free Enterprise in Mexico City and Carolina de Bolívar, president of the Ludwing Von Mises Cultural Institute in Mexico City—both conservative institutions closely tied to the Heritage Foundation (Wilson and Smith 1992).

Another meeting that captured the attention of the Washington community was a conference organized by the Brookings Institution, CSIS, and the Fraser Institute (coordinated mainly by Nora Lustig and Delal Baer) held in June 1993 on Capitol Hill. Entitled "NAFTA Summit: Beyond Party Politics," the conference featured Sen. Bill Bradley (D–NJ), Rep. Bill Richardson (D–NM), Sen. John Kerry (D–MA), Rep. Kika de la Garza (D–TX), and Sen. Alan Simpson (R–WY). CSIS also organized a congressional study group on Mexico, cochaired by Sen. Lloyd Bentsen (D–TX), Rep. Ronald Coleman (D–TX), and Rep. James Kolbe (R–AZ) (see Table 6.3).

Table 6.3 CSIS Congressional Study Group on Mexico

Senate	House
Bill Bradley (D–NJ)	Tom DeLay (R–TX)
Dennis DeConcini (D–AZ)	E. Kika de la Garza (D–TX)
Pete Domenici (R–NM)	William Goodling (R–PA)
Wyche Fowler (D–GA)	Richard Gephardt (D–MO)
Bob Graham (D–FL)	Robert Lagomarsino (R–CA)
Phil Gramm (R–TX)	Dave McCurdy (D–OK)
John McCain (R–AZ)	John Miller (R–WA)
Barbara Mikulski (D–MD)	Bruce Morrison (D–CT)
Paul Simon (D–IL)	John J. Rhodes III (R–AZ)
Alan Simpson (R–WY)	Charles Schumer (D–NY)
	Lamar Smith (R–TX)

Thus, with these types of events, Mexico sought to affect the political environment and to sway public opinion in favor of NAFTA. However, despite the innumerable conferences, publications, newspaper and journal articles, and appearances on radio and television talk shows, the ultimate impact of think tanks in NAFTA's final outcome was limited, as the following section will show.

The Limited Influence of Think Tanks in the Approval of NAFTA

Think tankers and university-based scholars agree that there are at least two general indicators of the impact of think tanks on American public policy: their presence in the mass media and their access to politicians and business groups. To test the degree of media saturation of think tanks, I conducted an electronic search of approximately 580 U.S. newspapers from 1990 to 1994. I examined the number of citations in which the five think tanks included in this study and two anti-NAFTA think tanks were quoted in relation to NAFTA. I also conducted an electronic search of the names of witnesses who appeared before congressional hearings on NAFTA. The purpose of this inquiry was not to find conclusive evidence regarding the impact of selective think tanks on NAFTA. Rather, the aim was to find measurable indicators of the pervasiveness of think tanks in the media and before Congress. Figure 6.1 summarizes the appearance of think tanks in newspapers.

The Institute for International Economics had 150 citations (38 percent), the highest number of citations. This outcome is understandable, as IIE was the only think tank in the pool that specializes in international economics. The Economic Policy Institute, an anti-NAFTA organization, was second with more than 100 citations (27 percent). Notwithstanding the Mexican government's efforts, this shows that anti-NAFTA organizations received wide coverage in American newspapers. The Heritage Foundation was a distant third, with fewer than 50 citations (14 percent). Heritage has often claimed that its researchers are not often cited in the electronic media, but their analyses are frequently cited in local newspapers. The search shows that the number of citations in American newspapers are not as numerous as think tanks usually assert. Finally, CSIS, which claims to be a frequent media source, received fewer than 20 citations (3 percent).

Another way to evaluate the impact of think tanks during the NAFTA debate is to observe how many think tank representatives testified before Congress. Figure 6.2 summarizes the outcome of an electronic search.

Figure 6.2 reveals that only 5 percent of congressional witnesses were from think tanks. This finding, and the unimpressive appearance of think tank quotes in newspapers, contradicts, at least in part, the traditional view of think tanks as key actors in the American decisionmaking process. This is not to say that these

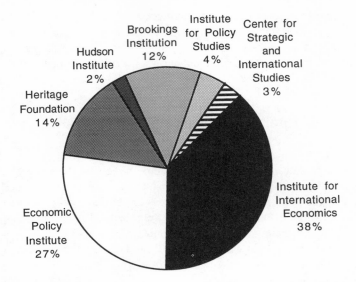

Source: A Lexis-Nexus search was conducted in the "papers" file, covering approximately 580 U.S. newspapers from the period 1990–1994. The search was constructed to identify all think tank names appearing within twenty words of "NAFTA."

Note: The Institute for Policy Studies and the Economic Policy Institute were anti-NAFTA; the remainder were pro-NAFTA.

Figure 6.1 NAFTA-related References to Selected Think Tanks in Major U.S. Newspapers, 1990–1994

institutions had no influence during the negotiations. Organizations such as Heritage and CSIS, and to a lesser extent Brookings, had significant access to congressional staff and legislators. During NAFTA's negotiation process, politicians received numerous think tank publications and were invited to luncheons, conferences, study groups, lectures, and meetings organized by think tanks. However, the think tanks studied here did not have an overwhelming presence in newspapers or in congressional hearings.

Another interesting finding was the significant difference in available testimony from business and labor. Among the different sectors of the population included in this search, businesspeople were the largest group of witnesses, with 36 percent of the total, while labor unions held a distant fifth place with only 10 percent of the total, a difference of more than three to one. If it is true that business groups generally favored NAFTA (there *were* sectors of the business community against the agreement) while the labor movement opposed it, business groups had more opportunities to present their views to Congress than did labor.

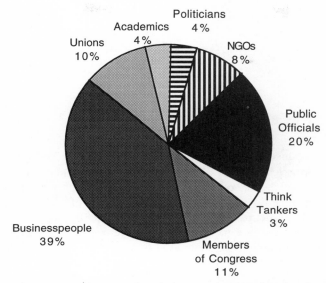

Source: A Lexis-Nexus search was conducted of congressional hearings focusing on NAFTA in 1993.

Figure 6.2 Witnesses at NAFTA Congressional Hearings, by Sector

There is a general consensus among analysts that a few weeks and even days before the final congressional vote, the Clinton administration developed an impressive campaign to obtain the support of undecided members of Congress for NAFTA's passage. For example, Treasury Secretary Lloyd Bentsen and other members of Clinton's cabinet tried to convince Rep. Richard J. Durbin (D–IL) that NAFTA would benefit corn growers and other farmers in his district. The administration approached Rep. Estéban Torres (D–CA), offering millions of dollars for the poor who were expected to be harmed by NAFTA. To obtain the support of the Louisiana delegation, the Clinton administration made a deal with Mexico to limit imports of Mexican sugar. The measure indirectly helped Rep. Benjamin L. Cardin (D–MD), whose Baltimore district was the site of a sugar refinery. Similar deals were made with Florida's delegation to protect citrus and vegetable growers. To gain the support of Rep. Lewis Payne (D–VA) the administration supported protections for the domestic textile industry (Hook 1993: 3014–3015). Likewise, Rep. Eddie Bernice Johnson (D–TX) obtained a promise from the Clinton administration for more purchases of the flawed C-17 cargo plane in return for her vote for NAFTA (Maggs 1993).

Indeed, the final vote for NAFTA was obtained not through ideological persuasion but through political bargaining. Money and politics, as usual, were ultimately decisive in NAFTA's approval. Nevertheless, in the negotiation process and the final congressional authorization different political actors intervened, each one at a different level and with their own resources. In this regard, think tanks did an impressive job: their intellectual lobby helped build pro-NAFTA public opinion. Their role in the approval of the treaty was not decisive, but was certainly indispensable.

Final Considerations

Throughout this paper, I have tried to show that modifications to the American political system since the 1960s have enabled think tanks to develop as important actors in American politics. I noted the substitution of political parties with the mass media and the rise of candidate-centered politics to indicate why today ideas and ideological forces now have a greater chance of affecting policy outcomes than in the earlier period of U.S. history when parties were very strong.

In the case of the free trade negotiations between the United States and Mexico, think tanks helped set the tone of the political debate over NAFTA as well as mold American public opinion. From the beginning of the negotiations, the Mexican government understood the importance of think tanks and actively sought them out.[7] This alliance was possible for two main reasons. First, during the 1980s Mexico moved to the Right on economic policy issues. Second, as I have argued, NAFTA's passage was in the interest of these think tanks and their supporters—corporations, conservative foundations, and conservative advocates. Perhaps for the first time this century, Mexico was more conservative than the United States. In general terms, most of the think tanks studied in this paper— with the exception of Brookings and IIE—were always in favor of a free market. They did not change their views, but Mexico changed its policy beginning in the mid-1980s. Thus, what facilitated this "marriage of convenience" was Mexico's shift to the Right.

The debate over NAFTA was a learning process for Mexico. Mexico's strategy showed that Mexican officials were able to successfully identify the main political actors in the United States and learn how the decision-making process could be influenced. The days in which Mexican politicians negotiated exclusively with the U.S. president are over. Now, Mexico has many tools for dealing with the American political system.

During the NAFTA negotiations, Mexico discovered the utility of having contacts with think tanks and academics. The techno-elites who have governed Mexico over the last decade are aware they can sell Mexico's image in the United States not only through advocacy advertising or by contracting a public relations agency but also through think tanks. It was an easy task for Mexican authorities to deal with these institutions. The nature of think tanks and their particular place in American politics was compatible with two strong points of Mexican politicians: the ability to maintain personal contacts and the use of rhetoric.

Significantly, Mexico learned to use its money in the United States. The millions of dollars it spent on its lobby, its economic support to the Hispanic community, and its financial support of think tanks demonstrated that it was willing to use its money to obtain the approval of NAFTA. At the same time, U.S. organizations and interest groups learned that Mexico was a good source of income. If the Mexican government wanted to be heard in the American political arena, they had to pay the price—literally. American intermediaries were happy to charge for their services. In this regard, Mexico followed practices honed by countries like Japan and South Korea.

NAFTA's negotiation process also significantly favored American academics who specialize in Mexican affairs. In the 1990s, Mexico became a domestic policy issue for the United States. The U.S. government, interest groups, and society in general sought out the expertise of those with knowledge about their future commercial partner. Moreover, the Salinas administration at least temporarily enhanced the status of these academics, especially those who were relatively unknown. By organizing events with academics and think tank scholars and establishing a special relationship with these specialists, Mexico increased their visibility and influence. The level of attention Mexico conferred on U.S. scholars was a unique episode in recent Mexican history.

The authoritarian nature of the Mexican political system permitted the implementation of a political strategy with clear political and economic goals, regardless of Mexico's political problems. Mexico was able to sell itself in the United States as interested in development, progress, human rights, and the environment, and as committed to democracy and free trade. Think tanks played a crucial role in selling that image. They spread the notion that NAFTA was, in the words of Delal Baer, an "insurance policy that may guarantee a stable, friendly, and prosperous Mexico into a foreseeable future" (Baer 1993a: 2). The think tanks and their spokespeople proclaimed that free trade was, in a nutshell, the answer to both Mexico's economic and noneconomic issues (Baer 1991).

Certainly, there are many lessons to be learned from the NAFTA experience by Mexicans, Americans, and U.S. think tanks. It is true that the events in Chiapas in 1994 and 1995 have been a painful experience for Mexicans and have disturbed observers in the United States. The post-NAFTA interdependence era—I hope—has also been a very educational and humbling period for think tanks and U.S. scholars. But this new era presents a difficult test for think tanks' hypotheses that predicted a prosperous and stable Mexico. Once again, history has been the tyrant of social scientists and their theories.

Notes

I would like to express my gratitude to Marisa Studer for sharing her knowledge on American think tanks. Victor Godínez made valuable observations on the first draft of this paper. Imtiaz Huzein and Pilar Domingo also made insightful comments. Finally, Mauricio Tenorio helped me revise my arguments.

1. "Think tank" is an imprecise term and specialists disagree on its definition. For Nelson Polsby and Kent Weaver, think tanks are basically universities without students. For Robert K. Landers they are "organizations that do research bearing on public policy." For Samantha L. Durst and James A. Thurber "six characteristics help distinguish think tanks from other kinds of research organizations: 1) organizational purpose; 2) focus of study; 3) intellectual independence; 4) sources of funding; 5) type of expenditures; and 6) role." In this chapter, I use the term "think tank" to refer to non-profit public policy research institutions dedicated to the dissemination of ideas and policy recommendations to the media and government, and to the formation of American public opinion. On the issue of the difficulties in defining think tanks, see Weaver (1989); Polsby (1983); Smith (1989); and Durst and Thurber (1989).

2. Traditionally the IIE has been considered a liberal think tank associated with the Democratic Party, but in the case of NAFTA it was identified with conservative organizations.

3. I focus on these think tanks because, according to the Mexican officials I interviewed, they were the most relevant to NAFTA. These five think tanks differ substantially from one another. The Brookings Institution is more academic-oriented and less ideologically committed than Heritage. Throughout its more than 75 years of existence, Brookings has gained national and international recognition for its scholarly work. Its staff consists of respected academics and its books are often required in university courses. Heritage, on the contrary, is an advocate-oriented organization designed to market conservative ideas. Its goal is to influence the view of government officials, the media, and above all, members of Congress and their staffs on current issues. Most members of Heritage do not hold a Ph.D. Its professional staff is not career academics, and they typically spend a few years in the organization before moving on. "We are not an academic institution by any means," asserted Michael Wilson, a senior policy analyst at Heritage. "Brookings and AEI are academic institutions to some extent. They write books, do long studies, and look at issues over the long run. We try to get ahead of the curve on issues. We try to forecast what is going to be important next month, next year, or next week. Then, either we write a paper or put together a study group, or working group, or go over and meet with some members of Congress" (Wilson 1993).

CSIS and IIE are dedicated to analyzing international issues. CSIS focuses on topics such as military affairs, security, and economic and political issues. IIE concentrates on the analysis of international economic topics such as finance, trade, and debt. However, what these think tanks have in common is that they supported NAFTA, and some of their staff were key in improving Mexico's image in the United States.

4. For Burnham, two other features of current politics are what Nelson Polsby calls the institutionalization of the House of Representatives, a phenomenon that is manifested in the high rate of returning incumbents seeking reelection and divided government in a postpartisan era. See Burnham (1989).

5. This document was provided to me by a former staff member of a think tank who chooses to remain anonymous.

6. In the report of activities of the Mexican Embassy in Washington in 1990 I found the following note: "The intense participation of officials of this Embassy in different forums, seminar, conferences, etc., organized or cosponsored for universities in collaboration with Mexican entities or the Embassy have represented one of the main tools of the integral promotion of our country in the United States" (Secretary of Foreign Affairs n.d. - c).

7. Ambassador Petricioli expressed as much after attending a seminar organized by the Center for U.S.–Mexican Studies and the Overseas Development Council: "the value of this type of seminar for the negotiation process is very important" because these institutions and "others of the same nature decisively affect both the Administration and Congress" (Secretary of Foreign Affairs 1990).

References

Abelson, Donald E. 1992. "A New Channel of Influence: American Think Tanks and the News Media," *Queen's Quarterly* 99, no. 4.

Adams, Bruce. 1979. "The Limitations of Muddling Through: Does Anyone in Washington Really Think Anymore?" *Public Administration Review*. 39, no. 6, November–December.

Aldrich, John, and Richard G. Niemi. 1990. "The Sixth American Party System: The 1960s Realignment and the Candidate-Centered Parties." Unpublished paper.

Baer, Delal. 1991. Statement by M. Delal Baer before the Committee on Foreign Affairs, Subcommittee on International Economic Policy and Trade, Subcommittee on Western Hemisphere Affairs. Washington, D.C., 6 March.

———. 1993a. "NAFTA and U.S. National Security." In *NAFTA Summit: Beyond Party Politics*. Conference sponsored by the Brookings Institution, The Center for Strategic and International Studies, and the Fraser Institute. Washington, D.C., 28–29 June.

———. 1993b. Interview by author. August.

Bernal, José Luis. 1995. Interview by author. Mexico City, October.

———. 1996. Interview by author. Mexico City, 20 February.

Burnham, Walter Dean. 1989. "The Reagan Heritage." In Gerald M. Pomper, ed., *The Election of 1988. Reports and Interpretations*. Chatham, N.J.: Chatham House Publishers, Inc.

Critchlow, Donald T. 1993. "Think Tanks, Antistatism, and Democracy: The Nonpartisan Ideal and Policy Research in the United States, 1913–1987." In Michael J. Lacey and Mary O. Furner, eds., *The State and Social Investigation in Britain and the United States*. Cambridge, Mass.: Cambridge University Press.

Durst, Samantha L., and James A. Thurber. 1989. "Studying Washington Think Tanks: In Search of Definition and Data." Paper prepared for delivery at the 1989 annual meeting of the American Political Science Association. 31 August–3 September.

Feulner, Edwin J., Jr. 1985. "Ideas, Think Tanks, and Governments." *The Heritage Lectures*, No. 51.

Franc, Michael. 1993. Interview by author. Washington, D.C. 27 June.

Ginsberg, Benjamin. 1984. "Money and Power: The New Political Economy of American Elections." In Thomas Ferguson and Joel Rogers, eds., *The Political Economy: Readings in the Politics and Economics of American Public Policy.* Armonk, N.Y.: M.E. Sharp, Inc.

——— and Martin Shefter. 1990. *Politics by Other Means: The Declining Importance of Elections in America.* New York: Basic Books.

Heritage Foundation. 1991. *The Heritage Foundation 1991 Annual Report.* Washington, D.C.: Heritage Foundation.

———. 1992. *The Heritage Foundation 1992 Annual Report.* Washington, D.C.: Heritage Foundation.

Himmelstein, Jerome L. 1990. *To the Right: The Transformation of American Conservatism.* Berkeley: University of California Press.

Hook, Janet. 1993. "The Uphill Battle for Votes Produces a Whirl of Wooing and Wheedling." *Congressional Quarterly Weekly Report.* 6 November.

Howell, Leon. 1995. "Funding the War of Ideas: The Role of the Four Sisters." *Christian Century* 112, no. 22, 19–26 July.

Hoynes, William, and David Croteau. 1990. "All the Usual Suspects: McNeil/Lehrer and Nightline." *Extra* 3, no. 4.

Kondracke, Morton. 1980. "The Heritage Model." *The New Republic.* 20 December.

Langston, Thomas S. 1992. *Ideologues and Presidents. From the New Deal to the Reagan Revolution.* Baltimore, Md.: Johns Hopkins University Press.

Maggs, John. 1993. "Planes for Votes Swap Illustrates Rising NAFTA Price-tag Byline." *Journal of Commerce.* 8 November.

Matlack, Carol. 1991. "Marketing Ideas." *National Journal.* 22 June.

Nobel, David F. 1981. "The Foundation Trap. Corporatist Culture Ministries." *The Nation.* 21 March.

Ojeda, Rosalva. 1995. Interview by author. Mexico City, 28 September.

Polsby, Nelson. 1983. "Tanks But No Tanks." *Public Opinion* 6, April–May.

Ranney, Austin. 1983. *Channels of Power: The Impact of Television on American Politics.* New York: Basic Books.

Ricci, David. 1993. *The Transformation of American Politics: The New Washington and the Rise of Think Tanks.* New Haven: Yale University Press.

Salinas de Gortari, Carlos. 1994. "Intervención del Presidente Carlos Salinas de Gortari en la Reunión Anual de la Business Roundtable, June 11, 1990." In Carlos Arriola, ed., *Documentos Básicos Sobre el Tratado de Libre Comercio de América del Norte.* Mexico: Porrua.

Secretary of Foreign Affairs. 1990. Letter from Ambassador Gustavo Petricioli to Secretary of Foreign Affairs Fernando Solana. "Seminar on Free Trade Agreement." General Archive of The Mexican Secretary of Foreign Affairs. III/110 (VIII). 39738.

———. n.d. - a. "Grupo Intersecretarial para el Seguimiento y Coordinación de las Relaciones de México con Canadá y Estados Unidos." General Archive of the Mexican Secretary of Foreign Affairs. III/ 352 (72: 73: 71)/ 42900 6.

———. n.d. - b. "Scholars for a Free Trade With Mexico." General Archive of the Mexican Secretary of Foreign Affairs. III/ 352 (72: 73: 71)/ 42900. Tratado Trilateral de Libre Comercio.

———. n.d. - c. Informe Mensual de la Embajada de Mexico en Washington, Julio de

1994. General Archive of The Mexican Secretary of Foreign Affairs. 42247 General 7a Parte Pasa 8a Parte.

Schulman, Beth. 1995. "Foundations for a Movement: How the Right Wing Subsidizes Its Press." *Extra* 8, no. 2.

Smith, James A. 1989 "Think Tanks and the Politics of Ideas." In David C. Colander and A. W. Coats, eds., *The Spread of Economic Ideas.* New York: Cambridge University Press.

———. 1991a. *The Idea Brokers. Think Tanks and the Rise of the New Policy Elite.* New York: Free Press.

———. 1991b. *Brookings at Seventy Five.* Washington, D.C.: The Brookings Institution.

Suárez Mier, Manuel. 1993. Interview by author. Washington, D.C., 21 July.

Velasco, Jesús. 1995. "The Influence of Ideas on Policy Realignments: The Neoconservative Case." Ph.D. dissertation, The University of Texas at Austin.

Vogel, David. 1983. "The Power of Business in America: A Re-appraisal." *British Journal of Political Science* 13. part 1, January.

———. 1989. *Fluctuating Fortunes. The Political Power of Business in America.* New York: Basic Books.

von Bertrab, Herman. 1993. Interview by author. Washington, D.C.,16 August.

Waldman, Steven. 1986. "The King of Quotes: Why the Press Is Addicted to Norman Ornstein." *The Washington Monthly* 18, no. 11, December.

Wattenberg, Martin P. 1990. *The Decline of American Political Parties, 1952– 1988.* Cambridge, Mass.: Harvard University Press.

———. 1991. *The Rise of Candidate-Centered Politics: Presidential Elections of the 1980s.* Cambridge, Mass: Harvard University Press.

Weaver, Kent R. 1989. "The Changing World of Think Tanks." *PS: Political Science and Politics* 22, no. 3, September.

Wilson, Michael. 1993. Interview by author. Washington, D.C., 19 May.

——— and Wesley R. Smith, eds. 1992. *The North American Free Trade Agreement: Spurring Prosperity and Stability in the Americas.* Heritage Lectures No. 400. Washington, D.C.: The Heritage Foundation.

Chapter 7

The Negotiations between the Mexican Government and the U.S. Financial Community: A New Interpretation

Victor M. Godínez

> There is only interdependence among independent ones.
> Otherwise there is only servitude.
>
> Carlos Fuentes, *El Fin del Sistema Mexicano*

> I wonder whom we should thank for having dealt so ably with the
> spiritual realm of which no one any longer has a personal understanding.
>
> Fyodor Dostoyevsky, *Devils*

Since August 1982, when Mexico's external debt crisis began, financial matters have become the central focus of economic relations between Mexico and the United States. Since then, interaction between Mexican officials and the American financial community has become a routine aspect of Mexico's economic life. This sort of interaction was not previously lacking; it simply was more episodic and had less direct influence over the design of Mexico's economic policy. The nature of Mexico's financial crises since 1982 has established a pattern of recurring negotiations with specialized agencies of the U.S. government and large banking and financial institutions in the United

States. One of the central theses of this chapter is that the impetus for economic change that Mexico is now undergoing and the impetus for the political emergence of "technocrats"[1] were defined at the height of these negotiations.

The Emergence of Bilateral Cooperation

The recurrent pattern of financial negotiations between Mexico and the United States since 1982 has been largely unavoidable due to the considerable economic and monetary instability that has characterized Mexico's economy. The continuous interaction between officials on both sides of the border has been characterized by a growing level of coordination and mutual understanding. Unlike other spheres of bilateral relations in which disagreement and even conflict are the norm (such as with immigration, drug trafficking, the environment, and extradition), in the financial sphere the parties involved seem to have agreed on a basic platform that has facilitated their decision making. This level of coordination was one of their most notable attributes. There has been an absence of fundamental differences during times of crisis. Naturally, this degree of cooperation has reduced the potential for conflict. A common framework of values and socioeconomic and economic perspectives (or, as Shelling would say, of a shared universe of representations) among the actors is one of the factors—but not the only one—that has helped defuse the environment within which such crises tend to occur. That the negotiators share a single frame of reference has facilitated and allowed these actions to be effectively carried out according to the logic of solutions and strategies that each case requires.

The political and structural causes of this regime of cooperation and understanding are varied. The nature of these causes is diverse and they are a function of changes occurring at international, binational, and national levels. It is not my intent to discuss such matters here,[2] my concern is the underlying reasons behind the negotiating positions of the Mexican government. These probably include the one factor that has strongly influenced the development of this cooperation. In the many bilateral rounds that have taken place since 1992, Mexico explicitly avoided confrontation by searching for solutions that would coincide with the views and initiatives of the United States. The origins of this stance stem from the highly pragmatic considerations of Mexican authorities about Mexico's place in the international power structure. However, as I have suggested elsewhere (Godínez 1988), it is important to add that this type of posture also stems from a deliberate choice of Mexican negotiators, born of their own economic and political philosophy. This posture also results from the requirements of the rapid, distinctive, and conflictual ascendancy of the current ruling elites (who in essence are conducting Mexico's financial negotiations).

An Intellectual Revolution or an Overstatement Regarding Political Changes in Mexico?

The strategies and tactics deployed by Mexican negotiators have exhibited an understanding of the national economy—and of market dynamics—that is totally congruent with the approach of the principal financial actors in the United States. This change has possibly had the greatest impact on Mexico over the course of its economic relations of the past decade and a half. The intellectual revolution that, according to U.S. observers, occurred in the 1980s (a notion that has been immodestly accepted by some Mexican academics), has as its mainstay this new approach. The origins of this new approach, however, are less inauspicious than an intellectual revolution. Rather, its origins are just one of many outcomes of an ordinary political fact that, given Mexican politics, some would consider to be vulgar: the rise to power of a close-knit political group. This group is characterized by a homogeneous economic perspective that was forged in the context of what Albert Hirschman has called a process of ideological upsurge[3] (Hirschman 1981).

My argument is that, in the context of the crisis of the postrevolutionary development model, this process gave rise to a period of ideological political maneuvering in the 1980s. This maneuvering was to promote the so-called modernization project. The project's main objective was to advance a total reorganization of society based on efficiency imperatives determined by small teams of specialists or technocrats. The decisions made by these teams have become, with surprising ease, public policies whose only foundation is the economic science of their authors.[4] Given this context, a discussion about whether such public policies were appropriate or unavoidable—or whether there were alternatives—is less interesting and perhaps unknowable in the face of such polarized positions. What is interesting to highlight is that the technocrats' modernization project was imposed from the highest levels of power and carried out with the help of traditional (and not very modern) resources from the old postrevolutionary Mexican regime. The authoritarian aspect of the modernization project, which certain individuals tried to justify using the metaphor of "perestroika without glasnost,"[5] was ignored by political, financial, and academic elites in the United States, who instead enthusiastically supported the political ascendance of the new ruling group in Mexico. In fact, one of the staunchest supporters mobilized by this ruling elite when implementing its project was the U.S. financial community. These links have evolved during successive phases of interaction. Gradually, they have led to a marriage of interests between the political group trying to consolidate power and the institutions and public and private financial agencies that have bet heavily on the outcome—and on something else.

Economic Precariousness and Urgency:
The Primary Features of the Financial Negotiations

Table 7.1 presents a summary of macroeconomic indicators in Mexico before and during each of the main financial negotiating rounds between Mexico and the United States.[6] Some observations can be drawn from this data. The first observation is that the financial negotiating rounds that have taken place in the past fifteen years have occurred amid fragile economic conditions in Mexico. One exception to this was, to some extent, the 1989 round finalized two years later with the Brady Plan. On the other hand, in the 1982, 1986, and 1995 negotiating rounds, Mexico's economic vulnerability was extreme. At these three times the bilateral talks took place against a backdrop that undoubtedly influenced the content of the negotiations: the greatest economic and monetary crises in Mexico's history since the Great Depression occurred in these three years. In these three cases, the decline of economic activity combined with high inflation and the effects of a devaluated peso. The 1982 and 1995 crises were preceded by growing and unsustainable imbalances in the country's balance of payments.

During these periods of economic and financial crisis, a sense of urgency permeated the financial negotiations. Accordingly, José Angel Gurría argues that one of the lessons of the past fifteen years is that "a timely reached agreement is better than an optimal solution" (Gurría 1995a). Paraphrasing a game-theory formulation used in international relations: to Mexican government officials, the specific outcomes of the negotiations (financial costs and commissions, terms, conditionalities, domestic recession, unemployment, drop in income) are in line with the rewards obtained (the timely support of the financial markets in order to consolidate their conflictual rise to power). It is important to ask one question about such notions of timing and optimal solutions. Did they mean the same thing to Mexican and U.S. negotiators?

Table 7.1 Mexico's Macroeconomic Conditions During the Four Main Rounds of Financial Negotiations with the United States

Round	GDP Growth		Inflation*		CA/GDP		Exchange Rate[†]	
	Before	During	Before	During	Before	During	Before	During
1982	9.0	−0.6	23.3	57.5	−5.9	−3.6	3.7	133.2
1986	3.1	−3.7	71.9	131.8	1.7	−1.4	45.5	105.0
1989	1.5	2.9	123.0	20.0	0.8	−3.0	91.7	8.5
1995	2.1	−7.0	8.4	34.8	−7.1	−0.1	13.3	89.1

GDP: gross domestic product; CA: current account; Before: average previous biennial figure in which the negotiating round started; During: year of the negotiating round.
*Consumer prices intra-annual average rate
[†]Annual percent devaluation rate vis-à-vis the dollar
Source: Banco de México figures

The Political Manipulation of the Economy

The second observation is that, in the three cases mentioned above, the financial negotiations between Mexico and the United States were not the consequence of explicit designs of international economic policy. In these three rounds the negotiations were imposed out of necessity: the crises that precipitated the negotiations made it impossible for Mexico to ignore its payment difficulties. Domestic economic decline, financial and monetary instability, and restrictions imposed abroad simply compelled the government to look for help and support from the United States. More importantly, in the configuration of these crises the Mexican government's economic, financial, and foreign exchange actions played a primary role. This was especially true in the case of the debt crisis that began in 1982. The responsibility of this crisis is almost universally attributed to the incongruent economic policies of the so-called financial populism of President López Portillo's administration. There is less agreement, on the other hand, over who bears responsibility for the macroeconomic policy—and the underlying reasons for—the crises that precipitated the negotiating rounds of 1986 and 1995. Regarding the 1986 crisis, José Angel Gurría (1995b) says:

> in 1985 the initial efforts (of the economic adjustment begun in 1982) did not produce the desired results, particularly in public finances. Yet, such efforts were overridden by two events: the 1985 earthquake that demanded enormous expenditures on reconstruction and the fall in oil prices, from an average of $25 a barrel in 1985 to $12 in 1986.

As some have suggested, other factors explain the 1986 crisis (Bendesky and Godínez 1986; Godínez and Ruprah 1988). Certainly, the decline in oil prices was key, but this alone was not a determining factor. Prior to this, the government had revised its economic policy, inducing an internal recession (with its financial and monetary consequences) as an attempt to regain control over the adjustment program implemented at the end of 1982. This program had been shelved due to a miniexpansion brought about by public expenditures during the second quarter of 1984 and the first quarter of 1985. This departure from what had been a restrictive fiscal policy was not included in the government's economic policy. The main motivation of this public spending was to give political support to official government candidates in the federal elections of 1985. This deviation from the economic program for political purposes caused a macroeconomic disequilibrium and an obvious loss of control over the adjustment process. It also produced the virulent rebirth in international banking and financial circles, especially in the United States, of the topic of the Mexican crisis. The increase in public spending in an election year caused financial agencies to respond with rigid measures and forced an expansion and acceleration of the so-called structural change in the economy.

Evidence of the Mexican government's deteriorating ability to persuade the international financial community before the 1985 earthquake and the 1986 drop in oil prices is shown in the following examples. First, the initial part of the multiannual debt programming, formalized in March 1985, was left technically invalid for five months due to some European banks' reticent responses to the first signs of instability in the adjustment program. Second, the Mexican government's inquiries in early 1985 into the possibility of reentering, even marginally, the voluntary international credit markets were categorically rejected by international banking and financial institutions. Third, on the eve of the September 1985 earthquake, the International Monetary Fund (IMF) decided to suspend the delivery to Mexico of nearly $450 million that was part of a $3.4 billion loan arranged at the end of 1982.

In an effort to reestablish the confidence of its creditors, the Mexican government took various measures. Four weeks before the earthquake, the government announced a number of measures intended to reorient the economy toward adjustment: a 20 percent currency devaluation; the dismissal of thousands of public employees; a reduction of fiscal expenditures the second half of the year; the virtual elimination of import licenses; and a relaxation of its foreign investment policy. Further, at the end of 1985 (after the earthquake), the government undertook a number of radical measures designed to satisfy the conditions imposed by the international financial community. In the space of a few weeks, the government requested membership into GATT; adopted a reduced 1986 budget; raised the price of fuel by 50 percent; reinitiated the sale of nonstrategic public companies; ratified for the fourth year its policy of limiting wage increases; and finally, sent the IMF a new letter of intentions requesting the IMF's cooperation in order to continue its "economic reordering" begun in 1982 (Bendesky and Godínez 1988: 104–105; Godínez 1986; Castañeda 1985).

A similar parallel to the events of 1985 occurred with the December 1994 devaluation crisis. The memory of this experience is still fresh and recalls an economic policy that fed a growing and unsustainable deficit in Mexico's balance of payments. This policy overvalued the exchange rate and allowed the supposedly autonomous Central Bank to rapidly expand credit in 1994. The Central Bank financed—instead of impeded—capital outflow and allowed, through development banking, the channeling of credits that totaled nearly 4 percent of the GDP.[7] The political use of those economic resources by the Salinas de Gortari administration is not subject to debate. In any case, both in 1986 and in 1994 the government's role in unleashing the crisis was not due to errors of calculation, as it was claimed,[8] but rather to the manipulation of fiscal, monetary, and financial variables for political and electoral purposes. Scientific knowledge, technical skills, and the obligation to change took a back seat to these ends.

From Negotiation to Executive Agreement?

A third observation is that the effective ability of Mexican negotiators to intervene in the design of the final agreements seems to be declining with each round. Rather, the basic engineering of such arrangements and the accompanying assistance packages seem to originate from the United States. In fact, the negotiating rounds that followed the August 1982 meeting took place under the protection of initiatives whose names are telling: the Brady Plan, the Baker Plan, and the Rubin Plan.

The trend towards passivity on the part of Mexican participants was particularly noticeable in the 1995 round. This round of talks seemed to be equivalent to treaty talks, in the literal sense of the word: "the meeting of one government authority with one or some of its immediate collaborators or subordinates in order to jointly make decisions over specific issues." In fact, the negotiations that produced an emergency finance package, announced by President Clinton in January 1995, took place in other spheres and among other actors. The most difficult negotiation was, perhaps, between President Clinton and the U.S. Congress. Although both the terms and results of the package are well-known, it is important to emphasize certain of its features. President Clinton's proposal to lend Mexico $40 billion was opposed by Democratic members of Congress who had earlier opposed NAFTA. Joined by the isolationist and conservative wing of the Republican Party, the Democrats tied the package's approval to a number of demands on Mexico regarding immigration, drug trafficking, labor rights, policy toward Cuba, financial guarantees through oil revenues, increased sales of public companies, and the creation of an independent monetary authority modeled on the Federal Reserve system (or turning the Bank of Mexico into a monetary board) (Doherty 1995). In the face of opposition to the package—and in the face of rapidly falling international reserves in Mexico—President Clinton finally opted to use the stabilization funds of the U.S. Treasury and negotiated a substantial increase in loans already committed by the IMF and the Inter-American Development Bank (IDB). The total amount of this package, nearly $51 billion, has no international precedent.

It is precisely in the international arena where President Clinton began the second front of negotiations to lobby for the financial package to Mexico. This negotiating front was sponsored by the U.S. government prior to the launching of the scheme that was finally adopted.[9] Treasury Undersecretary Lawrence Summers first proposed the plan at a meeting in Paris of the G7 in January 1995. Two days later, the director of the IDB was notified by the Federal Reserve and was obligated to obtain the credit for Mexico. The IMF was notified the night before the package was announced and it confirmed its participation (with a loan three and half times greater than any loan for a single project to any individual member country in its fifty-year history). This confirmation was received at 7 a.m. on 31 January 1995 during a telephone call between IMF Director Michel Camdessus, Subdirector Stanley Fisher, Secretary Rubin, and Undersecretary Summers. The haste of the agreement prevented the U.S. government from consulting its European allies, who only learned of the package when Clinton publicly announced it. This upset some individuals in European political and financial circles. As a result, several meetings of the executive council of the IMF took place in order to earn the support of the main European powers—particularly the British and the Germans—who did not share the United States' concern that Mexico's crisis was a risk to the international financial community. In the view of European officials, the crisis was instead a problem for American investors who had made imprudent investments. To the Europeans, the United States seemed to be transferring its regional responsibilities onto an international playing field. At the IDB, similar questions were asked. Finally, the U.S. government was able to reduce the tension, which in some way tested transatlantic economic cooperation, and was able to obtain support for its aid package from its main European allies. I recognize that for many academics this brief description may just be an insubstantial anecdote. However, as Charles Kindleberger responded to critics of his *Manias, Panics and Crashes*: "anecdotes are proof and what counts is whether they are representative or not." So, what are these anecdotes of this aid package representative of? They exemplify the relative passivity of Mexican negotiators, who on this occasion had a secondary role, since the majority of the work was performed by the U.S. government. What were Mexican negotiators doing in the meantime? They were lobbying for the Clinton-Rubin solution.

Getting Mexico's Economic House Back in Order

The fourth and final observation is that the United States was not moved to action out of philanthropy nor out of pure politics. President Clinton himself expressed this clearly in his 1995 address to Congress. He said it was necessary to offer guarantees to protect loans made by the American private sector to Mexico. This, the president added, was of great importance to the United States' strategic interests. He then added:

> Now, there will be tough conditions here to make sure that any private money loaned to Mexico on the basis of our guarantees is well and wisely used. Our aim in imposing the conditions, I want to make clear, is not to micro-manage Mexico's economy or to infringe in any way on Mexico's sovereignty, but simply to act responsibly and effectively so that we can help get Mexico's economic house back in order (Clinton 1995).

As in 1986, the urgency of a crisis that no one responsible for economic policy expected or could anticipate was what forced Mexico to redefine its public policy. These modifications—though they are congruent with the ideological and economic choices of the government—were not the result of an original program nor were they adopted autonomously. This subject is undoubtedly very polemic; it upsets, irritates, and in some cases provokes intolerance in close government circles. My interest is not whether such policies were appropriate, but in pointing out the origin of their adoption and instrumentation.

I wish to pose one last point as a question. Who in Mexico truly knows the financial cost to the country for the last aid package? Not a single authority has offered any figures, nor is there an official report that details this. However, according to explanations the U.S. government has given to Congress and the American public, the most recent aid package will have important benefits for the United States. Treasury Secretary Rubin has made assurances that these benefits will exceed the benefits had the government invested these funds via conventional financial methods. Do we have to wait for these benefits to be accounted for in the United States in order to learn their costs to Mexico?

Notes

1. I use the term "technocrats" to identify the individuals whose ascendance to power was promoted by President Miguel de la Madrid and who generated an internal struggle with the old cadres of the PRI during the presidential terms of Salinas de Gortari and Zedillo. These technocrats do not comfortably accept being called this. They assume that as professional economists they are distinct from the generation of PRI politicians that preceded them. Yet, they have substantially maintained the most nefarious government practices of their predecessors.

2. Regarding this point, see Godínez and Ruprah (1988). See also Bendesky and Godínez (1988).

3. The usefulness of this concept to discuss the dominant economic ideology in the United States and its transfer to the political elites of other countries is illustrated in Valdés (1989). In other words, it is a process in which "political parties or organized groups have decided to use the power of the state and mobilize their followers on the basis of doctrinaire discourses in order to reorganize society and drastically modify its rules, thus changing the behavior and lifestyles of its people" (Valdés 1989).

4. A widely respected professor has this to say: "Salinas and his *equipo* represented a new cast in Mexico. *Técnicos*, as opposed to *políticos*, is the usual description. This shorthand is inadequate, however, because the technical expertise of the persons holding the key economic positions was of a high quality. The most prestigious U.S. universities rarely turned out as many first-rate Ph.D.s in economics for a single foreign country, other than earlier in Chile under the Chicago boys. These experts were committed by conviction, and by what they deemed to be necessity, to a new structure for the economy" (Weintraub 1995: 40).

5. Conspicuous, such technocrats in power explained on various occasions that they were learning from the experiences of reform in the former Soviet Union under

158   Bridging the Border: Transforming Mexico–U.S. Relations

Gorbachev. In their view, economic reform must precede political reform and, it would be a mistake to carry them out simultaneously. Of this, they are right: an economic modernization of the kind carried out in Mexico would have been unthinkable—in terms of timing, methods, and content—had it occurred within the context of competition and political pluralism.

6. For a detailed account of the process of Mexico's financial negotiations in the 1980s, see Godínez and Ruprah (1988). See also see Godínez and Ruprah (1990), and Bendesky and Godínez (1988). For an official account of the decade of the 1990s, see Gurría (1995b).

7. Sidney Weintraub (1995: 41) observed that if such resources were considered, and were not accounted for in the federal budget, the public deficit figures would be less positive that what was officially presented.

8. That is how those responsible for economic policy explained it in 1985 (see the respective communiques of the SHCP) and in 1995 (see the declarations of Secretary Blanco at the annual meeting in Davos, Switzerland, in February 1995).

9. This information was obtained from the February 1995 editions of the *New York Times*, the *Wall Street Journal*, the *Financial Times, Le Monde, El País*, and the *Economist*.

References

Bendesky, L., and Victor Godínez. 1986. "Deuda y Disuación Financiera: la Experiencia Mexicana." In A. Borón, ed., *Crisis y Regulación Estatal: Problemas de Política en América Latina y Europa*. Buenos Aires: Grupo Editor Latinoamericano.

———. 1988. "The Mexican Foreign Debt: A Case of Conflictual Cooperation." In Riordan Roett, ed., *Mexico and the United States. Managing the Relationship.* Boulder, Colo.: Westview Press.

Castañeda, Jorge G. 1985. "Mexico at the Brink." *Foreign Affairs* 64, no. 4, Winter.

Clinton, William J. 1995. Remarks at the Department of Treasury, 18 January 1995. U.S. Department of State Dispatch, vol. 6, no. 4, 26 January.

Doherty, Carroll J. 1995. "Rank and File Draw a Line Against Aid for Mexico." *Congressional Quarterly*, 21 January.

Godínez, Victor. 1986. Carta Mensual. *Estados Unidos: Perspectiva Latino-americana* 11, no. 2, February. Mexico City: Centro de Investigación y Docencia Económicas.

———. 1988. "Mexico's Foreign Debt: Managing a Conflict (1982–1987)." *International Journal of Political Economy* 18, no. 14, Winter.

Godínez, Victor, and Inder Ruprah. 1988. "Evolución y Perspectivas de la Deuda Externa de México. Elementos para una Interpretación de la Estrategia Negociadora y de sus Costos." In R. Bouzas, ed., *Entre el Ajuste y la Heterodoxia. Negociaciones Financieras Externas de América Latina (1982–1987)*. Buenos Aires: GEL.

———. 1990. "En Busca del Descuento del Mercado: México y el Enfoque no Convencional de la Deuda Externa." In R. Ffrench-Davis, et al., *Conversión de*

Deuda Externa y Financiación del Desarrollo en América Latina. Buenos Aires: Grupo Editor Latinoamericano.

Gurría, José Angel. 1995a. "The Mexican Debt Strategy." *Challenge: The Magazine of Economic Affairs,* March–April.

———. 1995b. "Corrientes de Capital: el Caso de Mexico." In R. Ffrench-Davis and S. Griffith-Jones, eds., *Las Nuevas Corrientes Financieras hacia América Latina. Fuentes, Efectos y Políticas.* Mexico: Fondo de Cultura Económica.

Hirschman, Albert O. 1981. *Essays in Trespassing: Economics to Politics and Beyond.* New York: Cambridge University Press.

Schelling, Thomas C. 1956. "An Essay on Bargaining." *American Economic Review* 46, June.

Valdés, J. G. 1989. *La Escuela de Chicago: Operación Chile.* Buenos Aires: Editorial Zeta.

Weintraub, Sidney. 1995. "Mexico's Foreign Economic Policy: From Admiration to Disappointment." *Challenge: The Magazine of Economic Affairs,* March–April.

Chapter 8

Discord in U.S.–Mexican Labor Relations and the North American Agreement on Labor Cooperation

Edward J. Williams

The North American Free Trade Agreement (NAFTA) has contributed to significant new departures in U.S.–Mexican cooperation. The two governments grow ever closer; business communities in the two nations evolve a more intimate relationship; police forces on both sides of the international line develop cooperative accords; environmentalists in Mexico and the United States work hand in glove; and a host of other collaborative initiatives combine to define a new cooperative reality for the bilateral relationship.

Organized labor in the two countries provides a glaring exception to the general trend. The coming of NAFTA seems to deny the age-old ambition for working class solidarity once again as organized labor in Mexico and the United States concocts programs that frustrate bilateral cooperation. The framing and initial implementation of the NAFTA labor side accord, the North American Agreement on Labor Cooperation (NAALC), has not made matters any better.

A description and analysis of those initiatives define the purpose of this chapter. The discussion emphasizes the significant divisions between the two labor union movements and the implications of the NAALC as it has been conceived and initially applied in Mexico and the United States. This chapter divides into four parts. After this introduction, the first section sets the scene by explaining two contextual foci: a short interpretation of the trends and forces that have diminished the political punch of the Mexican and U.S. labor movements and a discussion of other binational groups that have been successful in evolving cooperative initiatives. The discussion proceeds to the crux of the matter: 1) an examination of the influences that have impeded Mexican and U.S. labor from seeking cooperative strategies; and 2) a description and analysis of the NAALC and its initial execution, highlighting the conclusion that the agreement will not contribute to bilateral cooperation between the Confederación de Trabajadores Mexicanos (CTM) and the AFL-CIO. The final section of the chapter sets out some projections and conclusions.

The Context: Union Debility and Bilateral Cooperation

Two contextual factors suggest the need for cooperative initiatives between organized labor in the United States and Mexico. In the first instance, the labor movements in both countries become ever weaker as neoliberal ideologies wax increasingly formidable. International solidarity should be a strategy to revive organized labor's waning political potency in Mexico and the United States.

Second, other forces pursue binational initiatives quite successfully. Governments cooperate, businesspeople launch joint ventures, environmentalists offer mutual assistance, human rights groups collaborate, drug mafias co-conspire, etc. In the process, singularly and in tandem each of those binational groups prospers and increases its influence in each country.

The logic of the analysis suggests that those flourishing binational initiatives provide a pattern to be embraced by organized labor in Mexico and the United States. Solidarity, of course, defines the rallying cry and fundamental principle of the labor movement. Yet, organized labor in the two nations remains divided as its political influence sinks into further decline.

Labor Union Debility

The decline of the Mexican and U.S. labor movements is far too obvious to spark serious debate. The causes differ to some degree in the two countries, but they also share several common origins: the global ideological fashion of neoliberalism, the changing characteristics of the two nations' economies, and the disreputable image of labor leaders.

As both cause and effect of the neoliberal movement, governmental and private interests in the United States and Mexico have been reorganizing their economies in a spree of downsizing, privatization, liquidation, and restructuring. An abbreviated litany of business and governmental strategies in the United States captures the sense of the influences chipping away at labor's position.

Downsizing and mergers by the nation's largest companies eliminated 4.7 million jobs in the decade stretching from 1984 through 1993. In 1994, another half million jobs were cut. The clear majority of those millions of lost jobs came from relatively well-paying, labor-organized industries (Genasci 1994; Hunger Awareness Resource Center 1995).

When American business enjoyed prosperity, overtime and temporary workers frequently filled the positions eliminated earlier while subcontracting programs expanded. Temporary employees are almost totally unorganized, and subcontracting frequently replaces well-paid organized workers with unorganized, lower-wage labor.

While those strategies contributed mightily to organized labor's relative debility, the U.S. labor movement's own sins weighed in the balance. U.S. labor unions have been frequently corrupt, arrogant, and out of touch with the changing characteristics of the U.S. and world economies.

Table 8.1 sets out the data on U.S. organized labor's decline. Absolute membership increased from 1945 to 1975 with marginal increases continuing through 1980, when the absolute numbers of union members went into decline. The data on membership as a percentage of the overall workforce tell the more important tale. After a peak relative membership in 1945, the percentage figure dropped ten percent in 30 years, and another ten percent in about another ten years.

Like the United States, Mexican organized labor is in decline. The causes of the decline of Mexican organized labor emanate from a series of post-1982 and post-1994 policies and programs designed to overcome the ravages of economic crisis and "modernize" the economy and the polity. The policies included wage fixing under government-sponsored *pactos*; a series of privatizations, liquidations, and restructurings; and the negative economic fallout of trade liberalization.

Wage fixing began with the austerity programs initiated immediately after Miguel de la Madrid's accession to power in 1982. As the government's programs were applied, real wages fell precipitously (de Palma 1994: C1; *Mexico Business Monthly* 1993: 22; Tierney 1994: 3). The economic crisis beginning in late 1994 signified more misery for Mexico's workers as the screws tightened and the workers sacrificed.

Table 8.1 U.S. Union Membership, Selected Years

Year	Union Membership*	Membership as a % of Workforce
1945	14,300,000	35.5
1975	19,600,000	25.5
1992	16,400,000	15.8

*Rounded to the nearest one hundred thousand.
Source: The World Almanac 1994: 141.

In the same mold as downsizing in the United States, Mexico's liquidations, restructurings, and privatizations spelled another series of negative impacts upon workers and organized labor. One source quoted 400,000 jobs lost from 1982 through 1993. That figure seems rather low. Other sources count 160,000 jobs cut at Petróleos Mexicanos (PEMEX), another 20,000 to 25,000 from the privatized railway system, and 35,000 from business downsizing in the city of Monterrey alone, not to mention significant cutbacks at Fertimex, Tabamex, Teléfonos de México, and the auto and steel industries. Whatever the exact count, the numbers were clearly large. Moreover, the ranks of the unemployed multiplied again with the economic downturn sparked by the crisis of 1994–1995 (*El Mañana* 1989; *New York Times* 1993; *Mexico Update* 1990; *Latin American Weekly Report* 1994: 316; *La Jornada* 1992: 17; Bierma 1996: 32; Nauman 1992: 4).

Threatening demographic trends also contributed their negative influences to the problems of Mexican organized labor. The Mexican labor force more than tripled between 1950 and 1990 while available jobs trailed behind, particularly since 1982. Projections predict another increase in the labor force of nearly 50 percent between 1990 and 2005. Mexico's labor force increases by about a million workers each year, as worker supply far outstrips demand (Pick and Stephenson-Glade 1994: 82–87).

In response, Mexican organized labor has pursued a series of strategies ranging from opposition through collaboration with the government, but the Mexican labor movement has repudiated a policy of international solidarity with its U.S. counterpart. The conservative, parochial posture of Mexican and U.S. labor appears all the more puzzling in the context of binational initiatives by other groups.

Binational Cooperative Initiatives

As U.S. and Mexican labor unions shirk international cooperation and see their influence wither, other binational groups embrace cooperative initiatives and increase their wealth and influence. Those initiatives include business ventures between U.S. and Mexican interests and governmental cooperation between Mexico City and Washington. Even more germane for the analysis of labor union solidarity, the ventures also count successful binational cooperation among public health proponents, environmentalists, human rights organizations, and labor rights advocates. In every case, those groups champion many of the same causes and argue many of the same issues as organized labor in Mexico and the United States. On the focus of this analysis, their effective collaboration accentuates the failure of labor unions to evolve similar success on similar problems and issues.

The 1994 NAFTA accord consecrates official governmental cooperation, of course, but the partnership is both more mature and more enveloping than reciprocal trade and investment. The intimate bilateral relationship has been evolving at least since the Carter administration issued a Presidential Review Memorandum (PRM 41) in 1978 elevating Mexico to the first dimension of U.S. foreign policy interests.

Myriad joint ventures by Mexican and U.S. businesses flourish, defining a trend quite different from the void of cooperation between labor union groups. The trade and development corridors evolving in the binational borderlands provide especially cogent examples. The economic logistics of NAFTA have catalyzed intriguing initiatives between Mexicans and Americans as they unite in the borderlands to compete with other groups of Mexicans and Americans in the binational corridors. The cities of San Antonio, Laredo, Nuevo Laredo, and Monterrey stand as the most powerful binational coalition in the mid-1990s, but other groups also compete. An example is the Arizona-Sonora corridor composed of Phoenix, Tucson, both Nogales, Hermosillo, and Guaymas (Mexican Investment Board 1994; Williams 1994: D4).

Governmental and business cooperation form dimensions of the larger scenario, but they really have less relevance for the case at hand than other cooperative ventures that strike closer to the analysis of binational organized labor. Mexican–U.S. binational public health, social action, human rights, and environmental groups also cooperate widely and effectively.[1]

Binational cooperation among environmentalists began in the early 1980s, but moved into a new stage with the broaching of NAFTA in the early 1990s. NAFTA riveted attention on the environmental degradation of the binational borderlands, sparking the formation of organizations on both sides of the international line and linking several into effective examples of international cooperation.

A catalog and description of those binational organizations goes beyond the ken of this essay, but a listing of several serves the point. In Texas and Nuevo León, the Texas Center for Policy Studies has joined with Bioconservación of Monterrey to pursue the Binational Project on the Environment. In West Texas and southeast New Mexico, the International Environmental Alliance of the Bravo groups more than ten organizations from both sides of the Rio Grande. In New Mexico, the International Transboundary Resources Center (Centro Internacional de Recursos Transfronterizos) works with like-minded Mexican counterparts in several locations.

Similar groups contend environmental and health issues in Arizona and California. The Northeastern Sonora-Cochise County Health Council (NSCCHC) cooperates with the Red Fronteriza de Salud y Ambiente, based in Hermosillo, Sonora. In southwestern Arizona, the International Sonoran Desert Alliance boasts three national affiliates: Mexican, U.S., and Native American Tohono O'odham living on both sides of the border. In California, the San

Diego Environmental Health Coalition cooperates with the Tijuana-based Comité Ciudadano Pro Restauración del Cañon del Padre on a series of environmental issues.

A number of Mexican–U.S. binational organizations also cooperate in the defense of human rights. Amnesty International includes chapters in Mexico and the United States. In the 1980s, the sanctuary movement encompassed adherents in both countries. The American Friends and Mexican Amigos are probably the best known of these human rights organizations (American Friends Service Committee 1992).

Binational public and environmental health advocates also form part of the collective of groups and organizations that mobilize voters, monitor human rights, protect the environment, and nurture cross-border cooperation. The United States–Mexico Border Health Foundation defines the most significant recent progress in the field. It began functioning in 1996.

Finally, binational labor rights groups also illustrate examples of collaborative initiatives that cover the territory. Although it goes beyond the single issue of labor rights, the binational Coalition for Justice in the Maquiladoras (CJM) forms the most important of these groups. In the labor area, the CJM concentrates on measures to implement new policies governing hours, working conditions, safety standards, and the like.

In contrast to the mainstream of organized labor in Mexico and the United States, every one of these initiatives represents binational cooperation. Furthermore, every one reflects the dynamic toward international collaboration symbolized by NAFTA. They include bureaucrats, businesspeople, environmentalists, social activists, and human rights advocates (not to mention drug mafias), but not the peak representatives of organized labor in Mexico and the United States.

Internationalism in Mexican and U.S. Labor Thought and Practice

Mexican and American trade unionists betray a series of cultural, socioeconomic, and political attitudes and positions that militate against an internationalist position. In both countries nationalism and political alliances with government play into the mix. In the United States, labor's traditional commitment to protectionism assumes significance. In Mexico, the authoritarian characteristics of the system help explain organized labor's reluctance to push international solidarity with its U.S. counterpart. In both countries, finally, jobs for working men and women play mightily in the analysis. In the United States, the specter of jobs lost to Mexico significantly influences organized labor's strategy. On the other hand, the hope of jobs gained in Mexico informs the strategy of organized labor. In both countries, NAFTA and the side agreement on the NAALC have complicated the calculation.

The United States: The Cold War and Protectionism

Examining first the U.S. side of the binational equation, the inhibitions to international cooperation run the gamut from the general to the particular, from attitudinal disposition to political calculations. At a macro level of analysis, labor chieftains in the United States share the isolationist prejudice that weaves its way through the American historical tradition. That feeling reflects a certain arrogance in the minds of Americans that has convinced many that the United States needs no allies. In the context of organized labor, the prejudice contributes to the U.S. rejection of solidarity with its fraternal organization in Mexico, or elsewhere.

The major thrust of U.S. labor's foreign trade policy aims at the protection of U.S. jobs. With the exception of a short-lived foray into internationalism when it supported President Kennedy's Trade Expansion Act of 1962, labor's position has been staunchly protectionist. For others, the expansion of trade may imply positive contributions like economic growth, lower consumer prices, and increased international understanding, but for U.S. labor the implications are quite different. Expanded international trade spells the loss of American jobs and the erosion of organized labor's influence (Cowie 1993). Moreover, the postwar international experience of U.S. organized labor has been preoccupied with its role in the U.S. anticommunist crusade. U.S. unions have occasionally cooperated with their foreign brethren, but not necessarily to increase wages or improve working conditions. Rather, the thrust has been to battle communist-dominated unions in Chile, Costa Rica, Ecuador, France, Italy, and elsewhere.

From another analytical perspective, U.S. labor's long-lived repudiation of consciously articulated theoretical formulations also diminishes its proclivity to offer serious consideration to the advantages of international solidarity with its Mexican counterpart. With occasional exceptions best exemplified by the United Auto Workers and the International Longshoremen and Warehousemen's Union, American labor's concentration on bread-and-butter issues inhibits a larger vision of the meaning of working class solidarity and its many nuances and extrapolations, including international cooperation.

Combining the sense of a couple of the previous perspectives, U.S. labor's attitude toward working men and women in less developed countries (LDCs) like Mexico also reflects contradiction and ambivalence. On the one hand, a genuine sympathy for poor and exploited Mexican workers characterizes the U.S. response. On the other hand, of course, Mexican and other Third World workers strike at the very heart of U.S. organized labor's priority interest. Foreign workers define competition and the loss of U.S. jobs.

In the best of the analytical critiques, the self-aggrandizing practices of multinationals in league with weak, pliant, and corrupt Third World governments offer a context to explain the competition from poor working men and women in LDCs and suggest the wisdom of international solidarity. But the sophisticated analysis frequently gets lost in the translation, and Mexican and other Third World workers become primarily competition for scarce jobs.

Finally, American racism forms part of the complexity of the response. As always, racial prejudices frequently complicate American and other international actors' attitudes and negatively impact the inclination and/or the ability of Americans to evolve fruitful cooperation with Africans, Asians, and Latin Americans.

All of those factors have combined to constrain U.S. organized labor from moving toward a policy of authentic and comprehensive cooperation with Mexican labor in previous times and in the mid-1990s. Several factors weigh just as heavily from south of the Rio Grande where Mexican labor has been equally reluctant to embrace a policy of proletarian solidarity.

Mexico: Authoritarianism, Nationalism, and Developmentalism

Similar and different factors compose an analysis of Mexican organized labor's position on cooperation with its U.S. counterpart. In a somewhat comparable nationalistic context, Mexico's labor union leaders remain ill-disposed to join their U.S. counterparts. In a rather different political context, furthermore, Mexico's labor union leaders operate in a semiauthoritarian system; the heavy hand of governmental power comes quite close to dictating the policies and programs of Mexico's labor movement.

The analysis from Mexican authoritarianism runs straight forward. Mexico's governing elites mandate the formulation and implementation of the policies and programs formally promulgated by Mexican organized labor. Indeed, the role of government became more assertive during the 1980s and 1990s. The Mexican government purged a number of Mexican labor leaders and imprisoned others in a campaign launched by de la Madrid and intensified by Salinas de Gortari. Mexico's labor leaders fell into line, pledging their support to the modernization of the Mexican economy. NAFTA formed a keystone of the modernization program. To the person, Mexico's labor leaders promoted the trade agreement, admittedly some more enthusiastically than others. In that context, they contradicted their U.S. counterparts who vociferously opposed the free trade treaty. Mexico's labor leaders continued their support of the treaty in the mid-1990s.

In the mid-1990s, U.S. labor leaders continue to seek the cooperation of their Mexican brethren to raise wages and improve working conditions for Mexican workers, thereby increasing production costs in Mexico. The de la Madrid, Salinas de Gortari, and Zedillo administrations have opposed the goals of U.S. unions. Mexico's labor leaders support the government, at least partly because uncooperative labor leaders in Mexico are purged and/or end their careers in jail.

Hence, Mexican labor leaders eschew cooperative arrangements with U.S. organized labor. A Mexican analyst gets to the point in complaining that Mexican organized labor suffers from a state of limbo. While the *sindicatos* claim formal representation of working men and women, "their interests and their activities continue to be defined by the will of the politically powerful, especially the federal government" (Trejo 1994: 2).

But, that fact forms only part of the picture. The analysis also needs to emphasize that personal authoritarianism, nationalism, and developmentalism define the values of Mexican labor leaders. An evaluation of labor chief Fidel Velásquez captures a component of the analysis. In the words of Kevin Middlebrook, Fidel is "heavy on discipline, including for himself and in relationship to the government and to the president." Such a personality shirks from challenging governmental elites (Middlebrook 1989: 201).

Perhaps even more importantly, Velásquez and other Mexican labor leaders are nationalists. Middlebrook defines Velásquez' political beliefs as being characterized by conservative nationalism (Middlebrook 1995: 112). Hence, Mexican labor protects national dignity and promotes national development. As early as 1954, the dominant CTM officially pronounced its obligation to the nation over its duty to support class struggle (Ryan 1970: 365). As nationalists, Mexico's labor leaders share a deeply ingrained antigringoism, particularly among the older cadre of labor leaders. They have experienced the humiliation of U.S. imperialistic muscle flexing. Gringos are not to be trusted. Hence, collaboration with gringos does not come easily.

Developmentalism also weaves its way into the analytical scenario. Like other Mexicans, labor leaders strive to contribute to the nation's economic growth. Economic growth translates into the creation of jobs for Mexico's massive number of unemployed and underemployed workers. Mexican organized labor correctly predicts new and better jobs emanating from NAFTA. Hence, Mexican organized labor counts several splendid reasons to support NAFTA and to refuse cooperation with U.S. unions bent on its destruction. Prudent self-interest in an authoritarian political system counsels the wisdom of supporting the government on important issues. Moreover, a history of binational interaction teaches that gringos should not be trusted, no matter the color of their shirt collar. Finally, NAFTA promises to create jobs for fellow Mexicans, a desirable goal for Mexico's organized labor.

Comparison of Unions and Social Action Groups

Unlike binational environmental, human rights, and public health groups, therefore, significant tension defines the relationship between U.S. and Mexican organized labor in the mid-1990s as NAFTA continues to test the ambition to move to working-class solidarity. The differences between labor and other social action groups' characteristics and agenda add another increment to the analysis.

On the one hand, social action groups tend to be analogous to labor unions in their concentration on socioeconomic issues, but the two also diverge in significant ways. In the first instance, environmental groups and their brethren tend to be far more independent of government than are traditional unions or *sindicatos* in the United States and Mexico. They are also more flexible than traditionally hidebound, hierarchically organized labor unions. Consequently, they are less politically compromised and more free to act as their predilections and perceived interests guide them (Kidder and McGinn 1995: 14–21).

Furthermore, environmentalists and human rights activists wax passionate and are ideologically committed to their respective causes, and they enjoy a following that facilitates mobilizing political support. Environmentalism, especially, defines the social message of the mid-1990s. To be sure, millions of dedicated trade unionists and *sindicalistas* continue their struggle for social justice, but their cause no longer catalyzes the political support of fifty years ago. However moral and right organized labor's call for social justice may be, its political resonance has waned; its potential for political mobilization diminished; its mass popularity declined.

Moreover, environmentalists and human rights advocates tend to be more sophisticated, more highly educated, and more cosmopolitan then their counterparts in the *movimiento sindical*. In that sense, they move easily to international cooperation and alliances. Hence, the sociocultural and political attitudes of the proponents of environmentalism and human rights prepare them better than trade unionists for international cooperation.

Finally, and perhaps most significantly, the perceived self-interests of Mexican and U.S. *sindicalistas* contribute mightily to divergence and mutual suspicion. As noted previously, the crux of NAFTA for unionists and *sindicalistas* is the perception of a zero-sum calculation of jobs lost in the United States and jobs gained in Mexico. For many environmentalists and human rights advocates (and business interests), on the other hand, NAFTA provides the promise of allies gained and resources added to pursue their mutual self-interests in both countries.

In sum, NAFTA divides U.S. and Mexican organized labor. Furthermore, the labor side agreement to NAFTA does little to reconcile the alienated union movements. In truth, the theory and practice of the North American Agreement on Labor Cooperation appears to belie the promise of labor cooperation, or at least labor cooperation interpreted as collaborative initiatives by the major federations in Mexico and the United States—the CTM and the AFL-CIO. Indeed, the NAALC may be working the opposite effect in the mid-1990s. The early skirmishes over the unionization of several *maquiladora* plants in the borderlands and a manufacturing plant near San Francisco exemplify the influences at work dividing U.S. and Mexican labor and highlight several other points explicated in this chapter.

The NAALC and the NAFTA Connection

Neither the theory nor practice of the NAALC promises to overcome the divisions between Mexican and U.S. organized labor. Rather, an analysis of the text of the agreement combined with a review of its initial practice suggests that the NAALC may well exacerbate hostility between the two movements.

Looking first to the origins and its major thematic principles, it is clear that the North American Agreement on Labor Cooperation has virtually nothing to do with labor unions cooperating to do much of anything. Of twenty-five central foci set out in the accord under the rubrics "Objectives," "Obligations," and "Labor Principles," one of the "Objectives" alludes diffusely to the need to "pursue cooperative labor-related activities on the basis of mutual benefit." Furthermore, the labor agreement offers no potential for the harmonization of the several national labor codes. Hence, cooperation is difficult since the three national movements are operating in different legal contexts. Finally, the NAALC defines an infinitely complex and lengthy appeals process clearly designed to obviate the imposition of sanctions against any of the three governments and obviously calculated to maintain national foci of decision making (U.S. Department of Labor 1993).

The lack of protocols designed to nurture international proletarian collaboration should come as little surprise, given the original impetus for the NAALC. In large part, the agreement evolved from the politics of the U.S. presidential campaign of 1992. Candidate Bill Clinton charged incumbent George Bush with failing to protect jobs (and the environment) in the original NAFTA accord. Clinton promised, if elected, to negotiate side agreements to remedy those flaws. Along with other promises, the pledge assured U.S. labor's support in the election, contributing to Clinton's electoral victory. In turn, U.S. organized labor called in its political chips by demanding the protection of labor rights in the side accord.

A major goal of the resultant NAALC reflected the fundamentals of a long tradition of unionism in the United States; it sought to protect American jobs, not to foster cooperation with Mexican *sindicatos*. Following the strategy inaugurated as early as the Caribbean Basin Initiative of 1983, the NAALC clearly included worker rights provisions designed to encourage better working conditions, child labor protection, the right of free association, etc. in Mexico (Commission for the Study of International Migration and Cooperative Economic Development 1990: 73–74).

Those worker rights define goals in themselves, of course, but to the point of this analysis, they also pursue a tactic designed to preserve American jobs. Their long-range goal seeks to equalize wages and working conditions in foreign countries, thereby making U.S. workers more competitive with their foreign counterparts. To reiterate, the major purpose of the agreement does not pertain, even indirectly, to labor union cooperation.

On the contrary, the NAALC is state-centered. It concentrates on the governmental policies and programs of the three sovereign signatories, not on the activities of unions, labor rights groups, or any other nongovernmental organization. In the process of pursuing a complaint about the freedom of association, for example, the original "plaintiff" may be union or *sindicato*, but its standing formally disappears if the issue gets adopted by its government and is pursued within the context of the agreement. After the initial petition, the actors become governmental officials, not unionists or *sindicalistas* (Mumme and Stevis 1995: 35–36). In sum, the original impetus for the NAALC, the more proximate purpose for its drafting, and the document itself, are not concerned with binational labor union cooperation. Whatever "labor cooperation" in the title may mean, it certainly does not specifically encourage organized labor in the United States and Mexico to band together to increase their influence and/or to serve their constituents.

Furthermore, the initial practice of the agreement offers little reason to believe that the NAALC will encourage binational labor union cooperation, certainly not between the CTM and the AFL-CIO, the labor peak organizations in the two countries (International Labor Rights Fund 1995; Inter-Hemispheric Education Resource Center 1995b; U.S. Department of Labor 1995). As of mid-1996, three complaints under the NAALC have been filed and decided in the United States. Another petition was withdrawn. One case has been decided in Mexico. All of the U.S. complaints revolved around collaborative attempts by U.S. and Mexican groups to organize *maquiladoras* in the borderlands. Two of the three U.S. cases evolved from disputes in the state of Chihuahua; the other from the Mexican state of Tamaulipas. The Mexican case deals with a complaint against Sprint, the telecommunications company, for firing U.S. workers in a plant near San Francisco.

The Chihuahuan disputes took place in Ciudad Juárez and Ciudad Chihuahua. They contributed to three petitions brought to the U.S. National Administrative Office (NAO) for the NAALC. The NAOs from each of the three signatories to the NAALC are the first agencies to receive and adjudicate petitions brought under the agreement. The NAOs also perform other functions not germane to this discussion.

After having unsuccessfully solicited the cooperation of Mexico's dominant CTM, in 1994 the United Electrical, Radio, and Machine Workers of America (UE) and the International Brotherhood of Teamsters (IBT) recruited Mexico's small Frente Auténtico del Trabajo (FAT) to launch efforts to organize two *maquiladora* plants, owned by General Electric and Honeywell (U.S. Department of Labor 1994; Myerson 1994a and 1994b; *El Financiero Internacional* 1994: 3). The organizing efforts failed, and the UE and IBT appealed the cases to the U.S. NAO on grounds that the Mexican government frustrated the organizing efforts because it did not correctly apply its own labor code. The U.S. NAO denied two of the three petitions; the third was withdrawn.

Significantly, Mexico's CTM and other important Mexican unions guarded their silence throughout the entire process. They did not support the FAT. Likewise, the AFL-CIO took no active role in the process.

The final case brought to the U.S. NAO ended in qualified success for the Mexican and U.S. petitioners. It dealt with workers in a Japanese-owned Sony *maquiladora* in Nuevo Laredo, Tamaulipas. The Mexican workers attempted to replace their CTM union, but were denied an election by the government-dominated Conciliation and Arbitration Board (CAB). In this case, four U.S. and Mexican human/worker rights groups filed a petition with the U.S. NAO: the International Labor Rights Fund, the American Friends Service Committee (AFSC), the CJM, and the Asociación de Abogados Democráticos (National Association of Democratic Lawyers).

The U.S. NAO found the Mexican CAB in violation of Mexican laws and called for ministerial-level consultations between Mexico and the United States, in accordance with the NAALC. The ministerial consultations, in turn, specified a series of remedial measures, including three seminars to educate interested parties on union registration procedures. In this case, the CTM went beyond indifference and actively opposed the binational petitioners.

After the U.S. NAO had held against the Mexican government, the Sindicato de Telefonistas de la República Mexicana (STRM) and the U.S. Communications Workers of America (CWA) brought a case to the Mexican NAO. It charged the lack of a prompt remedy in U.S. labor law and practice for Sprint's subsidiary's firing of 177 (mostly Latino) workers in San Francisco. The U.S. National Labor Relations Board found that Sprint committed more than fifty violations of the law (Inter-Hemispheric Education Resource Center 1995: 6). The Mexican NAO found for the petitioners and recommended the case to the ministerial level. The Mexican and U.S. Ministers of Labor ordered hearings and analyses of the implications of the rapid closing of plants.

The initial round of cases under the NAALC implies significance for an analysis of labor union internationalism. It confirms that the most important labor organizations in Mexico and the United States remain uncommitted to binational cooperative efforts. The Mexican CTM continues to withhold its cooperation from its U.S. counterparts, and the AFL-CIO is lukewarm about lending its support to binational organizing efforts.

On the Mexican side, the CTM eschewed participation across the board. Indeed, the local CTM affiliate in league with the local authorities in Nuevo Laredo in the Sony case actively opposed the binational organizing effort. On the Mexican side, the FAT has been the most significant participant in the binational efforts. The STRM, the Democratic Lawyers Association, and Mexican members of the AFSC and CJM have played less important roles.

None of those organizations represent the CTM, the most significant of organized labor's peak organizations in Mexico. The FAT is small, fairly radical, independent, and as much social movement as *sindicato*. The *telefonistas* and their leader, Francisco Hernández Juárez, nurture a well-earned reputation for progressive unionism and maintain something close to a hostile relationship with the CTM. Hernández Juárez is often mentioned as the next *líder máximo* of Mexican organized labor, replacing the long-lived Fidel Velásquez, who turned ninety-six years old in 1996. The *telefonistas* do affiliate with the Congreso del Trabajo (CT), a loosely knit national labor confederation. The Democratic Lawyers Association has no connection to the CTM.

The lineup on the U.S. side tends to be more complex, but the essential conclusion much the same. The AFL-CIO remains aloof from the binational organizing effort. Beyond that point, the motives of the U.S. partners shade from international solidarity to calculating self-interest.

Human rights/labor rights/social action groups and unions made up the U.S. participants in the initial round of cases under the NAALC. Groups like the AFSC and the CJM maintain an ambivalent relationship with the AFL-CIO. The UE is not affiliated with the AFL-CIO and, according to Barry Carr, "the influence of the old Communist party culture still exercises some influence" within the union (Carr 1994: 17). The Teamsters maintain a tension-filled relationship with the AFL-CIO and often see themselves as an alternative rather than an affiliate. Like the Mexican *telefonistas*, finally, the U.S. Communications Workers of America cultivate a progressive internationalist agenda and find it easy to maintain cordial relations with the progressive leader of the telephone workers' *sindicato*, Hernández Juárez.

The point is clear enough. The exceptions prove the rule. While the CTM and the AFL-CIO disdain binational cooperation, the several groups that pursue the strategy are either nonunion social action groups or, if unions, are small, radical, consciously progressive, or competitive with the peak organizations— the CTM and the AFL-CIO. To carry the argument one step further, the positions assumed by the AFL-CIO and the CTM may well stem from a perfectly rational analysis of their self-interest. On the side of the AFL-CIO, the explanation is straightforward. Its leadership has been sidestepped by the CTM so frequently that it has about given up all attempts to nurture genuine cooperation. The explanation of the CTM's position is rather more complicated, but certainly not irrational. The AFL-CIO's support of the FAT subverts the hegemony of the CTM and other official and semiofficial unions in Mexico. It is unreasonable to expect the CTM to cooperate with a group apparently bent upon weakening its position.

Mexican organized labor also may question the motives of its U.S. counterpart as U.S. unions pursue the organization of U.S.-owned industry located in Mexico. That is, U.S. labor's strategy of organizing in Mexico may well be advantageous for Mexican workers, but it is also designed to narrow the wage differential between the two countries. Thus, it reduces the incentive for U.S. businesses to move south in search of lower labor costs. In the process, the strategy preserves jobs in the United States, always a primary objective for the

U.S. labor movement long steeped in protectionist principles. A recent study crystallizes the point: John Hovis, president of the United Electrical Workers union, said he plans to build strong, independent Mexican unions by defending workers whose rights have been violated by U.S. firms operating in Mexico. "Strong Mexican unions stop job flight," Hovis said (Carr 1994: 30).[2]

Moreover, U.S. unions tend to be uncertain allies of their Mexican counterparts. Their position reflects their interpretation of their interests. For example, the Teamsters have supported the unionization of *maquiladora* workers to drive up wages in Mexico in hopes of diminishing the two nations' wage differential. But, the same Teamsters have vehemently opposed Mexican truckers operating in the U.S. border states because they fear the competition of lower-wage Mexican truckers (*Business Week* 1996: 51).

Conclusions

While the North American Free Trade Agreement contributes to flourishing interaction among numerous groups in Mexico and the United States, it has done precious little to nurture cooperation between the CTM and the AFL-CIO. Moreover, the special side agreement pertaining to labor in the NAFTA countries has made no significant contribution to labor union solidarity. If anything, the North American Agreement on Labor Cooperation may complicate the relationship as it provides a forum that highlights differences between the Mexican CTM and the U.S. AFL-CIO.

The unsuccessful outcome of initiatives to further international working-class cooperation in the context of NAFTA flows all too clearly from the history, the ideological persuasion, and the contemporary power position of organized labor in both the United States and Mexico. In both countries, organized labor is comparatively weak, more or less nationalistic, and relatively unschooled in the ways of proletarian internationalism.

NAFTA, furthermore, gets to both movements' fundamental interests in crystallizing the issue of jobs. In the United States, the AFL-CIO intransigently opposed the trade agreement because it implied the loss of jobs—and, of course, the potential erosion of union membership and influence. In Mexico, the CTM and other labor organizations followed the lead of the government and their own self-interest in supporting the NAFTA because it implied an increase in Mexican jobs—and, of course, a potential increase in union membership and influence.

Moreover, the NAALC makes no contribution to binational union cooperation. The document's origin evolved from a politically inspired effort to protect U.S. jobs. Its basic principles define a state-led process designed to reduce conflicts that threaten commerce. Its provisions set out a hopeless appeals process and offer no way to harmonize labor codes to facilitate cooperation.

As the initial practice of the NAALC has evolved, furthermore, it has threatened the power position of the CTM in Mexico. The CTM's enemies coalesce with U.S. groups to challenge a system of Mexican labor law and practice fashioned by the CTM and the government that guarantees the continued primacy of the CTM, the official labor federation. Agitation from the several U.S. groups adds to the insecurity of the CTM, further exacerbating longtime divisions between organized labor in the two countries.

Furthermore, the mixed motives of U.S. labor are questioned in Mexico. While the principles of working-class solidarity may be served and the position of Mexican dissident labor strengthened, the U.S. union movement is equally interested in decreasing wage disparities to reduce the incentive for U.S. companies to relocate in Mexico. The issue of jobs, to reiterate, stands at the core of the tension-filled relationship.

In the future, the jobs equation is not liable to change dramatically, but three other factors may influence the relationship between the two movements: the increasing influence of binational social action groups in the relationship; an evolving sense of community encompassing U.S. and Mexican workers; and a change of leadership and policies emanating from the top of the two union movements.

The growing influence of binational social action groups tends toward what Barry Carr calls labor internationalism as distinct from trade union international-ism. Another analysis gets to the same point by distinguishing between traditional unionism and social movement unionism (Carr 1994: 4; Kidder and McGinn 1995). The discussion of binational cooperative initiatives presented in this chapter analyzes some of the considerations of that calculation.

A sense of evolving community is also struck in that same discussion. Many of the examples emanate from borderlands groups where the partici-pants enjoy ongoing physical and social interaction with one another, thereby bonding in a genuine feeling of solidarity. A variation on that theme comes out of binational cooperative initiatives launched by auto workers and farm workers in Mexico and the United States. In this variation, similar vocational and job site experiences substitute for the physical proximity of the borderlands bonds.

Finally and most obviously, a change in national union leadership may nudge the respective movements toward increased collaboration. In the United States, John J. Sweeney assumed the presidency of the AFL-CIO in the fall of 1995. His platform hinted at a change in international policy, and he moved in 1996 to replace the director of the American Institute for Free Labor Development (AIFLD), a key component of the AFL-CIO's international presence. Still, significant new directions await definition (Greenhouse 1995: A12; Weiss 1995: 3; Inter-Hemispheric Education Resource Center 1996: 8). In Mexico, meanwhile, Fidel Velásquez continues to hold forth. He promises to step aside, but the move is uncertain. This is not the place to offer an extensive analysis of the succession to Fidel, but more sympathy toward binational cooperation with the United States would certainly be forthcoming if Hernández Juárez emerges as the leader of Mexican organized labor.

Notes

1. This discussion leans heavily upon a series of articles in *BorderLines*, published by Albuquerque's Inter-Hemispheric Education Resource Center. See especially Volume I: 2, 3; and Volume II: 1, 2, 3.

2. Of course, the ambition to nurture "strong, independent" *sindicatos* should not be despised, whatever the motivation. Along with other positive developments encouraged, that fact implies that the NAALC probably has some redeeming qualities. But, those positive characteristics of the Agreement remain beside the point of this analysis.

References

American Friends Service Committee. 1992. *Sealing Our Borders: The Human Toll. Third Report of the ILEMP.* Philadelphia: American Friends Service Committee.

Bierma, Paige. 1996. "Joaquín Hernández Galicia: Bum Rap." *Mexico Business*, May.

Business Week. 1996. "Kantor's Truck Stop." 22 January.

Carr, Barry. 1994. "Labor Internationalism in the Era of NAFTA: Past and Present." Paper presented at the conference on "Labor, Free Trade, and Economic Integration." Duke University.

Commission for the Study of International Migration and Cooperative Economic Development. 1990. *Unauthorized Migration: An Economic Development Response* (Ascencio Report). Washington, D.C.: Commission for the Study of International Migration and Cooperative Economic Development, July.

Cowie, Jefferson. 1993. "U.S. Labor and NAFTA: Reflections on the Past and Future of Economic Integration." *Latin American Labor News* 8.

de Palma, Anthony. 1994. "Mexico's Pack for Stability in Economy." *New York Times*, 27 September.

El Financiero Internacional. 1994. "Unions Pressure U.S. on NAFTA Labor." 19–25 September.

Genasci, Lisa. 1994. "Tired Workers Revolt against Forced Overtime." *Arizona Daily Star,* 30 September.

Greenhouse, Steven. 1995. "A Big Job for Labor." *New York Times*, 27 September.

Hunger Awareness Resource Center. 1995. "Where Have the Good Jobs Gone?" An offprint of *U.S. News and World Report*, (3 July). Tucson: Hunger Awareness Resource Center. Fall.

Inter-Hemispheric Education Resource Center. 1995a. *First NAFTA Labor Rights Complaint in Mexico. Borderlines,* 3, no. 3, March. Albuquerque: Inter-Hemispheric Education Resource Center.

————. 1995b. *Borderlines* 3, no. 7, July. Albuquerque: Inter-Hemispheric Education Resource Center.

————. 1996. "AIFLD Chief Asked to Leave." *Borderlines* 4, no. 1. Albuquerque: Inter-Hemispheric Education Resource Center.

International Labor Rights Fund. 1995. "Mexican Authorities Betray Sony Workers Again." *News from ILRF*, 1 August.

La Jornada. 1992. "Amplian 21 Días Más el Programa de Retiro Voluntario en Ferronales." 5 August.

Kidder, Thalia and Mary McGinn. 1995. "Transnational Workers Networks." *Social Policy*, Summer.

Latin American Weekly Report. 1994. "Rural Alert." 21 July.

El Mañana. 1989. "Cananea Seguirá Funcionando." 23 August.

Mexican Investment Board. 1994. "Case Histories in Success: Joint Ventures in Mexico." Mexico City: Mexican Investment Board.

Mexico Business Monthly. 1993. "Mexico: Economic Indicators." *Mexico Business Monthly,* November.

Mexico Update. 1990. "More Parastates on the Block." 10 June.

Middlebrook, Kevin J. 1989."The Sounds of Silence: Organized Labor's Response to Economic Crisis in Mexico." *Journal of Latin American Studies* 21, part 2.

————. 1995. *The Paradox of Revolution: Labor, the State, and Authoritarianism in Mexico.* Baltimore: Johns Hopkins University Press.

Mumme, Stephen, and Dimitris Stevis. 1995. "NAFTA and International Social Policy." Unpublished manuscript. Fort Collins: Colorado State University.

Myerson, Allen R. 1994a. "Big Labor's Strategic Raid in Mexico." *New York Times,* 12 September.

————. 1994b. "Reich Supports Mexico on Union Organizing." *New York Times,* 13 October.

Nauman, Talli. 1992. "Modernization Takes Heavy Toll in Both Private and Public Sector Jobs." *El Financiero Internacional,* 21 September.

New York Times. 1993. "Mexico Sells Off State Companies." 27 October.

Pick, James, and Skye Stephenson-Glade. 1994. "The NAFTA Agreement and Labor Projections: Implications for the Border Region." *Journal of Borderlands Studies* 9, no. 1, Spring.

Ryan, John Morris et al. 1970. *Area Handbook for Mexico.* Washington, D.C.: Superintendent of Documents.

Tierney, Jennifer. 1994. "New Wage, Price Pack Signed." *El Financiero Internacional,* 3–9 October.

Trejo Delarbre, Raúl. 1994. "El NAFTA en Mexico: La Renovación Sindical no Llegará de Fuera." *Latin American Labor News* 9.

U.S. Department of Labor. 1993. National Administrative Office, North American Agreement on Labor Cooperation. Washington, D.C.: U.S. Department of Labor.

————. 1994. U.S. National Administrative Office, North American Agreement on Labor Cooperation. *Public Report of Review. NAO Submission #940001 and NAO Submission #940002.* Bureau of International Labor Affairs, 12 October.

————. 1995. *Foreign Labor Trends: Mexico, 1994–1995.* Mexico City: U.S. Embassy.

Weiss, Larry. 1995. "Sweeney Victory May Mean New International Policy." *Working Together*. Minneapolis: Resource Center of the Americas. September–October.

Williams, Edward J. 1994. "El TLC y La Oposición." *El Independiente*. 27 May.

World Almanac. 1994. Mahwah, N.J.: World Almanac.

Chapter 9

Mexico's New Foreign Policy: States, Societies, and Institutions

Jorge I. Domínguez

"Yes, yes, yes: how fortunate that our ideals coincide with our interests," Carlos Fuentes's Artemio Cruz recalled on his deathbed, once having spoken mendaciously to his U.S. partner (Fuentes 1964: 112). Feelings of joint interests, hopes, and deceit have long coexisted in U.S.–Mexican relations, defining the varied connections between the two countries. Those themes persist as the twentieth century ends, while the United States and Mexico ponder why the hoped-for Mexican miracle of the early 1990s was so short-lived and whether the ideals and the interests of the partners were incompatible and the truth-telling well-short of the standards of partnership.

And yet, much did change in U.S.–Mexican relations in the 1980s and 1990s. Consider just some economic examples. Mexico's exports of goods (including in-bond industries, or *maquiladoras*) nearly doubled from 1986 to 1990, and by the end of 1993 they again increased by over a quarter above the 1990 level. This growth reaped the gains from the wrenching reorganization of the Mexican economy after the 1982 financial collapse and from the associated reshaping of Mexico's international trade policy, including Mexico's adherence to the General Agreement on Tariffs and Trade (GATT).[1] The rate of Mexico's export growth, moreover, accelerated on the eve of, and immediately after, the enactment of the North American Free Trade Agreement (NAFTA). Mexico's exports surged by 12.3 percent in 1993, 17.3 percent in 1994 (NAFTA's first year), and 33.2 percent in 1995, aided in this last case by a sharp devaluation of the peso (Inter-American Development Bank 1995: 288; Economic Commission for Latin America and the Caribbean 1995: 55). Mexican trade, long concentrated overwhelmingly on the U.S. market, became even more focused on the United States during these years. As Jorge Chabat notes in his chapter, two-thirds of Mexico's exports went to the United States in 1988 but three-quarters did so in 1994. Similarly, Mexico was awash in the waves of international capital flows (at times it felt like a drowning). The net transfer of resources to Mexico was nearly $51 billion in 1991–1993 and about negative $30.5 billion in 1994–1995 (Economic Commission for Latin America and the Caribbean 1995: 62); that is, Mexico received a large inflow of funds in 1991–1993 and suffered a large outflow of funds in the two years that followed. This financial relationship, too, was particularly intense with the United States.

This book[2] is concerned with yet another change in the 1980s and especially in the early 1990s: the deliberate effort by the government of Mexico to influence the U.S. government to change its policies toward Mexico and, in so doing, to facilitate and speed up the economic changes noted above. This change in Mexican policy is noteworthy principally because, as Chabat's chapter makes clear, the Mexican government had long adopted a foreign policy of abstention from engagement in the major international issues of the day, and it preferred legalism as its principal procedure for the conduct of its foreign policy.[3] Mexico's new foreign policy sought to persuade the United States that, at long last, Artemio Cruz was right: their interests and ideals coincided.

U.S.–Mexican relations have never been limited exclusively to the inter-governmental arena, despite some of the Mexican government's efforts over the years to control such relations. Instead, the relations between the two countries have long engaged ordinary citizens, large business firms, and varied kinds of governmental and nongovernmental organizations. How might we assess, therefore, the composite effect of the actions of many actors, in addition to the Mexican government, as they seek to influence the U.S. government in its policies toward Mexico?

Finally, these Mexican efforts to change U.S. policy necessarily had many and varied effects upon Mexico. Mexican policy favored the free movement of labor and capital, of goods and people. Though the Mexican government focused its attention on the U.S. government, the consequences of liberalized trade, widespread migration, and larger capital flows contributed to reshape Mexico itself.

This chapter will argue that state-based explanations help to shed light on many of the most salient features of Mexican foreign policy and of U.S.–Mexican relations. Neorealism explains the contours of interstate relations; presidential-ism, neorealism's foreign policy–making counterpart, in turn, serves to explain the pattern of decisions at key moments in both governments. Presidentialism explains well the principal decisions with regard to NAFTA in the two countries, and the epochal change in each country's policies toward the other in the late 1980s and early 1990s.

Society-based explanations necessarily supplement state-based explanations. Millions of Mexicans have moved from one country to the other independent of the wishes of both governments. Their behavior has placed a key item on the binational agenda and constrained the capacity of both governments to deal with each other. Society-based explanations also illustrate the capacity of Mexican Americans to influence their communities of origin in Mexico. A different society-based explanation calls attention to the patterns of social class contact and experience between the United States and Mexico. The beliefs of elites in the United States and Mexico have converged, facilitating international cooperation, but the beliefs of nonelites have not, thereby deepening intranational conflict concerning U.S.–Mexican relations.

Finally, institutionalist explanations help to account for Mexico's relative success in raising the profile of its own agenda in Washington, D.C. They also unravel why and how Mexico has had to transform its own institutions charged with relations with the United States, permitting and encouraging more public agencies and private actors to become involved. And Mexico has also felt compelled to contribute to the creation of new international institutions to cushion and to channel the new U.S. influence in Mexico.

State-based Explanations

In the scholarship about international relations, so-called neorealist approaches insist that the most important actors in world politics are states, that their behavior is rational, and that states seek power and calculate their interests in terms of power in the face of an international system that lacks effective centralized authority, i.e., interstate anarchy.[4] States seek to balance against the one among them that might seek hegemony. Neorealist theories of international relations insistently eschew discussions of the process of foreign policy making and stay away from considering intersocietal relations.

Nonetheless, neorealism fits well with an approach to the study of foreign policy making that emphasizes the centrality of the president. Presidents seek to endow their governments with rational coherence: they choose cabinet ministers and their principal subordinates, they define their roles, and they set the rules whereby they may relate to one another (Krasner 1972). Presidentialism, consequently, is the policy-making face of neorealism.

The long-term pattern of U.S.–Mexican relations is consistent with a neorealist interpretation of Mexico's international relations and, more specifically, with a presidentialist approach to the making of foreign policy. In the nineteenth century and the early twentieth century, Mexico actively sought to balance the power of the United States in the Americas. After World War II, however, Mexico lacked the resources to confront the United States across all issue areas and, instead, balanced against the United States only on some key issues while bandwagoning on the rest. Mexico came to behave according to a pattern classically summarized by Ojeda: "The United States recognizes and accepts Mexico's need to dissent from U.S. policy in everything that is fundamental for Mexico, even if it is important but not fundamental for the United States. In exchange Mexico cooperates in everything that is fundamental or merely important for the United States, though not for Mexico" (1976: 93).

In our book, Alan Knight's chapter notes Mexico's delicate balancing against the United States on such important issues as international petroleum policy or relations with Cuba's revolutionary government. More generally, however, Knight argues that Mexican and U.S. politics have tended to march roughly in step throughout the twentieth century, certainly since the 1930s. Presidents of the respective countries, such as Franklin Roosevelt and Lázaro Cárdenas, Dwight Eisenhower and Adolfo Ruíz Cortines, Lyndon Johnson and Gustavo Díaz Ordaz, and George Bush and Carlos Salinas de Gortari, exemplify the extent of what Knight calls the fundamental though qualified congruence between Mexico and the United States. (The congruence is qualified because there were, of course, important differences as well.) The reason for this congruence has been Mexico's limited ability to play other international roles— exactly what Mario Ojeda's adaptation of realism to the Mexican case would lead us to expect.

Historically, Chabat reminds us, Mexico's traditional foreign policy was quite effective: not since the 1920s has there been a serious risk of U.S. military intervention in Mexico.[5] And after its revolution, Mexico was able to pursue a foreign policy that gradually widened the country's scope of action in international affairs (González 1989).

To behave rationally and coherently in the international system, Mexican foreign policy making rested firmly in the hands of the executive branch and, ultimately, in a highly centralized and powerful presidency. Explicitly or implicitly, all the authors in this book agree that the decision to seek NAFTA and to align broadly with the United States was made by President Carlos Salinas. Despite misgivings or opposition, one president—though building on the initiatives of his predecessor, Miguel de la Madrid—could reorient Mexican policy dramatically.

Interestingly, as Todd Eisenstadt and Jesús Velasco make clear, the Salinas de Gortari administration's diagnosis of the U.S. political system led it to emphasize a much more plural approach toward the United States, implicitly believing that presidentialist explanations did not apply equally well to the making of U.S. foreign policy.[6] Mere reliance on Mexico's traditional executive-to-executive relations, Salinas administration officials believed, would not suffice to advance Mexico's general interests in the United States or, in particular,

NAFTA's ratification by the U.S. Congress. George Bush had been defeated for reelection shortly after NAFTA's signing, and Bill Clinton seemed at first interested in everything except what occurred beyond the boundaries of the United States.

It was wise, and long overdue, for Mexican officials to develop a more sophisticated perspective on U.S. government decisionmaking. And yet, Eisenstadt argues accurately that NAFTA's passage through the U.S. Congress, in the end, would have been impossible without President Clinton's sustained commitment to its enactment and willingness to trade favors for votes to obtain the final segments of support for approval of this comprehensive trade treaty. A key explanation, therefore, for the signing and ratification of NAFTA was presidential initiative and commitment in both countries. Presidentialism, the policy-making counter-face of neorealism, imparted rationality and coherence to the process of U.S. policy decisions concerning Mexico once the NAFTA debate was cast as a crisis in U.S.–Mexican relations.[7]

Presidentialist explanations, moreover, shed considerable light on the workings of institutions associated with NAFTA's enactment. Edward Williams's chapter explores the context and relations around the North American Agreement on Labor Cooperation (NAALC), an agreement associated with NAFTA thanks to the Clinton administration's initiative. Williams points out that, notwithstanding its name, the agreement features very little cooperation between labor unions in the two countries; on the contrary, relations between the principal union federations have been adversarial.

The NAALC, Williams also notes, is state-centered. The original plaintiff may be a labor union, but its standing formally disappears once the complaint is adopted by its government and is pursued within the context of the NAALC. At that point, the actors become the government officials, not the labor unionists. The NAALC, consequently, is best understood as an example of the power of statist, not institutionalist or society-based, explanations.

In short, state-based explanations go a long way to explain past and current patterns evident in U.S.–Mexican relations when there are high stakes, including the main changes in Mexican foreign policy in the 1980s and 1990s. Neorealism, as modified in the particular Mexican case, captures well some key features of Mexico's international behavior. Presidentialism, neorealism's policy making counterpart, explains effectively both Mexico's decision to reorient its relations with the United States and NAFTA's final enactment in both Mexico and the United States. State-based explanations define well even the characteristics of some institutions created by NAFTA.[8]

Society-based Explanations

This book's chapters strongly demonstrate the insufficiency of state-based explanations to comprehend the long-term patterns and the recent changes in

U.S.–Mexican relations. There are two broad society-based explanations. The first stems from the movement of Mexicans to the United States over time. Millions of people have acted independently of state preferences over long periods of time; their behavior has also constrained the capacity of states to deal with each other over various issues. The second explanation derives from the pattern of social-class–tinged experiences that affect participants in U.S.–Mexican relations. In the 1980s and especially in the 1990s, there has been a convergence of beliefs between the elites of the United States and Mexico, but there has been little convergence among nonelites. This helps to explain intergovernmental collaboration and intranational conflict in U.S.–Mexican relations.

Millions of people of Mexican origin or ancestry live in the United States, and have done so since the boundary between the two countries "migrated" northwards in 1848. During the two world wars and the Korean War in the twentieth century, the United States and Mexico made special arrangements to foster temporary Mexican migration to the United States to replace the U.S. workers who had gone off to war: the *bracero* agreements born during World War II and continued, with variations, until 1964. These intergovernmental agreements fit state-based explanations, of course. Mexicans did not behave solely according to those agreements, however. Many temporary workers stayed indefinitely. Others migrated without regard for the laws of either country. By the early 1990s, the U.S. Bureau of the Census reported that over six million people lived in the United States who were born in Mexico. In the 1990s, immigration is one of the more divisive political issues in the United States and one of the more contentious between the Mexican and U.S. governments.

Rodolfo de la Garza's chapter shows some of the consequences of inter-societal relations. He notes the connections between migrants in cities in the United States and their home communities. The migrants, he reports, send not only funds but also seek to exercise their influence to reshape their home communities. Migrants in the United States also represent a market for Mexican exports. De la Garza mentions several Mexican export drives specifically targeting Mexican consumers in the United States; he also records some efforts, albeit limited, to develop business relationships between Mexican and Mexican American firms.

Intersocietal relations also limit government policy. For example, de la Garza explores the Mexican government's hopes to change U.S. immigration policies. The Mexican government favors increased legal migration, opposes crackdowns on illegal immigration, and supports the full participation of Mexican immigrants, regardless of their legal status, in U.S. social welfare programs. The Mexican government would surely wish to have the support of Mexican Americans in persuading the U.S. government but, de la Garza informs us, for the most part this is not the case.

Mexican Americans agree with the Mexican government regarding allowing legal and undocumented immigrants to participate in social services. The majority of Mexican Americans, however, have favored reducing the number of legal immigrants entering the United States and support wider efforts to prevent illegal immigration (in the latter two cases, support is stronger the closer one lives to the U.S.–Mexican border). In fact, de la Garza observes that California Latinos were divided over the wisdom of the referendum question, Proposition 187, until the debate increasingly took on an anti-Mexican tone; only then did Mexican Americans turn out strongly against this anti-immigrant measure.

Clearly Mexican Americans do not represent a ready-made lobby for the Mexican government in the United States even on issues that would seemingly bring Mexican Americans and the Mexican government closer together. In fact, in other work, de la Garza has shown that Mexican Americans have held views that are highly critical of the Mexican government and political system (de la Garza et al. 1992). Intersocietal relations limit the capacity of the Mexican government to influence the United States and legitimate U.S. policies contrary to those of the Mexican government, while they empower Mexican-origin peoples in the United States to affect their communities of origin in Mexico.

Intersocietal relations feature another dimension: the molding of the views of those who act across national boundaries. The chapters in this book suggest a certain social class patterning to these relations. Elite Mexicans have internalized market-oriented economic beliefs that are close to those held by U.S. elites. Víctor Godínez argues that the political group that seized government power in Mexico in the 1980s and 1990s adopted a perspective on the world and the domestic economy that was quite close to the dominant views held in the United States. As a result, Godínez proposes, the relations between U.S. and Mexican negotiators over trade and financial issues were not particularly adversarial. Rather, they resembled a team effort to produce a joint outcome consistent with the shared beliefs held by the elites of both governments.

Jesús Velasco's chapter presents supporting evidence. Velasco records the relative ease of collaboration between the Mexican government, on the one hand, and U.S. think tanks on the other. Beyond the particular efforts to finance think tank activities favorable to NAFTA's ratification, a striking finding in Velasco's chapter is the ease of collaboration between Mexican officials and intellectual policy elites in Washington, D.C. The Mexican government was able to collaborate with think tanks that spanned a wide ideological spectrum—from the Brookings Institution to the Heritage Foundation—perhaps excluding only those intellectual organizations close to U.S. labor unions or the political Left. The Mexican government's intellectual success, therefore, is not principally explained in ideological terms but in social class terms: dominant elites in both countries worked to sign and ratify NAFTA, even if these elites ordinarily differed on other matters.

Elsewhere on the social stratification pyramid, matters were different. Williams's chapter indicates that U.S. and Mexican labor union peak federation leaders disagreed sharply with one another over the wisdom of NAFTA and, for the most part, have continued to fight one another after the Agreement's implementation. Organized labor came to represent one of the pillars of opposition to NAFTA in the United States. The elites share beliefs and cooperate; the workers oppose the elites in the United States and each other across national boundaries.

In the same vein, de la Garza states that the Mexican government obtained little support in its effort to rally ordinary Mexican Americans to lobby the U.S. government on behalf of NAFTA's ratification. On the other hand, both de la Garza and Eisenstadt indicate a greater Mexican government success in rallying the political, business, and social leaders of Mexican American communities. Thus the policies of the Mexican government toward Mexican Americans may have widened the differences between leaders and members among Mexican American organizations.

Intersocietal issues, in short, complicate relations between the United States and Mexico, specifically over immigration. The principal effects of intersocietal relations have been: 1) to make certain problems between the two countries seem intractable and to limit the capacity of the Mexican government to influence the U.S. government; 2) to contribute to the gradual evolution of changes in Mexico's home communities; and 3) to facilitate reaching agreements between elites of both countries while fostering differences between leaders and ordinary citizens—an outcome shaped through social class effects.

Institution-based Explanations

The Mexican government's fundamental approach to the U.S. government in the 1980s and 1990s emphasized the latter's much greater institutional complexity. Institutionalist explanations call attention, first, to Mexico's relative success in inserting its own agenda in Washington's agenda by making effective use of rules and procedures in the U.S. political system. Institutionalist explanations also point, second, to several unexpected consequences of this change in Mexican foreign policy. In order to be effective in the United States, Mexico had to transform its own institutions charged with relations with the United States. Its government had to permit, even encourage, much greater and varied participation by public agencies and private actors in the implementation of Mexican foreign policy. And, third, Mexico had to resort to new international institutions to cushion and to channel the new impact of the United States on Mexico.

During the Salinas administration, Mexico's U.S. strategy sought to obtain NAFTA's enactment and also to improve Mexico's general image in the United States and create a better relationship with the Mexican American community. To accomplish these objectives, at the outset Mexico had to reshape its own institutions. First, the Foreign Relations Ministry was replaced by the Trade Ministry as the lead agency presiding over relations with the United States, as Chabat and Eisenstadt point out. Second, Mexican consulates were freed from many of the constraints imposed by noninterventionist ideologies and ordered, instead, to build bridges to Mexican-origin peoples in the United States and, more generally, to represent Mexican interests in the United States at the subnational level. The first decision marginalized the Foreign Ministry from a leadership role during a momentous transition in U.S.–Mexican relations. The second decision gave the Foreign Ministry a new and important mission, consistent with strategies familiar to Mexican diplomats from years of observing the work of French and Spanish diplomats. These two early decisions went on to have multiplicative consequences.

The Diaspora

One important Mexican government motivation for developing subnational activities in the United States was to rally Mexican American support for NAFTA. As noted earlier, these NAFTA-support programs made headway among Mexican American leadership groups, though not among the broader citizenry. Nonetheless, the actions of the Mexican government, especially through its consulates, may have transformed its relations with people of Mexican origin in the United States.

As Carlos González Gutiérrez explains in his chapter, the Mexican government had long been constrained by its commitment to nonintervention— its own neorealist perspective—from sustaining direct and active relations with Mexican-origin or Mexican-ancestry peoples in the United States. In the traditional view, states engaged each other directly; they did not engage the society of the other. (Nonetheless, as de la Garza indicates in his chapter, the Mexican government has reached out intermittently to Mexican Americans at various points since 1849.)

Beginning in the 1970s, the Mexican government developed a more coherent policy toward the various Mexican communities in the United States, but not until 1990 did it establish a formal Program for Mexican Communities Living in Foreign Countries and lodged it within the Ministry of Foreign Relations. As de la Garza and González Gutiérrez note, this program will facilitate dual nationality for Mexican Americans, enabling them to retain rights in both countries and thus a stake in each. It has simplified customs procedures to reduce corruption. It provides educational materials for schools in the United States and simplifies the transfer of school credits between U.S. and Mexican schools. It has created eighteen Mexican cultural institutes in various U.S. cities. It establishes collaborative relations with the Mexican American business community and other Mexican American organizations. It better staffs consular offices to speed up processing requests for legal documents. It provides better access for Mexicans in the United States to the Mexican social security system.

Consequently, a program begun to advance specific Mexican government interests in the United States, through the institutional logic of the decentralized work of consulates, may be evolving into a relationship between the Mexican government and its own citizens in the United States and, to a lesser degree, it may also involve some U.S. citizens of Mexican ancestry. Thus the Mexican government's principal gain from its new strategy may be to rediscover its own grass roots in a foreign land, even if its narrower foreign policy objectives remain unaffected. The decentralized design of the consulates enables them to develop a life of their own—an institutionalist explanation for the evolution of foreign policy and the remaking of aspects of Mexico's policy-making process.

Lobbying the United States

The Mexican government has lobbied the United States in the more distant past, as Alan Knight reminds us in his chapter. Mexican attempts to influence the U.S. government were important and sustained from the Mexican Revolution until World War II. The stakes were high; relationships were in flux. The same occurred after the 1982 financial crisis and, especially, in the 1990s though on a more institutionalized scale.

The institutional design of the U.S. government permitted, and even abetted, the Mexican government's generalized lobbying; it also shaped the pattern, contours, tactics, and relative effectiveness of Mexican efforts to influence U.S. policy. At its best, lobbying provides information not otherwise available to decision makers, or it organizes in a new way the information that might be available. Thus it can help to set the agenda. Mexican lobbying kept NAFTA on the congressional agenda and packaged it effectively as a national security issue for the United States; this was important during the first half of 1993, Eisenstadt reminds us, when President Clinton seemed to waver in his support for ratification.

The Mexican government's approach to Washington-based think tanks was one important tactic, as Velasco explains in his chapter. This intellectual lobby made the case on behalf of NAFTA's ratification on the grounds that it met U.S. interests. Intellectuals presented the proratification arguments in subtle and sophisticated language to members of Congress, staff, and the public accompanied, whenever appropriate, by econometric simulations that calculated the costs and benefits of the new agreement; the most professional among these, especially those of the Institute for International Economics (Hufbauer and Schott 1992, 1993) made a strong case for enacting NAFTA.

Lobbying can also build coalitions to instruct decision makers about the range and depth of support for given policy positions, thus helping to clarify the political underpinnings of the policy agenda. The intellectual lobby of the think tanks, Velasco notes, contributed to this aspect of the ratification process by providing credible nonpartisan pro-NAFTA arguments that helped to shape public opinion. The Mexican government's lobbying campaign performed best when it stayed close to these propositions. Its economic studies of NAFTA's impact on various congressional districts, and its alliance building with business and Mexican American leadership groups worked well.

On the other hand, the Mexican government, Eisenstadt informs us, may have been much less effective, and may have wasted lobbying money, when it seemed to believe that its lobbying could actually get NAFTA enacted.[9] And Mexican lobbying had the least effect the closer the U.S. decision came to the White House itself: only the president of the United States could obtain the final votes in Congress to enact NAFTA, and only he could fashion the 1995 financial rescue package.

In any case, Mexican lobbying in the United States had to adjust to U.S. institutions and, for the most part, could draw little intellectual or practical guidance from Mexico's own institutional arrangements. Mexican government officials could draw on Mexico's own experience only in their relations with the think tanks because the team of officials then in charge of Mexican government economic agencies drew liberally from such institutions as the Instituto Tecnológico Autónomo de México (Golob 1996). Otherwise, the institutional setting in the United States differed from Mexico's. The role of Congress, constituents, the press, and the various agencies of the U.S. government set the main patterns for Mexican activities. Mexican lobbying had to operate also within the confines of U.S. law and regulations; in that way, Mexico became not just a foreign government but also a domestic actor within the U.S. political system[10]—an institutional arrangement that the United States permits, regulates, and, to some degree, abets.

In this fashion, the institutional design of the U.S. government serves also as an institutionalist explanation for the partial transformation of the Mexican government. The Mexican government made a transition from its emphasis on its sovereign majesty, committed to nonintervention, because it wanted to influence the U.S. government; in order to succeed, it had to remake its foreign policy in the institutional image of the U.S. government.

There is a closely related change in the implementation of Mexican foreign policy, namely, the more direct engagement of Mexico's private business sector. As Chabat and Eisenstadt show, Mexican business provided significant funding for the pro-NAFTA campaign in the United States and hosted visits to Mexico by dozens of U.S. congressional staff members. Though the trends for greater business engagement in the implementation of Mexican foreign policy were already evident during the de la Madrid presidency (Chabat 1989), the activity and funding for these purposes increases markedly during the Salinas de Gortari administration.

New International Institutions

NAFTA, Mexico's central foreign policy accomplishment of the 1990s, created new international institutions and procedures to govern Mexico's trade and many other international economic relations for the years to come. NAFTA's substance is beyond the scope of this work, but this book's authors call attention to some related or additional institutional factors derived from this historic shift in Mexico's international relations that served to cushion and to channel the new U.S. impact on Mexico.

Chabat suggests that Mexico gained from Canada's inclusion in the free trade negotiations and eventual agreement. A purely bilateral arrangement with the United States might have been more difficult to defend within Mexico.[11] Complexity helped. In the same vein, Chabat notes that Mexico developed other international institutionalist responses to cushion the political impact of its closer alignment with the United States (a behavior also consistent with neorealist thinking). Thus President Salinas faithfully participated in the meetings of heads of state of the Group of Eight, which clusters the largest Latin American countries. Salinas was the founding host of the Iberoamerican Summit, which gathers the heads of state and government of Spain, Portugal, and the Iberoamerican republics. During the Salinas presidency, Mexico joined the Organization for Economic Cooperation and Development and the Asia-Pacific Economic Council.

New international institutions served also to channel the actions of contentious private actors in U.S.–Mexican relations. For example, Williams shows that the NAALC permitted labor unions in both countries to file suits against firms that violate the labor standards of the country that hosts them. The NAALC, in particular, facilitated the collaboration between a small, dissident Mexican labor union federation, the Frente Auténtico del Trabajo (FAT), on the one hand, and two U.S. labor federations, the United Electrical, Radio, and Machine Workers of America and the International Brotherhood of Teamsters, on the other. This cooperation enabled the FAT to challenge Mexico's dominant Confederation of Mexican Workers by filing suit through the NAALC channels against Honeywell, General Electric, and Sony for obstructing the FAT's organizing efforts. Although there have been instances in the past of collaboration between U.S. labor federations and dissident Mexican labor unions (Middlebrook 1982), the NAALC provides a novel vehicle for private labor union partnerships that can advance joint objectives through institutional means and contain conflicts.

Another mechanism to channel private and public interactions has been Mexican government funding for certain U.S. private business activities. Chabat reports on Mexican government funding for the AmeriMex Maquiladora Fund L.P., an investment fund that sought to lure in-bond industries to the state of Yucatán. Though that project was discontinued in 1993, Chabat and de la Garza also comment on similar actions by Mexico's national development bank, Nacional Financiera. In 1992, NAFINSA created a $20 million fund to finance investment activities in Mexico by Mexican American business firms and, in

1993, it loaned $35 million to the Los Angeles–based Hispanic Capital Fund for its investments in Mexico.

Finally, as Godínez notes, the evolution of bilateral U.S.–Mexican institutions and procedures also subtly altered the style of Mexican foreign policy and channeled relations between the two governments. In part because of the shared beliefs noted earlier, Mexican negotiators, Godínez argues (quoting José Angel Gurría, Mexico's long-time debt negotiator who became foreign minister in 1994), thought that a timely agreement was more important than an optimal agreement. This perspective led Mexican negotiators away from confrontation and toward a certain bargaining passivity. The high point of this transformation in Mexican foreign policy behavior, Godínez notes, was reached during the discussions over the Mexican financial bailout in early 1995: Mexico, in effect, delegated to the U.S. government to bargain on their joint behalf before the International Monetary Fund and the Bank of International Settlements. Through shared ideas and the adoption of new practices for the conduct of foreign policy, Mexico and the United States came to coordinate their foreign economic policies to an unprecedented degree.

Conclusion

Mexico's new foreign policy is still guided by reasons of state and still shaped by the preferences and will of its presidents. To a substantial degree, the same remains true of U.S. foreign policy. Though the Congress and private actors play a much larger role in making U.S. foreign policy, Presidents Bush and Clinton were the key actors in the redesign of U.S. policies toward Mexico. The much closer collaboration between the two governments has been assisted by the convergence of elite beliefs and experience in both countries; U.S. and Mexican elites became much more likely to look for the "team outcome" in bilateral relations.

This dramatic shift in U.S.–Mexican relations has also been accompanied by significant changes in the institutions and practices of Mexican foreign policy, which is no longer conducted just by the president and the Foreign Ministry. Mexican foreign policy making and implementation now engages many and varied public and private actors, even giving new life, meaning, and significance to Mexican consulates in the United States. Mexico has resorted more proactively to new international institutions and procedures to cushion the new impact of the United States on Mexico and to channel the conflicts between contentious private actors from both countries.

Not all is well in U.S.–Mexican relations, however. Immigration looms large in this book as an issue marked by dispute, where Mexican Americans, to the chagrin of Mexico's government, side with the government of the United

States over most of the important bilateral issues. And, whereas elite beliefs and experiences have converged, the nonelites have become increasingly adversarial toward one another, providing the political foundations for intergovernmental conflict.

The ghost of Artemio Cruz's mendacity, finally, still haunts U.S.–Mexican relations in the second half of the 1990s. Even as the powerful in both countries proclaim that the ideals and interests of the United States and Mexico coincide, a great many people do not believe it. Many Mexican and U.S. citizens think that their governments fooled them when NAFTA was signed; Mexicans blame NAFTA for their economic troubles while U.S. citizens fear illegal immigration from Mexico and oppose bailing out its economy. Elite mendacity is a legacy from the history of U.S.–Mexican relations. It received a new lease on life by the manner of lobbying on behalf of NAFTA, which promised that the gates of paradise were about to open to all. Elite mendacity remains a threat to the continued improvement in relations between the two governments, and to the future prospects for building widespread public support for constructive and transparent relations to the long-term benefit of both countries.

Notes

1. For Mexico's previous trade policy, see Balassa (1983).
2. This is not a freestanding chapter. Instead, it calls attention to, and to some degree summarizes, themes that emerge in the chapters in this book. This chapter relies occasionally on textual references to other chapters, but my debt to the authors in this book is much greater than these citations suggest. The views expressed here are mine alone. The authors are at liberty to claim that all the errors in this chapter are mine and all the insights are theirs.
3. The classic study of this period of Mexican foreign policy is Ojeda's (1976).
4. The most influential neorealist scholar has been Waltz (1979).
5. By wider measures of effectiveness, however, Mexico performed less well. In a study of twenty-two conflicts with the United States over various issue areas at different moments in the twentieth century, Mexico performed generally well before World War II but much less well thereafter; in particular, Mexico lost most trade disputes with the United States from the mid-1940s to the mid-1970s (Wyman 1978: 121–125).
6. This is a reversal of the Mexican government's characteristic approach to the U.S. government. See the analysis in Rico (1989: 119).
7. For the distinction between "crisis" and routine conditions in U.S. policy making toward Mexico, see Rico (1989: 122–125).
8. For an extended critique of the applicability of neorealism to Mexican foreign policy, see Domínguez (1996).
9. Nonetheless, at $37 million (see Eisenstadt's chapter) the total cost of the Mexican lobbying effort may well be worth the price. From 1993 to 1994, NAFTA's first year, Mexican exports jumped by $9 billion. Some of that increase would surely

have occurred thanks to the dynamism of normal trade interactions, even without NAFTA. But if one assumes that, without NAFTA, the rate of Mexican export growth for 1994 would have been the same as for 1993, then NAFTA still added about $2.6 billion to Mexican exports in 1994 alone—despite the many troubles that ailed Mexico that year including the insurgency in Chiapas, the assassination of the most important presidential candidate and, later, of the ruling party's secretary general, and an overvalued peso that would contribute to a financial shock in December.

10. This was also a change. In the mid-1970s, a study of the behavior of Latin American diplomats (including Mexicans) in Washington, D.C., shows that they did not behave at all like this (Sack and Wyman 1976: 244–245).

11. For other discussions of the politics of NAFTA in Mexico, see Pastor and Wise (1994), Poitras and Robinson (1994), and Smith (1992).

References

Balassa, Bela. 1983. "Trade Policy in Mexico." *World Development* 11 (9): 795–811.

Chabat, Jorge. 1989. "The Making of Mexican Policy toward the United States." In Rosario Green and Peter H Smith, eds., *Foreign Policy in U.S.–Mexican Relations*. San Diego: Center for U.S.–Mexican Studies, University of California at San Diego.

de la Garza, Rodolfo, Louis DeSipio, F. Chris García, John García, and Angelo Falcón. 1992. *Latino Voices: Mexican, Puerto Rican, and Cuban Perspectives on American Politics*. Boulder, Colo.: Westview Press.

Domínguez, Jorge I. 1996. "Widening Scholarly Horizons: Theoretical Approaches for the Study of U.S.–Mexican Relations." *The David Rockefeller Center for Latin American Studies: Working Paper Series* 96-1. Cambridge, Mass.

Economic Commission for Latin America and the Caribbean. 1995. *Preliminary Overview of the Economy of Latin America and the Caribbean, 1995*. LC/G.1892-P. Santiago, Chile: United Nations.

Fuentes, Carlos. 1964. *The Death of Artemio Cruz*, trans. Sam Hileman. New York: Farrar, Straus, and Giroux.

Golob, Stephanie R. 1996. "'Making Possible What is Necessary': Pedro Aspe, the Salinas Team, and the Next Mexican 'Miracle.'" In Jorge I. Domínguez, ed., *Technopols: Freeing Politics and Markets in Latin America in the 1990s*. University Park: Pennsylvania State University Press.

González, Guadalupe. 1989. "The Foundations of Mexico's Foreign Policy: Old Attitudes and New Realities." In Rosario Green and Peter H. Smith, eds., *Foreign Policy in U.S.–Mexican Relations*. San Diego: Center for U.S.–Mexican Studies, University of California at San Diego.

Hufbauer, Gary, and Jeffrey Schott. 1992. *North American Free Trade: Issues and Recommendations*. Washington, D.C.: Institute for International Economics.

———— 1993. *NAFTA: An Assessment*. Washington, D.C.: Institute for International Economics.

Inter-American Development Bank. 1995. *Economic and Social Progress in Latin America: 1995 Report*. Baltimore: Johns Hopkins University Press.

Krasner, Stephen. 1972. "Are Bureaucracies Important?" *Foreign Policy* 7 (Summer): 159–179.

Middlebrook, Kevin J. 1982. "International Implications of Labor Change: The Automobile Industry." In Jorge I. Domínguez, ed., *Mexico's Political Economy: Challenges at Home and Abroad.* Beverly Hills: Sage Publications.

Ojeda, Mario. 1976. *Alcances y Límites de la Política Exterior de México.* México: El Colegio de México.

Pastor, Manuel, and Carol Wise. 1994. "The Origins and Sustainability of Mexico's Free Trade Policy." *International Organization* 48 (3) (Summer): 459–490.

Poitras, Guy, and Raymond Robinson. 1994. "The Politics of NAFTA in Mexico." *Journal of Interamerican Studies and World Affairs* 36 (1) (Spring): 1–35.

Rico, Carlos. 1989. "The Making of U.S. Policy toward Mexico: Should We Expect Coherence?" In Rosario Green and Peter H. Smith, eds., *Foreign Policy in U.S.– Mexican Relations.* San Diego: Center for U.S.–Mexican Studies, University of California at San Diego.

Sack, Roger E., and Donald L. Wyman. 1976. "Latin American Diplomats and the United States Foreign Policymaking Process." In *Conduct of Routine Economic Relations.* Commission on the Organization of the Government for the Conduct of Foreign Policy, vol. 3. Washington, D.C.: U.S. Government Printing Office. Appendix I.

Smith, Peter H. 1992. "The Political Impact of Free Trade on Mexico." *Journal of Interamerican Studies and World Affairs* 34 (1) (Spring): 1–25.

Waltz, Kenneth. 1979. *Theory of International Politics.* Reading, Mass.: Addison-Wesley.

Wyman, Donald L. 1978. "Dependence and Conflict in U.S.–Mexican Relations, 1920–1975." In Robert L. Paarlberg, ed., *Diplomatic Dispute: U.S. Conflict with Iran, Japan, and Mexico.* Cambridge, Mass.: Center for International Affairs, Harvard University.

Index

Acheson, Dean, 18, 24
activism, consular, 55–56
Adolph Coors Foundation, 128, 130
AEI. *See* American Enterprise Institute
AFL, 22–23
AFL-CIO, xxi, 114, 170, 173–75
AFSC. *See* American Friends Service
  Committee
AIFLD. *See* American Institute for Free Labor
  Development
Akin, Gump, Hauer & Feld, 118n4
Alcoa Foundation, 129t
Alemán, Miguel, 12
Alfred P. Sloan Foundation, 129t
Allard, Wayne, 109t
Alliance for Progress, 28n5
ambassadors: private sector, 106–7; regional,
  103–6. *See also specific ambassadors*
American Enterprise Institute (AEI), 126, 132,
  144n3
American Express Foundation, 129t
American Friends Service Committee (AFSC),
  166, 173–74
American Institute for Free Labor
  Development (AIFLD), 176
The American Spectator, 128
AmeriMex Maquiladora Fund L.P. (Fondo
  Maquiladora AmeriMex), 38, 192
Amnesty International, 166
Amoco, 129t
Amway Corporation, 130
Anaya, Toney, xix, 80, 94t, 101t, 102, 105
anticlericalism, 9

anti-imperialism, 14
APEC. *See* Asian Pacific Economic
  Cooperation
Apodaca, Jerry, xix, 80, 102–3
Apodaca and Sosa, 94t
Arca Foundation, 129t
Aronson, Bernard, 119n11
Asian Pacific Economic Cooperation (APEC),
  40, 192
Asociación de Abogados Democráticos
  (National Association of Democratic
  Lawyers), 173–74
Aspe, Pedro, 12, 112
Association of Exporting Companies. *See*
  Coordinadora de Organismos
  Empresariales de Comercio Exterior
AT&T, 106, 129t
Avila Camacho, Manuel, 5, 12
Aztec Eagle, 84

Bacchus, Jim, 109t
Baer, Delal, 136–38, 143
Baker, Howard H., Jr., 100
Baker Plan, 97
BancOne, 130
Bank America Foundation, 129t
bankers, 22
Bank for International Settlements (BIS), 111,
  193
Becerra, Xavier, 109t
Bennett, Brian Timothy, 96, 138
Bentsen, Lloyd, 100, 138, 141
Bergsten, Fred, 138

---

*Page references followed by *t* or *f* indicate tables or footnotes, respectively. Page references
followed by n indicate notes.

206   *Bridging the Border: Transforming Mexico–U.S. Relations*

About the Contributors

Jorge Chabat received his Ph.D. in International Studies from the University of Miami. He is the director of the Division of International Studies at the Centro de Investigación y Docencia Económicas (CIDE) in Mexico City. He is the author of more than thirty articles on Mexico's international relations, relations between Mexico and the United States, drug trafficking, and national security. He has served on the political science and sociology faculty at the National Autonomous University in Mexico City and has taught at many other universities in the Americas and in Europe.

Rodolfo O. de la Garza is Mike Hogg Professor of Community Affairs in the Department of Government at the University of Texas at Austin. He also serves as vice president of the Tomás Rivera Policy Institute. Professor de la Garza combines interests in American and comparative politics. In American politics he specializes in political behavior and ethnic politics, with particular expertise in the study of Latino populations. His area of concentration in comparative politics is Mexico; his substantive interests are in political development, ethnic politics, and U.S.-Mexican politics. He has edited, co-edited, and coauthored five books, including *Ethnic Ironies: Latino Politics in the 1992 Elections; Latino Voices: Mexican, Puerto Rican, and Cuban Perspectives on American Politics*; and *Barrio Ballots: Latino Politics in the 1990 Elections*. He has served on the editorial boards of the *Western Political Quarterly*, the *Journal of Politics*, the *Social Science Quarterly*, and the *Hispanic Journal of Behavioral Science*. Currently he is directing studies on Latino–African American relations, immigrant incorporation, and Latinos and U.S. hemispheric integration. He is a member of the Council on Foreign Relations and the Overseas Development Council.

Jorge I. Domínguez is the Clarence Dillon Professor of International Affairs and Director of the Center for International Affairs at Harvard University. His most recent book (with James McCann) is *Democratizing Mexico: Public Opinion and Electoral Choices* (Johns Hopkins University Press, 1996).

Todd A. Eisenstadt is a doctoral candidate in political science at the University of California, San Diego. A fellowship recipient in the U.S. House of Representatives' Foreign Affairs Committee during the debates over the North American Free Trade Agreement, Eisenstadt is currently a graduate research associate of the University of California, San Diego's Center for U.S.–Mexican Studies. He recently spent a year as a Fulbright scholar at the Centro de Investigación y Docencia Económicas (CIDE) in Mexico City.

Victor Godínez has taught at the National Autonomous University in Mexico City. He was director of the International Studies Department at the University of the Americas, and has taught at numerous universities in Mexico, Latin America, and Europe. He is the author of numerous works, including "Entre la croissance et la recuperation de la confiance: L'economie mexicaine, 1988-1993." He received his Ph.D. in economics from the University of Paris.

Carlos González Gutiérrez is the director of community affairs for the Program for Mexican Communities Living in Foreign Countries in the Mexican Ministry of Foreign Affairs. He is a graduate of the Colegio de Mexico and the University of Southern California, with degrees in international relations. He joined the Mexican Foreign Service in 1987 and has served in the Mexican consulate in Los Angeles. He is the author of various scholarly articles about Mexico-United States relations, including "The Mexican Diaspora in California: The Limits and Possibilities of the Mexican Government," in *The California–Mexico Connection* (Stanford University Press, 1993).

Alan Knight is a professor of Latin American history and a fellow at St. Antony's College, Oxford University. He is the author of the two-volume book *The Mexican Revolution*. He is currently working on a general history of Mexico and a study of state and society in Mexico during the 1930s. He has taught at the University of Essex and the University of Texas at Austin. He received his Ph.D. at Oxford University.

Jesús Velasco received a Ph.D. in political science from the University of Texas at Austin. He is a professor in the Department of International Studies at the Centro de Investigación y Docencia Económicas (CIDE) in Mexico City. His research focus is on the role of ideas in political realignments.

Edward J. Williams is professor of political science at the University of Arizona. Professor Williams teaches, researches, and writes on Latin American, Mexican, and U.S.–Mexican border public policy and politics. He has contributed numerous articles to professional journals and has written eight books and monographs on various aspects of these topics. At present, he is serving as the president of the Association for Borderlands Studies, as a member of a national advisory committee to the U.S. National Administrative Office of the North American Agreement on Labor Cooperation, and as a member of the board of directors of the Tucson Committee on Foreign Relations.

WITHDRAWN

WITHDRAWN